The
LEADING
EDGE

Holly Ransom is an expert in disruption and future leadership. The founder and CEO of Emergent, she was named one of Australia's 100 Most Influential Women by the *Australian Financial Review*. Holly has delivered a Peace Charter to the Dalai Lama, interviewed Barack Obama on stage, was Sir Richard Branson's nominee for *Wired* magazine's 'Smart List' of Future Game Changers to watch in 2017 and was awarded the US Embassy's Eleanor Roosevelt Award for Leadership Excellence in 2019. Holly is a Fulbright scholar and Harvard Kennedy School Class of 2021 Fellow. *The Leading Edge* is her first book.

hollyransom.com
@HollyRansom
@holly_ransom

The
LEADING
EDGE

**Dream big,
spark change and
become the leader the
world needs you to be**

Holly Ransom

VIKING
an imprint of
PENGUIN BOOKS

VIKING

UK | USA | Canada | Ireland | Australia
India | New Zealand | South Africa | China

Viking is part of the Penguin Random House group of companies
whose addresses can be found at global.penguinrandomhouse.com.

Penguin
Random House
Australia

First published by Viking, 2021

Cover design by Alex Ross © Penguin Random House Australia Pty Ltd
Typeset in 12.5/17pt Adobe Garamond by Midland Typesetters, Australia

Printed and bound in Australia by Griffin Press, an accredited
ISO AS/NZS 14001 Environmental Management Systems printer

A catalogue record for this
book is available from the
National Library of Australia

ISBN 978 0 14379 152 2

penguin.com.au

MIX
Paper | Supporting
responsible forestry
FSC® C018684

For Grandpa and Grandma, who taught me you only live once and you ought to behave accordingly: to live y(our) best life means leaving y(our) world a better place.

Contents

Preface

Every one of us is born with the ability to lead the change we care enough to make. And each of us can hone our leadership skills to better scale the impact we dream of having. Saying no to making a leadership contribution is saying yes to allowing others to shape our world for us.

There are those people who laugh shyly and say, 'Oh I can't sing. I've got a terrible voice . . . But I love music!' Leadership is similar. You were born with a voice, a beautiful voice. It's just whether (and how) you choose to use it.

However, wherever and whatever we lead, each of us leads every day. The world needs your unique offering, and it needs it now. Diverse approaches to intractable problems can change paradigms. Distinctive skills combining in new ways are essential to breaking new ground. Authentic stories from personal experience will spark a movement. And the great thing? You don't have to be ready.

Leading from the edge is about embracing not quite knowing. It's about having all the questions as opposed to all the answers. It's about allowing a bold vision to rise up and to harness it with elemental force. It doesn't mean avoiding the work or being comfortable with something embryonic or half-baked masquerading as a finished product. But it does mean experimenting, collaborating and diversifying, and committing to continually improving.

Leading at the edge requires us to take our scribblings, our new idea, our raw invention and show it to the world well before we're ready.

Because if we *were* ready, if we *were* sure, the moment will have passed, the movement will have begun, the trajectory will already be set and we will be too late to make the change we dreamt of.

Leadership is not for the faint-hearted. It is for the big-hearted. And when we look inside our chests, we've all got one of those. We've all got the pre-requisite that's needed to be the leader the world needs us to be and we are all capable of leading when it comes to change we care about.

A quest for the Leading Edge

I was inspired to bring *The Leading Edge* to life because I know from experience the challenge of moving beyond the feeling of *wanting* to lead and into the *action* of leading. While I pored over books, keynote presentations and leadership programs shining with uplifting ideas, I always found the inspirational afterglow short lived. For the most part, the ideas never bridged what I term the personal implementation chasm: how could I go from being someone with a will, a work ethic and strong ideals to someone able to catalyse new behaviour for a better tomorrow?

Growing up, I always had the big dream, the fire in my belly, the inner feisty social-warrior streak. What I didn't have, and longed for, was the science. On my journey, I have developed the mindset to choose my moment, deal with criticism and bounce back strong. The methods to back up my opinions, test my fledgling strategies and work through fear. And the mastery to set and achieve goals, to work 'on' as well as 'in' my mission and to build a tribe of allies equally restless for change.

But it's not about *what* I've done, or even *why* I've done it. I want to break open the notion that leadership is exclusive. It's not. And in today's world more than ever we simply cannot afford for it to be. I believe everyone was born to lead in some way, and *leading from the edge* means harnessing the state of mind, the processes and the artistry that will arm leaders like you for impact.

The Leading Edge approach

I've spent the best part of the last fifteen years in search of answers.
I've interviewed Barack Obama, Sir Ken Robinson, Condoleezza
Rice, Sir Richard Branson, Malcolm Gladwell and scores of other
leaders who've made their life's work living and leading from their
edge. I've worked with boards and leadership teams from cutting-
edge, noteworthy and influential organisations. And I had to stop
myself just then from writing 'I've been lucky enough to . . .'
Because leadership is not about luck. Leaders themselves are often
no less riddled with fear and anxiety than the rest of us. What great
leaders have learnt to do is build the mindsets, methods and mastery
that support their new ideas and turn their determination into real
traction. What *is* lucky is that so many of these people have been
only too happy to share their tangible insights to help more of us
achieve change. *The Leading Edge* is my opportunity to pass on
their wisdom and teachings to you, along with some of the realisa-
tions I've had during the past decade of pushing up against my own
boundaries.

In these pages I hope you'll find not just names you know,
but names you'll never forget. People from Kenya, Jordan, New
Zealand, Ireland, the Himalayas, Canada and many more corners
of the Earth. These leaders identify as Muslim, Black, transgender,
Indigenous, suburban, Jedi-warrior, LGBTQIA+, shy, fearless and
everything in between and are doggedly, intelligently seeking to be
the change they wish to see in the world. I wanted the people and
stories from the messy, challenging, vulnerability-inducing reality
that is working for impact every day. My aim has been to consolidate their lessons to illuminate a new path forward.

Before we venture further together, I'm keen for you to ditch any
notion you might have that I am preaching from a leadership pulpit.
I'm no better than anyone else who is striving to be a better person
and pushing for a better world. I wrote *The Leading Edge* to prompt
more questions, exploration and sharing. If I've learnt anything in

my life to date it's that leadership, like self-development, is an infinite pursuit – you never 'win' or 'arrive' – you just continue to try, learn and evolve. We often don't get it right first go and it requires continuous humility, curiosity and self-compassion. But there is no more noble pursuit than to choose our own adventure through life on the quest for better: better me, better us, better world.

What to expect from *The Leading Edge*

It starts from within. A common thread throughout the uncommon leaders, pioneers, trailblazers and change agents I've interviewed, is that their aspiration for a better world begins with a determination to be a better person. That's why the structure of *The Leading Edge* is dedicated to 'Leading Oneself' ahead of 'Leading Others': you can't run before you can walk.

Part One explores ideas, stories and actions to build our strength as an individual leader. This first section paves a pathway to enable us to be 'leading ourselves' at the edge of our comfort zone. Once we have taken these ideas on board, it's time to move to Part Two, 'leading others' at the edge of their own leadership capacity. Here's where we move from practising our own ability to make change to enabling collective impact.

You will see that both Part One and Part Two are divided into three collections of ideas: Mindset, Method and Mastery. Leadership is within everyone's reach, everyone's ability and everyone's power. It's simply about having the mindset to make change happen, the methods to progress change even when it gets tough and the mastery to own it like a leader.

I also encourage leaders to define success on their own terms. Something I've observed, without exception, from leading edge change-makers is that they've all done things in their own unique way. The tools and ideas discussed in these chapters are not professing a gold standard of human by which you should judge yourself (god forbid), nor are they intended to be a definitive list of qualities and capabilities. I hope that, like with any good DIY guide, you pick them up and give them a go. I'd love for you to make modifications, the way I do with my favourite recipes, and share them with me on social media so they can build on and enhance the foundations I'm seeking to lay here. Perhaps they'll spark some conversation and debate. I also hope that in the diversity of the stories and skills that follow you'll see your own strengths, find your own edges and feel emboldened to reach, believe and be. Because the world needs you – *all* of you.

Finding your leading edge

My message is simple:

I hope this meets you where you are and helps you reach a little higher, move a little faster, delve a little deeper or stand right where you are and make a little more real the change you want to see in the world.

Dream big.

Spark change.

Become the leader the world needs you to be.

Prologue

I was about four years old, shopping with my grandma Dorothy. We were waiting in the supermarket queue when the man in front of us launched into a verbal tirade at the young girl behind the counter. Evidently, she'd given him the wrong change. I watched as he towered over her and the girl's face began to match her flame-red hair . . . she looked like she wanted to melt into the floor. Before I knew it, my barely five-foot-tall grandma inserted herself between this giant of a man and the checkout, and brandished her finger at him, saying, 'How dare you speak to this young woman like that! You apologise this minute!' I will never forget the look of shock on his face as he stared down at her. Sheepishly he grabbed his things, mumbled 'sorry' under his breath and hurriedly rushed out of the supermarket.

Grandma proceeded as if nothing had happened – she bought her loaf of bread, thanked the girl and went to shuffle out of the store before she realised I wasn't with her. I was still back in the queue, superglued to the spot with my jaw on the floor. I couldn't fathom what I'd just witnessed. She motioned for me to follow her. 'Grandma, that was so brave!' I exclaimed, as I rushed forward to grab her hand. She paused for a moment as she wove my small fingers through hers and said, 'Honey, if you walk past things that aren't right, you tell the world it's okay.'

That was the first leadership lesson I remember, and the beginning of a fascination with our individual power to change the world we live in for the better.

Part One

Leaders who know themselves awaken to the question of 'How may I do better today than I did yesterday? Better for my family, my friends, my work and my community?' Part One of this book aims to share stories, insights and approaches that will allow you to do exactly that. Importantly, 'better' does not mean 'more'. When effective leaders say 'better', what they mean is deeper, fuller, more sustainable, more meaningful.

The leaders I've learnt from and admire are both masters of their sphere of influence and regular visitors to the territory beyond their comfort zone. These two ideas, in unison, are concepts we'll explore in Part One. Real leaders neither underestimate their power nor overestimate their importance. They focus on the problem at hand and on the people they're seeking to serve in ways that extend and challenge. In doing so, their sphere of influence expands, both through their direct action and the way they embolden and empower others. But it all starts from within.

We'll talk a lot about change. We are not passengers in our own lives, in our work or in this world. We want to shape these things. But as we'll see in Part One, we can't demand of others what we can't demonstrate ourselves. In an age where trust, transparency, vulnerability and authenticity are the order of the day we need to learn how to – as Gandhi so brilliantly put it – be the change we want to see in the world. This is ever-humbling work. The sort of work that requires you to actually act out and embody the mantra: 'Do what you can, with what you have, from where you are.'

Mindset

Leadership is a state of mind

1

Anchor to purpose

'If you don't know where you're going, you might wind up someplace else.'

Yogi Berra

Who's watching?

I've never thought more about my 'why' than on the starting line of my first Ironman. I was wearing an ill-fitting wetsuit, struggling to get my hair into a swimming cap and my goggles wouldn't stop fogging up. I was twenty-five and grossly undertrained. When I had signed up 100 days earlier, I could barely have run 10 km let alone the 3.8-km swim, 180-km cycle and 42-km run I was now facing.

As the gun cracked and we all surged forward, I was struck by the diversity of ages, accents, body shapes and fitness levels of the people around me. I began to wonder 'why' everyone else was here. The more I thought about it, the more ridiculous it seemed. Why were we all putting ourselves through a day of relentless pain?

In the time it took me to complete that course I pushed myself beyond my own limits in search of that bigger 'why'. I thought about it as I high-fived the oldest competitor in the field, a 78-year-old from Japan. I wondered 'why' as I passed a woman with a shaved head wearing a singlet that said 'survivor' underneath her race number. And I tried to guess it when I saw tears at the finishing line as family and friends yelled their guts out.

When people ask me why *I* raced the Ironman, there are two answers I give. The default is for people who ask without really wanting a proper answer. To these folks, I generally admit that I accepted a dare.

I was working as chief of staff to a banking executive at the time. At a company dinner, I was sitting next to the bank's legal counsel who told me that he'd completed twenty-eight triathlons. I told him I'd always wanted to do an Ironman, but hadn't the time to train. He immediately called 'bullshit'; he'd done all of his triathlons while holding an equally demanding job. I pulled out my phone and signed up.

But there's a second, deeper, answer to 'why' I did the Ironman, an answer I reserve for those who ask the question curiously, intent on listening to the reply.

About eighteen months earlier, as I recovered from depression, I had made a promise to myself. I swore that when I'd mastered a new mindset for living well, I'd test myself with the biggest physical and mental challenge I could imagine: the Ironman. I wanted to make a statement to myself, and to the world that there was nothing weak about depression. That what I'd been through hadn't broken me: it had allowed me to rebuild stronger than ever.

Having grown up in a household that wasn't big on showing emotion, I had initially perceived my breakdown as weak. I can still remember the day I fell apart in a mentor's office, saying, 'I just wish I could be stronger; I wish I could just push through this.' Because I always just had . . . until I hadn't. I'd found the wall and I couldn't go through it. I'd had to learn new ways to go around and over.

And lo and behold, here I was again, at a wall. It was riding into a headwind at the 88-km mark; my legs were burning. I could have walked faster. My head was screaming, 'Are you kidding that we have to do a whole other lap of this bike course and then run a marathon?!!' [Insert expletives freely!]

And then, divine intervention struck. One of the great things about marathons is the enthusiastic mix of people who line the streets all day cheering. Just as I was coming through town, I passed a mother on her front lawn, hanging over the fence with her two daughters: one looked about thirteen and the other about seven. As I approached, they began jumping. I heard the littler of the two shout wildly, 'Mum, Mum, look! It's a girl just like me.'

In that instant everything changed. No matter how much my body ached there was no chance in hell I wasn't finishing the damn race. I'd been oblivious that only about 20 per cent of the participants in an average Ironman are women, and not many were under thirty. I started to notice how the local girls would run alongside parts of the course with me, how they'd high-five me and not the boys. It made me realise that my real why was much bigger than me: it was about who was watching. I wanted those girls to believe they could do anything.

I crossed the finish line not long after the sun set, just shy of 14 hours after I started. I immediately descended into tears.

The infinite game

Unsurprisingly, having a strong sense of 'why' has application far beyond powering you round a triathlon course. On stage in San Francisco in January 2020, I was interviewing the man who propelled the 'why' into modern business parlance: Simon Sinek. I was keen to know if he thought leaders' mindsets had shifted since his record-breaking TED talk a decade earlier. Simon was quick to point out that we're still trying to motivate people with 'what'. Taking aim at KPIs, he said, 'It is much easier to simply keep giving people arbitrary goals and arbitrary dates with arbitrary numbers and bonus them when they hit those goals and just keep repeating and repeating and repeating – except that it sucks the life out of us.'

I watched the 7000-strong crowd nodding furiously.

Intrinsic motivation is routinely proven to be more powerful than an extrinsic reward, particularly when it comes to unleashing creativity and talent. In the why-how-what of a leadership mindset, the former is the only component of that three-part equation to activate the limbic part of our brains, the part that drives motivation and human behaviour, steels our focus, taps into extra-kilometre energy reserves and allows us to achieve extraordinary things.

Our continued focus on 'what' sees us dealing with overloaded inboxes daily, battling ourselves for heightened productivity week-on-week and prioritising the urgent over the important every quarter. Simon argues this approach destroys the culture of a company and annihilates trust and cooperation. He argues: 'Leading with "what" might be easier, but it's only a finite strategy.' His challenge to leaders is to start playing an infinite game. There are no winners or losers in an infinite game; the objective is to keep the game itself in play. But in business, as in life, too many leaders talk of *smashing* out a project, *killing* it in the boardroom or *destroying* the competition. Finite players are ruled by 'what' and will run out of resources, trust and cooperation quickly, whereas the game of the infinite leader is to keep moving closer to the why.

In the hundreds of interviews I've done with leaders, pioneers and record-holders to unpack their success, whenever I ask them 'how' they did it, they inevitably tell me 'why' they did it. The passion derived from being in pursuit of purpose is mission-critical, providing the resolve, the relentlessness, the resilience necessary to achieve major goals and impact.

What's *your* why?

If you can look out the window and articulate that right now, you already have a leadership mindset.

In my experience, few people have taken the time to define their true motivation, let alone to make a practice of regularly tapping into it. I don't say that to suggest it's easy (it's not!) but few things give us more bang for our buck than defining our why.

Next, we need to put our why to work. Do we have our why stuck somewhere we can see it? Have we embedded it into a daily self-talk ritual? When we introduce ourselves, do we clearly reference it? If you're answering yes to all of the above, in my experience you are a rarity. And yet it's the single greatest tool in our arsenal to enliven the best version of ourselves.

I've met people with universal whys and circumstantial ones, esoteric ones and ones that are deeply personal. Some call it their 'leadership philosophy' and others refer to it as a 'mantra'. But I've never come across an impactful person without one.

Connecting to why

We're in an age where authenticity and connection as leaders are paramount. Baby Boomers, Millennials, Gen Xs and Gen Zs alike prioritise a job with inspirational colleagues and culture. This trend sees us departing from command-and-control, hierarchical 'push' leadership cultures to more empowered 'pull' cultures.

To discover our purpose we need to live in a way that allows our purpose to find *us*. There seem to be two commonalities in how great leaders do this.

- **Deep introspection.** This involves getting off the grid to engage with material that will prompt challenging questions. You create space for meditation, journalling, disconnection from routine, demands and assumptions. Often, our purpose has left a trail of breadcrumbs through our lives: its essence lives in the things we most enjoy, the times we felt most ourselves, the moments we felt particularly engaged. If you haven't found it yet, create the space to go hunting for that trail.
- **Stand where lightning strikes.** Get far outside your comfort zones to seek out new experiences. Stand amid raging storms. Dare yourself to climb mountains. Volunteer, freelance, travel, interview and investigate . . . or sign up to a triathlon! If you feel you're living a life that is somehow not your own, try creating a collision course with purpose.

Deep introspection

New Zealand's All Blacks are something else. They are the most successful international men's rugby side of all time with a winning percentage of 77.41 per cent in 580 Tests (from 1903 to 2019). Equally impressive is the value attached to the All Blacks brand, which at last benchmarking in 2017 had soared past the US$200 million (NZ$282m) mark. The question that has perplexed many is 'how'? How has this team played a finite game with an infinite mindset? How do they not seem to have the boom-and-bust cycle we see in other teams and other companies?

The All Blacks draw on the spiritual teachings of their ancestors, their country's history, and the traditions of the Maori culture native to New Zealand. The sense of direction is needed to create belief and personal meaning in each player. Deep introspection is something that is not only encouraged in the players but mandated. When All Blacks legend Richie McCaw got his first All Blacks shirt, he spent time with his head buried in the jersey.

All Blacks players understanding their own why is part of a far greater narrative. Players are instilled with a respect for those who wore their jersey before them, and for those who will inherit the jersey after them. Richie wanted to take stock of that before he put the jersey on. He understood he was passing a baton of purpose from his ancestors to future generations. The jersey became an object(ive) representing pride, legacy and respect. Winning is the by-product. By tapping into each team member's 'why' and connecting it to a shared purpose, the All Blacks powerfully engage with each individual's intrinsic, rather than extrinsic, motivations. Without sticking your head in your jersey, without engaging in deep introspection, you miss the opportunity to widen your perspective.

Stand where the lightning strikes

There's no-one I admire more, or who I believe better embodies living authentically on purpose than Jane Tewson CBE. Jane is one of the most loving and remarkably impressive people you'll meet. She'd also go beet-red to hear me say that because she's one of the humblest.

Jane grew up in south-east England. She was profoundly shaped by her passionate activist parents: her dad was a pacifist in the World War II and her mum was a local doctor, motivated into medicine by her own mother, who was one of the first female doctors in London. Jane used to love going out on patient visits with her. She tells me in an interview: 'I would sit on the iron lung of one of her patients in the next village or ride horses with her so she could deliver morphine to patients dying with cancer . . . I loved the way she cared for people. It was always on an equal basis. Our house was always open to everyone.'

At school, Jane had an enormous appetite for learning, however she butted heads with her schoolteachers, having struggled with dyslexia all her life. She left Lord Williams's Grammar School without qualification and arrived in London around 1980, throwing herself into work as a secretary at a big London charity for children with intellectual disabilities. Thus occurred the first lightning strike; Jane discovered that the charity spent too much of the money raised on itself and no-one seemed to have anything to do with children with intellectual disabilities. Frustrated and fierce, she set out to create a new way of doing charity. Jane sought backing from a wealthy corporate. She chose the Saatchi Brothers and sat in reception at their office for two days until they finally agreed to see her. This was a bold move for a shy introvert who says she was 'scared shitless' but steeled by the purpose of helping others. She swore that 100 per cent of the money raised on behalf of any group would go to that group while the charity's costs were met by sponsors from the business world. Jane – 'not knowing what I didn't know' – founded Charity Projects in London in 1981, aged twenty-three.

Jane's life's work is a result of standing where the lightning strikes. Leading at the edge is a choice between death by BAU (business as usual) and the danger of doing something that really matters. While working in a refugee camp in Sudan in 1985, Jane was pronounced clinically dead after contracting cerebral malaria. She can vividly recall the sensation of looking down on her own body and then returning to it and surviving against the odds – there were no drugs left in the camp.

Think of the true leaders in your life. How many of them have looked into the face of their own mortality? To be clear, I'm not suggesting you put yourself in harm's way, rather that our 'why' exists outside our comfort zone. Western society has made living so comfortable, so convenient, that leadership is wrapped up in status so often signified by material comforts. When we lack the fulfilment of a why, we are hungry consumers of everything else. Jane has spent her life at the leading edge. 'I was just on fire' with passion, she says.

In response to the African famine, Jane founded Comic Relief with Richard Curtis, the organisation that kickstarted Red Nose Day in 1988. Initially a night where comedians donated their time to raise famine relief funds, the concept became an iconic global charitable drive. It raised £15 million in its first year alone and has raised more than a billion dollars to date. None of this would have happened if Jane had not put herself in the way of her why.

Today, Jane's Australian foundation, Igniting Change, has a mantra: 'Meet the people, feel the issue'. I've visited prisons and community groups, women's refuges and legal centres with Jane over the years and every time I've watched CEOs, politicians and people with no history of volunteerism or activism take up arms upon hearing her message. Jane says it's all down to three things: knowing your purpose, asking the right questions and listening with an intent to really hear the answers. Whether that's with people who have an issue you're trying to help solve or people who may be able to help you solve an issue for others, when you tap into purpose, you tap into a power source . . . and suddenly everything becomes clearer and brighter.

Who are you lighting up with your why?

Hold 'why' tightly and 'how' lightly

Mandela put it brilliantly when he said, 'Vision without action is just a dream, action without vision just passes the time, and vision with action can change the world.' Finding your 'why' and thinking your work is done is like thinking you've completed an Ironman once you've been given your race number.

The need to hold 'how' lightly reflects the dynamic nature of our world and the adaptive mindset required to lead. When I graduated from high school, I was told I would have ten jobs over my lifetime, many of which hadn't been invented yet. For kids graduating in 2021, we're talking to them about eighteen careers: not jobs, fundamentally different *careers*. To lead at the infinite edge, we must hold an intuitive grip on our 'how', flexibly tied to the anchor of our 'why', along the flowing reality of our 'what'. Oh, and keep your eyes on the horizon!

For me, 'how' means guiding principles. Some may use the term 'values' – whatever language you prefer. The important thing is we create a *meaningful* how. A meaningful how is proven by action and means you can check in with yourself at the end of a day and ask, 'Did I truthfully live according to my values today?'

Benjamin Franklin and enacting values

Benjamin Franklin was born in 1706. His parents were not rich; they had just enough money to send him to school for a couple of years and by the age of ten, he had left and become a print shop apprentice, sorting letters, mixing ink and tinkering with printing presses. From that humble background, Benjamin became a towering figure in the American Revolution. What we under-appreciate in this remarkable ascent is the effort Benjamin invested in his 'how': how he showed up, how he led, how he engaged with and for the people who loved him most.

Early in Benjamin's life, he took to carrying around a card that had a simple table with seven columns and thirteen rows on it.

Each column represented a day of the week and each row represented one of thirteen virtues that he wanted to work on. At the top, there was always one virtue Benjamin wanted to focus on overall. During the day, he looked at these virtues to keep them fresh in his mind. Each night, he'd ask himself if he'd practised the virtues during the day and mark the box if he had done so. His aim was to fill in as many boxes as possible; every week, he started anew with a fresh chart.

Through this disciplined process of enacting and reflecting, Benjamin was able to deduce some larger patterns around what he was most successful in upholding and eventually he found himself practising the virtues unconsciously. This is the practice Benjamin attributed as a common part of the success that he found in almost every facet of life.

Walking the talk; talking the walk

These days many leaders wouldn't dream of running an organisation without values, nor would most of us be keen on joining one. We care deeply about values in a collective context, and yet we often overlook the power of identifying, defining and embodying values within our personal lives.

How can you articulate your purpose and values in such way that they become embedded in your days? Can you make the language feel like your own? Can you choose words that stick in your mind and feel almost dangerous in their power and possibility?

Write down your purpose

What is the change you want to achieve before you die? What is the thing that gets you out of bed when you feel awful or gets you back up when you've been shot down? I think of it as, 'What is the one thing I can't not do?'

Create a set of values you will live by

Make them real. Don't just write 'integrity'. Explain what each means to you and in a way where you can check in with yourself every day and determine if you lived them. These are the codes that will guide your choices especially when things get tough. Place them where you can see them every day. Make sure they energise you, light you up and maybe even make you smile.

Let's make them realistic. I love a lot of what Franklin's virtue practice embodies: intentional practice, active self-reflection, a clear focus on the standards you want to hold yourself to account for. But let's be real about how little uptake there's going to be on developing a thirteen-strong virtue chart you carry around in your pocket today! We need a more practical way forward.

A lot of psychological research suggests we can remember things in threes, while many of our business models (as well as long-standing tools like a compass) operate in fours. I borrow from Franklin in making my starting point self-reflection. What virtues/values/principles will best serve me (and those who I seek to serve)? These need to be deeply personal and become the 'how' to our 'why'.

Every morning since that Ironman race, especially when I'm thinking, *Gee, it'd be nice to just curl up on the couch today*, my mind automatically goes to the girls running alongside me on the marathon and I hear the words, 'Remember who's watching.' I think about how I want to inspire young people every day to be the change they want to see in the world. I can only do that if I'm modelling being the change I want to see myself.

In 2018 I was given the opportunity to interview President Barack Obama on stage during his only engagement on his visit to Australia at that time. In front of 300 leaders at an invitation-only dinner, I had the privilege of delving into everything from innovation and leadership to decision-making under pressure and the importance of diversity and inclusion.

Acknowledging the platform and influence of the leaders in the room, I closed the interview by asking the president what his message would be to the leaders who sat surrounding us. He reflected on commentary he was hearing more frequently from leaders about the state of the world, warning every one of us to safeguard against complacency and asking, 'When did progress become a foregone conclusion?' He joked how Americans seem to be buying pockets of New Zealand real estate and hatching escape plans, jibing at former New Zealand Prime Minister John Key, who was in the front row, that it wasn't because of his economic management! He implored the audience to plant under their own feet, to invest in their communities, their companies and their countries. Capacity building and civic engagement were strong themes of our entire conversation. As President Obama finished, his tone turned serious. 'Progress starts with everyone in this room.'

Know your why, live your how.

A question from the leading edge:

What will be the legacy that you leave behind?

2

Frame
your choices

'There is a choice you have to make in everything you do. So, keep in
mind that in the end, the choices you make, make you.'

John Wooden

When I think about choices, I think about my grandmother
Dorothy. Few people have role-modelled choices for me the way
my grandmother has. She is the sweetest, most selfless woman you'll
ever meet. She's ninety at the time of writing and has been married
to my grandfather for seventy years. My grandma was a child of the
depression, a nurse during the polio pandemic, raised four kids and
co-wrote an international bestseller with my grandpa about (wait
for it) . . . sex. She's a baller. She has this unique ability to make
anyone she's talking to feel like they're the most important person in
the world. And she is a paragon of virtue – except when it comes to
poker. If you play poker with my grandma, I can promise you, you
will lose. Because nobody can bluff quite like she can.

One instance has always stuck with me. My grandparents live
four-and-a-half hours' drive south of Perth in a tiny country town
called Denmark. The population of kangaroos well outnumbers the
people, even during school holidays when kids like us would swarm
the place. One particular day, my two brothers, our cousin Patrick
and I had managed to talk Grandma into playing a game of poker

with us. We'd been going a few rounds and though the chips in front of Grandma had started to accumulate into a sizeable pile, we were still in it. Grandma probably decided she had to go tend to the garden and started to escalate the next hand; she kept bidding up and up and up until all of us folded. My younger brother spat the dummy and stormed off. Curious, I begged her to show me her hand. She had nothing more than a paltry pair of twos! She'd cleaned four of us out with *twos*. I felt a sense of injustice rising in me: I'd had a pair of queens! Grandma laughed at me, no doubt at the look of total indignation spread across my face, and then she stopped. 'Any hand you're dealt can be a winner, kid; it all depends on how you play it.'

Fifteen years later, in 2017, my grandma's feat was replicated by Josh Blumstein in the World Series Poker championship. The 25-year-old pocketed $8.15 million with *his* paltry pair of twos.

I've reflected on the lesson that lay beneath that poker game many times over. My grandma taught me two things that day:

1. There's always a way to get to the outcome we want; sometimes, it just requires a little more finessing.
2. We cannot afford to be complacent about the cards we think we're holding. As the saying goes, 'Hard work beats talent when talent doesn't work hard.'

My grandma's point: we *always* have a choice, but the art is in how we frame that choice, firstly to ourselves and then to others. Framing can help make the impossible seem entirely achievable.

Spoilt for choice – or spoilt by choice?

As Leslie Ye writes, ' Choice is the purest expression of free will – the freedom to choose allows us to shape our lives exactly how we wish.' As an idea this feels supremely liberating. But to take control of our choices we have to understand the influences that shape them for us, like the choices we inherently make by virtue of our unconscious biases. Or the choices shaped reflexively by the narrative we've been told growing up. Not to mention the 'choices' we are served on the internet. Choice is also difficult because it represents sacrifice: choosing one thing necessarily means not pursuing its alternatives, at least not right now. In taking one job, you choose not to take another. In devoting time to learning a new skill or concept, that time cannot also be used to watch Netflix or hit the gym. In our unprecedented age of options, unlimited choice can be overwhelming and, ultimately, limiting.

Comedian Aziz Ansari teamed up with sociologist and author Eric Klinenberg to write *Modern Romance*, an in-depth investigation into one aspect of modern choice: the reality of what it's like to date and look for love in the digital era. Thirty years ago, it took Ansari's parents less than thirty minutes to decide their marriage. Fast-forward to today, and Ansari admits it takes him more than thirty minutes to figure out what to order from UberEats! As he says in the book, 'The world is available to us, but that may be the problem.'

Like no other generation, the information we need to help guide our choices is right at our fingertips. The average Gen Z or Millennial will search at least ten sites before making a purchasing decision, but there's no data to suggest this behaviour actually leads to a higher level of purchase satisfaction. As Ansari explains, that's one of the challenges of the age of the internet, or the age of options: it doesn't simply help us to locate the best thing, it plants the idea that there is a *better* best thing to be found if we just search another moment more.

To make matters more complex, not making a choice is still making a choice. In Ansari's case, this means resorting to a peanut butter and banana sandwich in lieu of being able to make a take-out selection. The overabundance of choices can lead to stress, distraction, even paralysis. If you don't make choices for yourself, others will fill the void for you. Even the time spent searching can render us devoid of progressing a decision.

One of the cards on my wall reads, 'You do have time. You just need to make a decision.' Wise words from Seth Godin. Bringing ourselves to the leading edge requires the discipline to frame our choices as part of our bigger 'why'. How can we tighten our frame of reference so that the pursuit of a 'better best' doesn't leave us sitting on the sidelines of our own lives? When we're scrolling through countless social media sites, can we put tighter perimeters over which platforms, what content and for what purpose? Framing our choices is essentially zooming in on the why and how we mapped out in Chapter 1. Make a choice. Pause, evaluate, iterate. But don't choose not to choose and let others author your life for you.

Tuning into your choice algorithms

One of the most pioneering thinkers I've ever interviewed is Karen Palmer. I first met her when she stepped off a 24-hour flight to Australia, and her smile and enthusiasm could have powered a small city. Her field of endeavour is virtual reality: multidisciplinary immersive filmmaking. A real-life parkour champion, Karen realised the power of reframing our choices. She credits the parkour discipline of taking obstacles and turning them into springboards, supports and possibilities as a way of reassessing how our own choices shape our world. Inspired, Karen created *RIOT*, an emotionally responsive, live-action film that uses artificial intelligence and machine learning to navigate participants through a dangerous riot. In this neuro-game, participants are challenged to understand how their choices affect their lived experiences.

When you put on the *RIOT* headset, you are transported into a post-apocalyptic scene. There is smouldering debris and wreckage where buildings once stood. Smoke and haze are everywhere. Shots and loud crashes can be heard. Suddenly, there's a knock at your door. When you open it, a policeman dressed in full riot gear fills the doorframe. 'Get out of here,' he barks at you. He is physically dominant and intimidating. How you respond to this affects what happens next: if you stay calm, he backs off, but if you respond with fear or anger, that changes the film's ending. But you don't *consciously* respond to determine the outcome, at least not on your first go.

RIOT isn't like an old-school 'choose your own adventure' book where a series of options appear on the screen, and you select the most appealing. The film is watching you . . . and in the instant where the stimulus is introduced, it's watching your pupil, tracking your heart rate and bending the film arcs for you, based on your instinctive responses. The film is bringing consciousness to the default posturing each of us takes in our daily decisions: do we tend to be assertive, submissive, angry, fearful? Our path in *RIOT* will be determined by these micro responses. Karen points out, 'This is exactly what happens every day. By bringing greater awareness to our subconscious, I hope to provide people with the opportunity to more intentionally shape their future.'

Choosing wisely is a skill; like any skill, it can be improved. Karen believes bringing consciousness to our choices is the first step. Her work reminds me that the way we see the world is an imagined reality: we're all perceiving it differently. The choices we make as a result of our subjectivity are what create concrete outcomes. The second step is realising that we ourselves define our barriers and our limitations. Limiting our choices keeps our world feeling smaller, safer and more predictable – but that may prove the ultimate sacrifice to our ability to lead change.

The freedom of choice is the wonderful, messy, unwritten script underpinning our own autobiographical narratives. People will read their own stories and possibilities into our actions based on what we show the world. Our most important choice is to frame it or be framed by it.

The see-it-to-be-it challenge
We each construct a narrative of our choices through our own frame of reference. But what happens when our 'frame of reference' is based on fractured information or a narrative that continually tells you you're only built to play a supporting role?

When Geena Davis launched the Geena Davis Institute on

Gender in the Media in 2004, the goal was to research and advocate for equal representation. The institute's tagline? 'If she can see it, she can be it.' For Geena, an Academy Award–winning actor, the issue of gender bias hit home when she sat down with her two-year-old daughter to watch her first preschool television show. 'Surely, in the twenty-first century,' Geena told me, 'kids should be seeing that boys and girls share the sandbox equally.' Instead, the narrative lens appeared to be that girls and women have far less value than boys and men. The majority of characters were boys and they did most of the talking. When the celebrated actor shared what she saw as a mother with producers in the entertainment industry, she was met with denial. They said gender inequality had been fixed. Geena raised her eyebrows at me. 'I decided I needed the numbers.'

When the institute's first reports examined gender portrayals in G-rated movies in 2008, no other comprehensive study existed for kids' films. The institute analysed the numbers and nature of portrayals of male and female characters in 101 of the top-grossing G-rated movies from 1990 to 2005. The key findings showed that only 28 per cent of the speaking characters (both real and animated) were female, only 17 per cent of characters in crowd scenes were female and more than 83 per cent of the sample films' narrators were male. Gender was not the only aspect of imbalance in these films, either; the institute also evaluated the apparent ethnicity of characters. A full 85.5 per cent of the characters in G-rated movies were white; 4.8 per cent of characters were black, leaving 9.7 per cent as 'other' ethnicities. In short, the movies were deeply unrepresentative of the society they were being made for.

These imbalances are unsurprising. For as long as Hollywood and television have existed, the directors' chairs and company board rooms have been dominated by white men. We all have blindspots in situations where we are in the majority: Geena's data illuminates how imbalance compounds when autopilot decision-making goes unchecked. And how lack of choice works as an invisible reinforcer of dominant power structures.

When I interviewed Geena in 2019, she was interrogating the professions underrepresented groups are portrayed in, expanding beyond gender to look at age, sexual orientation, disability, body size and gendered values. The institute has shone a light on unhelpful stereotyping: characters of colour are more likely to be shown as violent (16.1 per cent versus 13.1 per cent for white character), and characters with disabilities are four times more likely to be depicted as worse than average looking compared to characters without disabilities (46.4 per cent compared with 11.7 per cent). Its most recent report explores masculinity with the provocative title 'If he can see it, will he be it?'

What I love about Geena's leadership is that she has broadened choices: for herself as an actor, for the industry as storytellers and for her daughter as a viewer. Talk about a reframe! And her rallying cry takes on ever-greater significance as we hurtle into the knowledge economy and the digital age. As aggregated and automated data becomes our currency, drives our conversations and permeates all aspects of commerce and community, we need to become hyper-alert to where autopilot choices might lead us. We need to check our choices for inbuilt biases: is the content we're consuming helpful or harmful? Is the environment we are choosing to operate in cutting us off from vital information? What are we not seeing? Whose voices are we not hearing? How can we actively seek out more positive frames of reference?

Let's look at some tools to help with intentionality in framing choices.

Reframing your choice of self

One of my favourite examples of tapping into our best selves came up when I interviewed Australian Football League premiership-winning coach Paul Roos. Paul is a legend on and off the field, having been a great player for Fitzroy in the 1980s before taking on his renowned role as a coach, in which he develops young talent, builds culture and was one of the first to introduce mindfulness practices to the hyper-masculine world of the AFL. In our conversation, Paul took me through a simple and powerful exercise that allows us to reframe how we actively choose to show up.

1. Pull out a business card (or for the digitally inclined, mock up a new LinkedIn profile) and write 'Chief Role Model' on it.

2. Underneath the role, where a traditional card might have the company name, write the context you want to define yourself in, or the people you see yourself playing that role for: your family, your company, your community group, or your kids, siblings, mentees.

3. Then think about what the behaviours are that exemplify playing this role, in that context, for you. For example, here's mine:

Holly Ransom
Chief Role Model
Master questioner, committed to helping
emerging leaders find their answers.
I never walk past it | I feel compassion first |
I start before I'm ready

This has been a game-changing exercise for me when it comes to keeping my choices in more conscious check. Would it help to write your version down and stick it somewhere you can see it? Can you start making choices today according to this simple frame?

The choices each of us make define the culture we live by. 'It's what's rewarded, what's challenged and it's what becomes a habit,' says Paul. His exercise invites us to ask questions around how we're framing options to ourselves, and be more aware of how we're actually measuring up against the important roles we play in our lives. We may find we need to take subtle interventions to shift our thinking.

Once we identify choice habits that no longer serve us we need to stop being a slave to them. There are two innate drivers we're kicking into gear here: our desire to be the best version of ourselves; and the desire to be consistent with the version of ourselves we announce to the world. When we know that our behavioural decisions, big and small, are true to our identities and helping us fulfil our potential, we can take a deep breath and trust the intuition of our choices.

Hell yeah or fuck no

One of the mental challenges I always work really hard to overcome is the 'if-not-now-never' frame. This is the mindset that sees us assume opportunities aren't plentiful, won't come around again or must be taken up with a 'yes' immediately as there may be nothing else. This gets the better of me often.

Seven-times world champion surfer, Surfing Australia chair, and motivational speaker Layne Beachley AO is well ahead of me on avoiding the pitfalls of the 'if-not-now-never' journey. Layne is one of the most powerful influences in my life and has taught me to have the courage to walk away from opportunities that don't light me up, no matter how much I wish them to.

From her home in Manly, watching the waves roll in from the Pacific Ocean, Layne tells me, 'I struggled with saying "no" for many years, even into retirement.' As an adoptee, Layne admits to a massive fear of rejection, which starts with not wanting to let anybody down. Layne tells me that upon retiring from championship surfing, she filled up her life with worthwhile commitments seeking to experience the feeling of being 'lit up' again. What she realised was that actually, she had to let things go, one by one, respecting the need to fulfil commitments but more so, respecting a commitment to herself. 'I needed to give myself permission, mentally and emotionally, to say no. And that's been a ten-year evolution.'

One of the many things I have learnt from Layne is that when an opportunity is presented to you, you look at it, you *feel* it and you ask yourself, 'Does this opportunity light me up?' When I tell Layne about a new endeavour, she often asks me, 'Does it excite you? Does it fill you with a sense of curiosity? If it does, hell yeah!' On the flip side, Layne cautions, 'If it's a shoulda, woulda, coulda, then it's a "fuck no".' Layne's advice for letting people down is simple. 'I have to start by knowing that if I'm saying "yes" to somebody else, I might be saying "no" to myself.'

As a result of our conversations, I've developed a strategy called 'filter criteria' for thinking through choices. I work out what the most important factors are and then hold every opportunity up against those criteria in the light of day to see which one delivers.

There are three key components to this strategy: when you set your criteria; stress-testing your criteria; and reviewing and updating them.

Set your criteria before you go opportunity hunting

Or at least do the criteria setting before you allow yourself to engage deeply in investigating an opportunity. For example, if someone calls you about a potential job, you set the criteria before you take the meeting rather than shaping the criteria afterwards. We are really good at post-rationalising (as Layne puts it 'telling ourselves rational lies') to make things fit, so to avoid that trap we need to check in with ourselves before we check into opportunities.

Have a conversation with your imaginary lovers and your haters

This means you can work through the worst-case and best-case scenarios going on in your head. These can be real people or faux adversaries and fans – whatever serves your purposes. A good way to do the latter is to do a take on a 'pro' and 'con' list and write down either side. Stress-test your criteria choices on your imaginary biggest supporter and then on your devil's advocate to hear what they've got to say. You may even want to write down the plausible points from each side so you can weigh them up in the clear light of day.

Change your filter criteria regularly

Just like you wouldn't want to drink coffee made with a filter that was months old, you don't want to be saying 'yes' to opportunities that are the result of older filter criteria. Your criteria will and should change as your experience, life circumstances, priorities, and capabilities change and so, too, should your decision-making.

Considering these filter criteria should surface the deeper questions below the choice itself. Are you answering the choice according to fear? Curiosity? Ego? What is holding you back in saying 'no'? What are you obligated to in saying 'yes'? Are you being true to the role model you know you could be?

For the record, I have still never beaten Grandma at poker, but I *have* learnt to back myself and play my own game with the hand I've been dealt.

> ### A question from the leading edge:
> When you next make a choice, consider:
> what are you really choosing?

3

Own your narrative

'There's a power in allowing yourself to be known and heard, in owning your unique story, in using your authentic voice.'

Michelle Obama

When I was twenty, I participated in a week-long global peace-building conference in Osaka, Japan, an incredible opportunity that culminated in presenting a Peace Charter to none other than the Dalai Lama. I was awestruck by the magnitude of the adventure as a kid from Perth, the world's most isolated capital city, who until the age of eighteen hadn't managed to travel beyond Bali (yes, I was a Western Australian cliché). When I arrived and found myself surrounded by people from dozens of other cultures and nations, there was one thought looming large in my mind: what on earth could *I* bring to the table to contribute to the meaning of peace? I felt like a deadset imposter.

After a week's worth of learning and activities, eight of the hundred of us were fortunate enough to be selected to draft the charter. I was incredulous. And more than a little daunted by the task at hand. We had a full day to do it, which quickly morphed into night . . . and then back into morning as we consumed copious amounts of average-quality hotel coffee and debated synonyms and phrases until 5.30 am. It was my ultimate inner-social-warrior-nerd's all-nighter and showed me the extraordinary power of diversity, the incredible challenge of diplomatic work and the heightened sense of accomplishment we get when building something with a truly global group of people. I had never been engaged in such passionate debate where the intricacies of language mattered almost as much as the subject itself. But we managed to find our common values and weave them into the text, and that alone made it feel like we had earned something of a right to chart a pathway to peace.

Later that morning the Dalai Lama entered the hall where we were all assembled and from the moment he did, you could feel his energy. He just seemed to unleash a positive vibration, as though he were radiating joy. Among his many words of wise optimism, he made a comment that I completely failed to understand at the time, but that struck me as being important enough to scribble down in my spiral-bound notebook: 'Until we're at peace with ourselves, we will never be at peace with others.'

His Holiness talked with animation about self-acceptance being step one on the journey to building a brighter, more peaceful future. He explained that we would never be able to constructively deal with conflict and work for peace if we hadn't first been able to undertake that process for ourselves. That if we could come from a place of love and self-acceptance, we didn't 'need' anything from our encounters with others: we didn't need to win, one-up or prove anything. He spoke about constructive disengagement – things like violence and hatred – so often stemming from unresolved personal turmoil. In contrast, inner peace removes the need to continually apologise or to doubt ourselves, which often robs the world of our fullest and most creative expression.

Much of this went way over my head. But I understood enough to come back to Australia with a different focus. I'd spent so many years doing so much outwardly that I'd neglected the internal work required to sit comfortably in my own skin, story, dreams and aspirations. I needed to make peace with my own narrative.

Jim Loehr, author of *The Power of Story*, says that the stories we tell ourselves are the only reality we will ever know in this life. 'And since it's our destiny to follow our stories,' he explains, 'it's imperative that we do everything in our power to get our stories right.' Given we are dynamic beings, this work is never done; we are continually evolving our story as we engage in new experiences and create new meaning. But, as Loehr argues, the most important story we tell is the one we tell ourselves: 'If you aren't the author of your own story, you're the victim of it.' Our purpose, the 'why' we talked about in Chapter 1, is at the heart of our story, closely followed by the plot line and suspense of our choices, as we discussed in Chapter 2. There's no story without a lead protagonist. That's you. Please prepare to take centre stage.

The storied leader

Many times I've challenged, defended or wished away the need to tell people more about myself. I'm a naturally private person and since being thrust into the spotlight at a young age when chairing the G20, I've always struggled to know how much of myself to give and how much to hold tight. It's a dance I know many leaders struggle with.

Ultimately, the parts of ourselves necessary to articulate our why must be shared. I never wanted to admit that my insatiable curiosity grew from an upbringing where answers weren't forthcoming. Or that my ability to connect with diverse and disempowered points of view was likely honed by the ostracisation I experienced when I first fell in love with a woman and came out. For a long time, I've resented the demand to have a public profile, maintain a social media presence, play out my personal narrative again and again . . . until I realised that leaders who have traversed the uncomfortable terri-tory of their internal selves and shared the map to self-acceptance are leaders who can be trusted to comprehend all aspects of the human condition as they shape a better world. To *own* one's narrative is to take pride in all of one's story. But to *lend* one's narrative when leading change is to take pride in all of humanity.

It wasn't until I came across Marshall Ganz, my academic mentor at Harvard, that I understood the connection between leading change and imparting truth. In his prolific work, Ganz writes about how powerful leaders, specifically powerful public leaders, tell new stories: 'a story of self, a story of us and a story of now'. He makes the case that we construct our identity through stories, and these stories are arranged around 'choice points' or story 'beats', times when we faced a challenge, chose a new path, experienced an outcome or learnt something pivotal. Reading Ganz's work, it struck me that our impact as leaders today lies in people choosing to follow us rather than in command-and-control structures where people are obligated to toe the line. Sharing our personal stories is absolutely critical to authenticity and vulnerability in leadership. Ganz describes the importance of personal stories as follows:

> Some believe their personal stories don't matter, that others won't care, or that we shouldn't talk about ourselves so much. But if we do public work, we have a responsibility to give a public account of ourselves . . . If we don't author our story, others will – and may tell our story in ways that we may not like. Not because they are malevolent, but because others try to make sense of who we are by drawing on their experience of people whom they consider to be like us.

The lines between our public self and our private selves are as blurred as work and home lives. Each of us must navigate boundary setting, drawing the line between what we share and what we don't in a way that aligns with our values and purpose. But I argue that our narrative is necessarily public; we will struggle to get engagement with others if we cannot share of ourselves. As Ganz puts it so well, 'If we haven't talked about our stories of pain very much, it can take a while to learn how to manage it. But if others are to understand who we are, and we omit the pain, our account will lack authenticity, raising questions about the rest of the story.'

What is the story you share of yourself, that enables people to trust you with theirs?

The science of story

Stories are fundamental to connection, trust and ultimately relationship-building. This makes sense intuitively and there is also some compelling neuroscience to back it up.

Stories provoke our emotions. In the 2014 *Harvard Business Review* article 'Why your brain loves good storytelling', neuro-economist Paul Zak revealed the powerful effect the hormone oxytocin has on the brain when we tell stories. Oxytocin is also often referred to as the 'trust hormone' because our bodies release it when we are with people we love and trust, when we hug or even when we shake hands in a business meeting. Crucially for us, it's released when we listen to stories. Oxytocin releases signals to the brain that everything is okay. In other words, it helps us to feel a higher level of trust than we did before hearing the story.

When we tell stories, all the different parts of our brain are stimulated and start to work together, combining words, logic, emotions and sensory images. In communicating our experience, we give it meaning, and we allow this meaning to become shared and to invite ownership and significance outside of us.

Believe

Eddie Ndopu is one of the United Nations Secretary-General's Global Advocates for the Sustainable Development Goals and the former head of Amnesty International's Youth Programme for Africa. He's a World Economic Forum Change-maker and has been named in countless lists of top thinkers, influencers and leaders for his age and region of the world. But Eddie self-describes differently. He prefers 'black, queer, disabled and brilliant . . . I embody all of the identities that position me at a disadvantage in society. But I am turning that on its head.'

Eddie's accomplishments are objectively phenomenal, but his story is all the more remarkable in context. Eddie was born in Namibia in 1990 to a single mother who fled apartheid in South Africa. At age two, he was diagnosed with spinal muscular atrophy and wasn't expected to live past five. Now wheelchair-bound, Eddie is the first black disabled person to graduate from Oxford, having completed a master's degree in public policy.

When Eddie is asked about his achievements, he speaks to the power of narrative, recognition and aspiration, and the way in which owning our personal narrative can be like creating a statement of intent: an aspiration story about all that we believe we are and can become. Eddie recognises his life was powerfully transformed after being selected for the prestigious African Leadership Academy as a teenager where he says that, for the first time, he was given the opportunity to think more expansively about himself and become a bigger, greater version of who he was.

Now, he flips the script on people's expectations of him and uses his aspiration to power him forward. 'It's not just an adventure; it's a political statement. It is possible for a young, black, disabled, queer person to achieve something.' Every promise Eddie makes to himself helps to reframe the 'otherness' that being different can invite from peers. 'I am not just fighting for access to get into the building – I'm fighting for joy, intimacy, belonging, self-determination. I want to open up talk about the emotional and personal, so we can experience the totality of our humanity.'

Listening to Eddie, I feel swept away with the scale of his narrative. He's now intent on becoming the first wheelchair-user in space, and you know what? With the way Eddie owns his narrative and shares his story, I'd back him to make that come true. The key to authentic leadership is to unlock the door and let people in. Only then do you create space for people to believe in you.

Playing 'me'

When I first tried my hand at this whole 'owning your narrative' process, I turned to the world of acting. I was inspired by world-renowned acting coach Larry Moss. One of my mentors took me to audit Larry's work (a process used to describe watching a coach 'work-up' a scene with actors) and I've been going back every year since. Sitting in the studio watching Larry in action, I was glued to the master and his craft. He worked his actors into the centre of themselves through the complicated matrix of defences, habits, pretences and distractions. He stripped them back to their own unique essence.

One of the hardest parts of claiming our own story is our fear of letting other people down. We perform a version of ourselves that stands up to social constructs, that smiles and nods rather than speaking out when we have a different viewpoint, that pursues a degree or job because our parents or significant other thinks we should, that bends over backwards to put the needs of others first. But every time we let someone down in the name of owning our personal narrative, there will be another we lift up – someone who sees us more clearly as a person they can relate to.

In his book, *Intent to Live*, Larry talks about the process of self-discovery as empowering actors to access *all* that they can be. As he puts it, 'If you don't have yourself, you can't give anything to the world.' Larry's book introduced me to the work of Uta Hagen, an acting teacher of biblical proportions who profoundly shaped twentieth-century theatre. She taught Larry and you might know a few of her other students – they include Al Pacino, Matthew Broderick and Jack Lemmon. Hagen says every actor should ask themselves nine questions framed from the premise: 'If someone was to play you as a character, what would they need to know?'

I had a go at working through the nine questions and honestly, it was one of the most powerful pieces of self-work I've ever undertaken. To answer them requires introspection, honesty and vulnerability. It demands more than the accomplishments you list in a LinkedIn bio or the rehearsed response to 'tell me a bit about yourself' you might roll out in a job interview or on a first date. This exercise requires you to contemplate the moments, experiences, perspectives and situations that make you 'you'.

Now, this isn't an exercise you need to share with anyone. In truth, I never have – maybe because it's too raw, but also because it's not the point. The point is to understand our own story better. Going through this process changed the way I told my story because it helped me honour significant moments that have shaped me that I'd overlooked – for better and for worse. Things like a particularly brutal early heartbreak that shattered aspects of my self-confidence; being given responsibility to lead teams with people three times my age at fifteen years old and the ways that matured my people skills; and being bullied in the workplace making me passionate about creating better cultures and better leaders. It also revealed the parts of my story I was struggling to come to terms with, which illuminated things I needed to work on.

If you're brave enough, pick up the pen (or strike the keys) and create the pivotal scene that will enable someone else to play you. Cast whatever Hollywood celeb you might like as yourself and then imagine you have to hand them answers to the following questions. Imagine, if they were to play you, where you're at in your life, right now, what would they need to know to truly own your narrative?

1. **Who am I?** Who is your character? Identify all the details: name/age, physical traits, education, personal opinions, likes, dislikes, fears, ethics and beliefs.
2. **What time is it?** The year, the season, the day, the minute. What is the significance of this particular moment in time?
3. **Where am I?** Identify the country, the city/town, the neighbourhood, the building, the room or the specific area of the room.
4. **What surrounds me?** What is happening in the environment around you? Weather, landscape, people, animate/inanimate objects?

5. **What are the given circumstances?** Identify events in the past, present and future. What has happened, what is happening, what is going to happen?

6. **What are my relationships?** This is more than your relationship to other people. Think about your relationship to objects, characters and events – what are the most significant relationships in your life?

7. **What do I want?** What do you want immediately? What does the character want overall?

8. **What is in my way?** What are the obstacles to getting what you want?

9. **What do I do to get what I want?** What actions do you take (both physically and verbally)? What tactics?

Playing ourselves is the greatest role of our lives. This one-off exercise provides some distance and perspective to an otherwise intensely personal character study! It can offer new insight and potentially show up aspects of our narrative we've not been owning. In the words of Brene Brown, 'Owning our story and loving ourselves through the process is the bravest thing we will ever do.' What have we got to lose? If we speak from the heart, and lose someone's approval, then in validating ourselves, we've still won.

The ownership of story is in the telling

The power of story can be seen in its centrality to the oldest continuous culture on Earth: Aboriginal Australians. Aboriginal Australians have more than 65,000 years of rich history passed down through storytelling.

Mikaela Jade, a Cabrogal woman from the Darug nation, is a powerhouse. She's attended the United Nations Permanent Forum on Indigenous Issues, advocated for Indigenous digital rights with Tribal Link Foundation and founded Indigital, a social enterprise that uses twenty-first-century technology to share ancient knowledge.

Mikaela initially developed the Indigital app out of the frustration that came from a lack of rightful narrative ownership by
Indigenous communities. In an interview, she tells me: 'While I was
a park ranger it really annoyed me that we put metal signs in front
of our cultural heritage places and the stories were always told
from someone else's perspective, not necessarily from the people
who the site was significant for.' Mikaela channelled her sense
of injustice into revolutionising technology to translate cultural
knowledge within Indigenous communities and to showcase their
cultural heritage to visitors using incredible, life-size holograms.
Indigital returns the ownership of story to Elders across Australia,
filming them on country and providing the resource to students and
teachers to extend Indigenous narratives and break down barriers.
The social enterprise was developed in collaboration with Indigenous Elders, who are paid for their involvement with Indigital
Schools and Indigital Storytelling.

In the process, Mikaela's personal story became amplified.
Mikaela had discovered her Indigenous heritage at twenty-nine.
'My story about finding my heritage is fairly common among Indig-
enous Australians,' she shared with me.

'A lot of the Stolen Generation during the '50s and '60s hid
their cultural heritage. They hid their stories. But when you lose
your story or your language, a whole way of being, a whole cultural
universe is lost forever.' At the time of white settlement, 250 Aboriginal languages were spoken around Australia, with many dialects
within each language group. Today, only 120 are still spoken, and
many are at risk of dying out.

In many ways, Indigital is an against-the-odds story. But stories
are often more successful the more unlikely they are. A lesson,
perhaps, for the prominent venture capitalist who liked the idea
of Indigital but argued that there was a fundamental flaw in the
business model: as he informed Mikaela, 'Indigenous people just
don't use technology.' Quite the opposite: by combining new

technology with ancient practices, new world leaders like Mikaela are able to restore narratives to their true owners and amplify our shared humanity. It's something I'm in awe of.

I've kept my spiral notebook from my meeting with the Dalai Lama and I've come to appreciate that, just like most things in life, self-acceptance is a journey and not a destination. There are parts of my story that fit like a comfortable glove and there are parts I offer much more timidly. There are also parts that I'm still scared to sit with. But what never ceases to amaze me is the power that's unleashed every time we're brave and vulnerable enough to face and own our story. It might just be the greatest thing we can do to truly discover what we're capable of.

A question from the leading edge:

Who were you before the world told you who you ought to be?

4

Build your bounce

'The greatest glory in living lies not in never falling, but in rising every time we fall.'

Nelson Mandela

I was living my dream. I was literally at the end goal of so many post-it notes, screensaver mantras and conversations with mentors. I should have been bouncing off the walls with excitement: I'd been lucky enough to get a scholarship to pursue my dream of studying a master's degree of public policy at Harvard. Instead I felt like someone had taken a sledgehammer to my guts. I was nearly 20,000 kilometres away from the newfound love of my life, in an empty Boston flat with the sound of other people's laughter wafting through the window. Anyone who knew me through the first twenty-five years of my life will tell you that I'm a fairly headstrong and unemotional person. I would have described myself as resilient. After all, I had been back to complete a second Ironman – still in someone else's wetsuit and this time with horrific levels of chafing – I had jumped off a boat in the Antarctic ice-studded waters, I could watch *Marley and Me* without shedding a tear . . . I know: I was a monster. And then I fell madly in love and unlocked this whole emotional side of myself, only to move a couple of months later to the other side of the world.

Many people have been through much worse than heartache. No-one is a stranger to pain and stress unless they're best mates with denial. Research on the epidemiology of trauma calculates that most of us – more than 70 per cent of us – will experience one or more traumatic event during our lifetimes. What will the universal trauma of the COVID pandemic do for our global resilience? The idea that great good can come from great suffering is ancient. Richard G. Tedeschi wrote extensively of post-traumatic growth, capturing the idea that disruptive events shatter our sense of 'normal' and enable some people to bounce back beyond their previous status quo. But when we are in the midst of trauma, it is hard to see the ocean for the tears.

As my flight arrived into New York, the city that never sleeps, neither could I. I had cried almost the entire way from Melbourne. I knew how incredibly fortunate I was to be studying at such a prestigious institution. But only when I acknowledged my pit-of-despair, ice-cream-eating, dream-doubting truth, could I start to reframe it and put strategies in place to help myself cope more effectively and build my resilience.

One of the things I find fascinating about stress is that often the worst part is being stressed about being stressed. Lying in bed unable to sleep should not in and of itself be stressful. If we are lucky, we're lying there warm, fed and comfortable, albeit staring at the ceiling. But the compounded nature of stress doubles us over on our worries. In her TED talk, Stanford psychologist Kelly McGonigal suggests it's our relationship to stress that is problematic as opposed to stress itself. Stress, she argues, gives us the opportunity to build strength. In one study she references details on how University of Wisconsin researchers tracked 30,000 American adults for eight years. They found that subjects with a lot of stress had a 43 per cent increased risk of dying – but only if they believed stress was harmful.

McGonigal also talks about a study from the University of Buffalo that found that every major stressful life experience increased an adult's risk of death by 30 per cent *unless* they also spent a significant amount of time helping loved ones and neighbours. Then, there was a 0 per cent increase in risk of death. 'When you choose to connect with others under stress, you can create resilience,' McGonigal said.

This is good news, because it means we can have far more influence over how we respond to events than over the events themselves. In life and in leadership, we can guarantee we're going to face multiple kinds of stressors. I believe resilience lies not in the first layer of stress – being time poor, resource poor or dealing with a difficult circumstance – but in how we decide to own that narrative and frame our choices. Feeling the victim and fuelling resentment can (literally) kill us. But aligning stress to effort can bring purpose to life. I've come to think of resilience as the springboard for bounce. It is a flexible reaction that enables us to move with the ups and downs of life, but always aim higher – and the stronger our springboard, or our sense of resilience, the greater the heights we'll be able to reach. The strength and flex of our springboard (resilience) is determined by the stories we tell ourselves.

The man in the iron halo

One of the best examples I've come across of someone building their bounce based on the story they tell themselves is British elite athlete Tim Don – also affectionately known as 'The Man in the Iron Halo'. In May 2017, Tim set a world record by completing an entire Ironman in seven hours, forty minutes, twenty-three seconds: something I can barely comprehend, given I would have been thrilled to have completed just my bike leg in that time! Over the years I've followed Tim's story with great curiosity. He was coming into the World Championships in Kona, Hawaii, off a real purple patch and pundits were speculating that another world record was on the cards. Then disaster struck.

On a training ride one morning, Tim was collected by a truck. He remembers locking his rear wheels, jamming his breaks and just skidding. At the time he was more concerned about ruining his brand-new tyres than he was about doing damage to himself. Even when his body finally came to a stop, in a heap on the side of the road, and excruciating pain in his shoulders and neck kicked in, Tim was still convinced he probably just had whiplash and would be able to race.

The reality was very different.

It took eight nurses to lift him off the MRI table, only to be told by the doctor that he had a broken neck (a C2 fracture).

Tim was given a choice: fuse his vertebrae (a better option in the short term but would likely rule out a return to competitive triathlons) or subject himself to three months in an iron halo. The halo would be more painful but offered a 90 per cent chance of complete recovery.

If you haven't watched *Tim Don: The Man with the Iron Halo* (you should, it's a ripper) let me paint you a picture of what choosing the halo option meant. Tim's head was screwed in place tighter than his bike seat. A circular metal framework surrounded his skull, with a brace reaching down to his stomach and back, to stabilise the neck. The painkillers he was on made him violently ill, but he couldn't jerk his neck to vomit. 'It was pretty horrific,' Tim says on camera. 'I almost went into the garage to get an Allen key to remove the halo myself.' For the first three weeks, Tim slept in a chair, upright. Any pressure leaning back on the brace put extra force on his screws, causing searing pain. At about three weeks, Tim was able to step off the strong prescription painkillers and moved back upstairs into a bed, but again was stuck upright, propped up by pillows. The problem with all of these sleeping positions was Tim's legs, which would pool with blood and swell up. Eventually, a bed was found that could almost imperceptibly move both his head and legs up and down, allowing Tim to sleep through the night.

Tim was forty at the time of the accident, generally around the age where Ironman careers peak. He worried his window had closed.

Then he realised wondering 'what if' didn't help anything because it didn't change anything. All he could do was focus forward. While he was in the halo, he spent most of every day in the gym or on some kind of cardio machine. About two months into wearing the halo, he set his sights on not just racing the Boston Marathon but on racing it in under three hours – something I couldn't dream of doing on a good day, let alone six months after a C2 fracture! Incredibly, he ran it in two hours, forty-nine minutes.

But the best was yet to come.

On 13 October 2018, Tim was back in Kona for the Ironman World Championships. Racing in the place where he'd been wiped from the field only one year earlier, Tim knew this startline was about closure. He finished fifty-third in a race of 2000. And while the time was well outside his personal best, finishing Kona was a personal best for so many other reasons.

When I think of Tim in his halo I think of him as an earth-bound angel, because there are so many lessons I've taken from his never-give-up attitude and the relentless focus on the process (not the goal) that made his comeback to professional racing possible. In terms of building bounce, I have three big takeaways from Tim's story.

Choose your attitude

Tim says the choice between fused vertebrae and the halo was a clear one for him. 'I didn't want to go out because of a careless driver,' he says. 'I'd rather try and fail than never try at all.' After three weeks, he started to challenge himself to become the Sherlock Holmes of hope: how could he hunt for the silver lining in his latest x-ray or the smallest bit of progress he made at the physio? 'I just kept telling myself, bones heal. I can heal. I can come back.'

Praise your progress

Every day was a challenge for Tim. Dividing the day into small segments was a helpful strategy. He says if he'd let himself think, 'I have two-and-a-half months left with this halo on', he would have gone mad. Instead, Tim said to himself, 'Okay, get up. I'll try to make my son some breakfast this morning. Right, the kids have gone to school, so I'm going to attempt the bathroom.' He broke the day down into micro-goals, and similarly broke his fitness routine into small chunks. 'I went to the gym and did five minutes on the exercise bike very easily. And then I was like, "Hold on, if I can do five minutes today, I can do six minutes tomorrow."' He tempered tenacity with caution. If Tim felt he could do an hour and a half of training he'd do an hour and a quarter. 'A little is good and, often, more isn't better.'

Connect to your purpose

After twenty years of training for thirty hours a week, returning to exercise was essential for Tim, physically and mentally. 'I felt a sense of purpose,' he says, adding that he also wanted to pay forward the goodwill he had been shown during his trying times. Tim is quick to heap praise on his wife, Kelly, in particular. 'She gave me sponge baths for months,' he laughs. The need to not let his family and friends down, and to show his kids how to be courageous in the face of disaster acted as powerful motivators. 'I thought, if I'm a miserable guy, that's just not cool for everyone who's supported me, especially in that first month. All those things that people did for me, I guess they kept me going.'

What is your metal halo? What are the shackles holding you in place right now and how can you use those restraints as a divine intervention to build your resilience and break free?

The triathlon world better watch out: Tim Don is back. And after honing the mental fortitude required to endure an iron halo I can't help but think the Ironman seems like a cakewalk.

Support structures enable resilience

It's important to challenge the idea that being resilient falls entirely on one's own shoulders. Rather than just expecting ourselves to 'be more resilient', how do we develop a set of resilience tools and relationships in order to bring that reality to life? Dawn O'Neil AM, the former CEO of two of Australia's most prominent mental health not-for-profits, Beyond Blue and Lifeline, spoke to me about the importance of having more than one support structure in our lives. She had a powerful way of conceptualising the idea: 'One of the strategies I love thinking about is our hand, and how we care for something by wrapping all of our fingers around it. Having one strategy is not enough. To me, our five fingers represent the need to have five support strategies to help us stay mentally healthy.'

Dawn speaks with the insight of someone who has spent more time listening than talking throughout her life. She points out that even for many of us who would consider ourselves mentally healthy, we exist on a sliding scale of wellness. Acute or chronic stress, brought on by something like a pandemic, can have the ability at any time to render our coping mechanisms null and void. When this happens, underlying issues of anxiety or depression that we may have normalised through routine coping strategies get thrown out of whack.

Dawn says that the strategies that form the 'Five Finger Support Strategy' model of wellbeing will shift and change depending on the circumstance and challenges faced, the key being the use of multiple approaches. When the COVID pandemic took hold of the world it brought a degree of focus to mental health and strategies for dealing with stress. One of the most simple and helpful checklists I found, which builds on Dawn's idea of having multiple strategies, was STREAM, from the Órama Institute for Mental Health, Wellbeing and Neuroscience at Flinders University.

S – Social networking
Keep in touch with people through social media, phone calls or a text message. Connection is critical to wellbeing.

T – Time out
Take time out, whether it's from long stints sitting down on your computer, endless zoom calls or extended time in close proximity with other people. This will help minimise the ongoing stress of being in a limited space with others.

R – Relaxation, mindfulness or yoga
Managing anxiety can be helped through breathing and muscular relaxation exercises, mindfulness training, dancing, singing and yoga.

E – Exercise and entertainment
Whether it's using the space available on your bedroom floor or going for a lap of the block, exercise is a great way to get endorphins going. Alternatively, catch up on some reading, digital or board games, hobbies or listening to music.

A – Alternative thinking
Understand uncertainty will lead to heightened tension and stress. It's often useful to think things through by talking to someone else, such as a friend or a counsellor. We are all in this together, with the benefit of different perspectives.

M – Mindful of others
Maintain caring relationships. Never forget that simple acts of kindness make us feel good about ourselves, the world and the future.

As leaders, we must be able to navigate our own mental health in order to recognise, destigmatise and model healthy behaviours for those around us. All too often, we have a 'one strategy' approach to helping people through adversity. For example, when I ask leaders what practical mental health support they have in place, an employee assistance program (EAP) phone line is often the only thing they can reference. Yet we know that while mental health costs Australian businesses $12.8 billion annually, only 4.4 per cent of employees use their EAP service. I encourage you to wrap your hand around Dawn's five-finger approach and know by heart the things that bring you back to yourself when you're not feeling okay. If we can start to self-correct on the smaller ebbs and flows, we will have strategies in place when the bigger punches of life occur. Just like you wouldn't build a structure with a single support beam and expect such a structure to bear a load, nor should we expect single points of strength to support the weight of our struggles.

Explaining stressful situations to ourselves

Martin Seligman is often referred to as the 'father of positive psychology'. One of his many fascinating findings has been around the topic of 'explanatory styles', the ways in which we choose to make sense of the world around us. Through his research, Seligman found that the way we deal with stress is more about nurture, less about nature. He began training people to 'change their explanatory styles from internal to external ("Bad events aren't my fault"), from global to specific ("This is one narrow thing rather than a massive indication that something is wrong with my life"), and from permanent to impermanent ("I can change the situation"), rather than assuming it's fixed, and found this made them more psychologically successful'.

Let's try putting this into practice. Start with a story you are telling yourself in which you are the victim. It could be about a disagreement you've had with your partner or an opportunity you've been passed over for at work. I find it even helps to say out loud 'the story I'm telling myself is . . .' Then try thinking about it in these three ways.

Widen the focus

How can you shift the narrative from internal to external? Try reframing your situation in terms of being an active choice rather than a passive condition.

For example, *I am half a world away from my other half because I have chosen to pursue my dreams.*

Enlarge the perspective

Expand the narrative so that it contextualises this particular situation within a much broader story about who you are and how you exist in the world.

For example, *Although I am half a world away from other half, I'm choosing to pursue my dreams because building my skills and capabilities will help me be the change I hope to see in the world, and I want to be a role model for the next generation, and hopefully for our own kids.*

Envision the change

Bring possibility and impermanence into your narrative, detailing the pathway to change.

For example, *Although I am half a world away from my other half, completing this study is going to seem like a small glimmer of gold when I look back at the end of my life. I will think how much the pain was worth it because it contributed to me becoming all that I am alongside my other half.*

Control plays into this, too. By shifting your narrative to give yourself a more internal locus of control and sense of empowerment, you'll perceive less stress, reframe any victim-narrative tendencies, and see positive changes in both your psychological wellbeing and objective work performance.

How can we use stress as a springboard for bounce?

In her latest book, *The Upside of Stress*, Kelly McGonigal argues that our stress mindset shapes everything from the emotions we feel about stress to the way we cope. I find her range of strategies for how we can better cope with and respond to stress really useful. To summarise:

- Acknowledge stress when you experience it. Simply allow yourself to notice the stress, including how it affects your body.
- Welcome the stress by recognising it as a response to something you care about. Can you connect to the positive motivation behind the stress? What is at stake here, and why does it matter to you?
- Make use of the energy that stress gives you, instead of wasting that energy trying to manage your stress. What can you do right now that reflects your goals and values?

Stress is a reflex but it's also a powerful energetic force that either pushes us down or propels us upwards, and with resilience we have the ability to flex our stress muscles in a way that makes us stronger. While we can't avoid stressful events or experiences in life, if we give ourselves the right framing, support structures and coping mechanisms, we can harness our stress to feed resilience, determination and curiosity.

Of all the incredible learnings I soaked up by moving overseas to study at Harvard, my pillow of tears perhaps brought me the greatest lesson of all: resilience is not about shutting out emotion and moving on, it's about allowing, acknowledging and reframing stress, trauma and pain in order to strengthen our resolve. I reframed the story I was telling myself: If I was going to be 20,000 kilometres away then I was going to make sure I worked ten times as hard to make this sacrifice worth it. In doing so, I turned frustration into fuel.

A question from the leading edge:

Are you helping or hindering your mindset when you talk to yourself about the tough stuff?

5
Stay hungry for feedback

'Feedback is a free education to excellence, seek it with sincerity and receive it with grace.'

Ann Marie Houghtailing

The first bit of feedback I can recall receiving was in my Year 2 school report. I'll declare it up-front: I was one of those types who loved school, but my Year 2 teacher did not love me. Mrs Roy had a brilliantly passive-aggressive way of giving feedback. The report said, 'Holly is a rather enthusiastic student who takes a very active role in class discussions and activities. She is still learning to respect quiet and independent working time.'

Subtext: *Holly has too much energy and is both an over-contributor and an over-talker. I'd appreciate it if she shut up occasionally and stopped distracting the other students.*

Fair serve, Mrs Roy.

It's funny how feedback sticks with us. Why on earth can I remember verbatim the entirety of the first letter to the editor in the local newspaper tearing me a new one at age eighteen, yet I can't seem to commit the capital of Mongolia to memory to save myself?

It seems we wear criticism like scars, whereas compliments brush past us as softly as feathers. Psychologists refer to this as the negative (or negativity) bias. Adverse events have a more significant effect on our brains than positive ones. The negativity bias is our tendency to register negative stimuli more readily and to dwell on these events for longer.

Feel familiar? Maybe you've posted something on social media, and while it got a bucket load of 'likes', you can't get over the one troll who felt the need to put the boot in. Or maybe you've received a generally positive performance review at work, but you find yourself fixating on the few constructive comments for areas in which you could improve. Maybe in the days following, you find yourself involuntarily cringing or feeling upset, even angry.

Right now, feedback is in transition as a concept. There is a tension between our professional formal feedback processes and the instant gratification mechanism provided by social media. Previously, company 'feedback' was conducted once a year in the form of a formal job appraisal. These meetings often induced palm-sweating trepidation whereby the entirety of our last 365 days was summarised in a single conversation that ran for somewhere between twenty and sixty minutes and could make or break our next twelve months. Managers tended to like them about as much as their employees. I had one boss who did seven back-to-back feedback sessions on the final day of the financial year, such was his impulse of avoidance.

Nowadays, we must contend with constant informal feedback in our lives and workplaces as well. Social media, real-time productivity scoreboards and company communication platforms are surging in uptake as companies look for ways to shift their culture into a real-time feedback model. Nearly all – 96 per cent – of employees say they want to hear feedback regularly, and Millennials and Gen Z have grown up on a diet of instant feedback. When feedback is timely and specific, we have a better chance at integrating the learning and moving on. Companies like Deloitte and Accenture have scrapped the annual performance review entirely, calculating that they spend approximately 2 million hours administering their yearly performance review process to wrap everyone around a bell curve anyway. Instead, they're opting to have an evaluation process that unfolds incrementally throughout the year. Approximately 6 per cent of Fortune 500 companies have followed suit and gotten rid of rankings.

While instant feedback is a good thing, the jury is still out on how constant feedback affects us. Given that in the last chapter we discussed how shifting our locus of control back inside ourselves positively affects mental health, the feeling of being continually measured via external judgement is likely to be detrimental to our wellbeing. Research looking at the way teens and younger generations consume social media suggests comparison to others causes us to live 'outside' ourselves, with a fractured experience of our place in the collective. For feedback to be effective, we must weigh it up against our why, own it in our narrative and use it as leverage in our resilience springboard to bounce even higher.

Being a leader will always attract criticism. Leading change at the edge will attract criticism from those whose power you are disrupting. Build your appetite for feedback, friends!

Gaming and the reality of instant feedback

When esteemed video game designer Jane McGonigal, who is, yes, the sister of Kelly from the last chapter (imagine the dinner conversation!), addressed the audience at TED in 2010, she had a thesis that most people instinctively wanted to resist. 'If we want to change the world,' Jane hypothesised, 'we need to get more people playing video games.' At the time she suggested the cumulative tally of hours spent playing games was 3 billion hours a week and challenged that the number needed to grow to about 21 billion hours. Why? She argued that many of us feel like we're not as good at reality as we are in games – not just in terms of accomplishments, but also in terms of our motivation to collaborate and cooperate. The instant feedback, clear scores to beat and next level adventures of games could seriously boost real-world feedback formats and performance.

After Jane's talk, Twitch Plays Pokémon (TPP) happened. TPP is a social experiment and channel on the video game live-streaming website Twitch, consisting of a crowd-sourced attempt to play Game Freak's and Nintendo's Pokémon video games by parsing commands sent by users through the channel's chat room. The stream became unexpectedly popular, and on 1 March 2014, the game was completed after more than sixteen consecutive days of gameplay. More than 1.16 million people participated, with peak simultaneous participation at 121,000, and with a total of 55 million views during the experiment. The cumulative effect of the game has become legendary in the media, described as 'mesmerising', 'miraculous', and a 'beautiful chaos'. Somehow, 1.16 million people collaborated to accomplish a task. Think back to your last company off-site high-ropes course . . . remember what a struggle it was to get ten people to achieve a goal?

As Jane points out, 'So far, collectively, the World of Warcraft gamers have spent 5.93 million years solving the virtual problems of Azeroth . . . to put that in context: 5.93 million years ago was when our earliest primate human ancestors stood up.' Imagine if we were to harness that energy to solve real world problems. How can we build this motivation to keep trying, to keep solution-building as a leadership mindset?

The continuous responsiveness of gaming almost programs players to win. Whenever you accomplish a task in a game, what happens? You get to level up! There's a new power, a new capability you've unleashed. You get a healthy bonus or a new tool to approach the next challenge with. I think, oftentimes probably unconsciously, that's what's happening in the workplace: when we accomplish a task, we sit ready and waiting to 'level up'. Only the workplace doesn't work like that. Feedback happens irregularly and feels disassociated from a particular task at hand. Career progression in many industries is broken into arbitrary timelines and advancement is not always reflective of performance.

Video games are predictable in their progression yet they never require players to perform the same tasks over and over again. Recent Mario games contain infinite continues or even mid-level checkpoints to ensure that, if the player dies, they don't have to replay the same content. Gaming architects realise that forcing a player to repeat content is where 'difficult' becomes 'tedious'. It seems remiss not to use this insight and to take digital collaboration tools, productivity maps or regular check-ins to create the same sense of progression in other areas of our lives, particularly our work lives.

I watch HR directors stiffen when I mention the notion of getting to level-up every time you complete a task. Disjointed feedback loops are a source of friction and resentment when it comes to society viewing Millennials' desire for advancement. We need to get better at delineating incremental sub-levels in our career journeys. One thing to note here: levels of progress don't necessarily need to involve title changes and more money.

Once upon a time, we got a job within an organisation and that organisation navigated our careers for us. Today, we must take ownership of our trajectory, which is likely to be through multiple organisations, sometimes simultaneously. I encourage you to get creative with how you level up at work. At your next performance review, why not provide some feedback on ways to optimise your motivation? How can we design our own feedback framework and propose small wins to support our milestones? Perhaps it's a company subscription to a new app, perhaps it's the opportunity to volunteer when a project is done, maybe it's a short course to upskill when ROI is met. As we deal with bigger and more complex issues, and less well-defined roles, what we learn from gamers is that motivation comes from feeling that we are continually progressing. That we are going somewhere. And increasingly, perpetuating that positive feedback loop is up to us.

Leading the feedback

Naomi Simson tells me she didn't understand her own potential until she actively sought out positive feedback loops. Naomi is the founding director of online experience retailer RedBalloon, which has had some 3.6 million customers and counting. She's the most followed Australian on LinkedIn. She was one of the first people I turned to for advice when I was starting my own company. When it comes to positive feedback loops, Naomi is a queen.

'It was only when I put myself out there to educate myself that I met other entrepreneurs and founders and I'd listen to their advice and think, I could do that!' Naomi believes that part of the positive aspect is reframing feedback as a story. She tells me, 'I find that the most constructive way to coach others is through experience-based storytelling. Speaking from experiences creates a different relationship [than] telling someone what they should do better.'

Another great tip from Naomi is in how she goes about seeking advice: 'I don't say, "Tell me what I should do." I say, "Tell me about a time, a time when you really struggled to engage customers in your journey." Or, "Tell me about a time when you lost supplies and had to improvise."' Naomi says this method extracts real value that can then be applied to her own circumstance, allowing her to make her own way forward.

I find a subtle but powerful shift in placing ourselves inside an active feedback loop. After all, feedback and stories go hand in hand. The use of story reminds us that feedback is always subjective, and allows our trust to lie in experience, rather than in opinion.

Getting away from all-or-nothing identities

According to Francesca Gino of Harvard Business School, 'People tend to move away from those who provide feedback that is more negative than their view of themselves.' Receiving honest criticism can be confronting; in her research with Paul Green and Bradley Staats, Francesca suggests that we do not listen to overly negative advice and prefer to stop interacting with these people altogether. It seems we tend to strengthen our bonds with people who see our positive qualities – natural, you'd think, since we want to protect our egos and sense of self. But as Francesca makes clear, we only will improve if we're willing to hear what our weaknesses are from others.

Why is doing that just so f*cking hard?

One of the most helpful books I've ever read on feedback is Douglas Stone and Sheila Heen's *Thanks for the Feedback*, which, unlike most of the books out there on feedback, isn't just focused on how to give it in an effective and productive way. The duo have spent the past fifteen years working across companies and communities to determine what helps us learn and what gets in our way. In their book, they explain why receiving feedback is so crucial yet so challenging.

Douglas and Sheila remind us that to harness the power of feedback, we need to be able to keep an open mind so we can 'find' the learning. To do that we have to identify how feedback acts as a trigger for us. These might be truth triggers, which happen when we view the feedback as wrong or unfair and become defensive, often rejecting the information entirely. They might be relationship triggers, which see us question the person giving the feedback or the relationship itself. Or they may come in the form of identity triggers, meaning something about the feedback causes us to question ourselves. We think of ourselves as a 'failure' and interpret that we should no longer try. These are often the most problematic triggers.

To avoid identity triggers, we need to depart from all-or-nothing identity labels and acknowledge that we are highly nuanced and complex creatures. This was a big light-bulb moment for me. I was able to identify why there were particular aspects of my character I found it significantly harder to receive feedback about or just flat out avoided seeking feedback on. I realised part of why I was feeling 'stuck', and broadly unable to metabolise feedback, was likely driven by the simplistic all-or-nothing identity label that I'd created for myself around 'achievement' and 'responsibility'. As such, feedback and conflict had served as binary light switches: any instance where it was suggested that I wasn't perfectly 'responsible' or responsibly 'perfect' amounted, in my mind, to egregious irresponsibility. This attacked the very core of my professional identity.

Douglas and Sheila stress that we have to give up simple labels if we are able to grow from feedback; we need to be more nuanced. They suggest we need to accept three things about ourselves in order to make it easier to hear and learn from feedback: we will make mistakes, we have complex intentions and we contributed to the problem.

Feedback is a critical component of self-growth and is essential in the toolkit of all leaders. Unless we understand our existing impact on others and outcomes, we will never be able to move closer toward our ideal relationship to both. But an important lesson here is that we need to be intentional about who we invite to provide their views. Not everyone will come from a place of wanting the best for us, and some will have a vested interest in the feedback they're giving us or the direction they're trying to point us in. Not everyone will be secure enough in themselves to be able to give feedback healthily.

By actively seeking out high-functioning feedback relationships in our lives, we can explore our own triggers, practise putting feedback into action and learn how to share feedback with others. The challenge is to find the feedback coach who will champion our journey.

Finding your healthy diet of feedback relationships

Darren Cahill is the tennis whisperer. On three separate occasions, with three completely different athletes, he's coached them to achieve and sustain world number one rankings. If you've ever watched Lleyton Hewitt, Andre Agassi or Simona Halep you have, perhaps unwittingly, come across some of the folklore of Coach Cahill, affectionately known as 'Killer'.

One of the things that fascinates me about Darren is his ability to repeat success with *very* different athletes. He guided Hewitt to become the youngest player ever to be ranked number one and Agassi to be the oldest player ever. He then coached Romanian Simona Halep to number one on the women's in 2017 and to her first Grand Slam victory at the 2018 French Open.

I ask Darren, as a coach of truly diverse players, how they manage feedback and how much it is a consistent or common framework that he draws from? Darren says, 'It has to start with honesty.' Attributing his framework to his father John (Jack) Cahill, a legendary coach of the mighty Port Adelaide Football Club in the Australian Football League (where Darren and I are fortunate to be on the board), Darren insists, 'You have to be honest on all occasions, but how you deliver that messaging is different for every single player and every single circumstance.'

Darren tells me, 'There are five things that determine whether or not you can be a champion.' Alongside the non-negotiables like speed, strength, size and weight, he insists, 'The five things that I've found every single great player in the world of tennis has are work ethic, purpose, belief, resilience and team.'

Losing sucks. Bad news sucks. Any competitive athlete or leader will tell you that. But how does a high-performance feedback relationship facilitate the bounce back? Darren tells me the story of Simona's loss in the 2017 French Open, a loss made all the more bitter by the fact it would have been her first Grand Slam victory and the clincher of her ascension to world number one. Sitting with a distraught Simona afterwards, Darren made the decision that he would become Captain Positive. He remained determinedly upbeat for weeks before Simona's fitness trainer pulled him aside and suggested he might be pushing too hard.

Darren dismissed him. 'She's so close. She just needs to keep believing and keep pushing and get to those big moments and just grind through them.' Back in training after her US Open loss,

Simona asked him, 'How do you think I played? What did I do wrong?' As Darren admits, 'I should have left it and said nothing . . . but I couldn't help myself, and as I'm talking about the handful of things she could have done better, I'm watching tears roll down her face.' As they walked back to the locker room, Simona's fitness trainer was shaking his head in that knowing I-told-you-so kind of way, Darren realised he hadn't created the space for Simona to just let that pain out. He knocked on her door and apologised for 'being a dickhead' and hugged her. She stopped crying and said, 'I've been waiting ten weeks for that hug.' Two weeks later, in Beijing, Halep annihilated the same player who bundled her out in the first round of the US Open (Sharapova) and attained the coveted world number one slot: 'All because I stopped pushing and gave her a hug,' Darren says with a smile.

Listening to Darren, I realise that a high-performance feedback relationship will always begin with where the other person is coming from, whether you're the giver or the receiver. Acknowledging feedback as a two-way conversation, Darren says there are certainly some common mistakes to avoid in feedback-based collaborations.

Focusing on the technical problems

Rather than fixing weakness, a good feedback conversation emphasises strengths.

Don't use the 'b' word

Darren says his biggest adjustment from a communication standpoint has been getting rid of 'but'. He believes when a person is waiting for a 'but' they will never hear what comes before.

Build accountability into the conversation

We all need people like Simona's fitness trainer who are not scared to tell us the truth. Givers and receivers of feedback can build this into their commitment to each other.

Don't be territorial and protective

Often the givers of feedback can act as the keeper of solutions rather than the enabler. It's far more important to connect other sources of expertise and inspiration.

What I took from Darren Cahill is that feedback works as a collaboration, where both parties are accountable for asking the questions and hearing the answers. And that unequal power dynamics do not make champions; trust and teamwork do.

Sitting down to a constructive feedback feast

If we want to reap the benefits of feedback, the most important thing we can bring to the table is a hunger for it. Some of you already will be, others might have to identify a goal or aspiration that puts the fire in your belly to make the pursuit worthwhile. Perhaps it's building a closer relationship with your child or the desire to reach the next rung of your career? When we view feedback in the context of the potential it's helping us to unlock or the impact it's helping us to achieve, we begin to change our relationship to it.

In his book *What Got You Here Won't Get You There*, executive coach Marshall Goldsmith challenges the premise of feedback with what he calls the 'feed forward' loop. In essence, Goldsmith focuses conversations not on reviewing the past but on nominating things we could change to become more effective in the future. It's a framework built on the idea that while we can change the future, we cannot change the past – and the real gem is that we take 'feed-forward' far less personally than feedback because it replaces judgement of past behaviour with suggestions for a more effective tomorrow. Put simply: it's less ego-bruising and more muscle-building!

The most successful feed-forward conversations I've been a part of have been regular, strategic, specific and factual. They'll often focus on the question, 'For this role to be maximally effective, what should we be doing more of and less of?' Vague concepts such as 'inspiring', 'fantastic', or 'not that great' are unhelpful. Instead, anchoring requests and responses in facts, actions, patterns of behaviour and impact allow an open and honest conversation.

I have developed my own approach to flipping feedback into feed-forward. Try it!

- Enter the conversation as an active participant.
- Prepare a list of questions that probe for specific feedback, based on any areas you feel aren't running so smoothly.
- Demonstrate that what you are after are suggestions for the future and that you are willing to change your approach or behaviour to give these a go.
- Be honest about what's not working and come to the table with solutions.
- Arm yourself with data so the conversation can be kept factual and grounded in reality.
- Receive feedback graciously and always take the high road, reframing negative feedback in a proactive light as necessary.
- Offer the person giving you feedback some constructive recognition on how they have performed through the process.

The research of neuroscientist Kevin Ochsner from Columbia University observes that only 30 per cent of people ever apply the feedback they're given. I find it helpful to set aside time separately from feedback conversations to reflect on what was shared and to come up with concrete action steps. For example, what are the new habits I want to form? How can I lift my intrapersonal communication to manage expectations better? What mindset do I need to apply to deal with similar situations differently in the future? Another helpful tip can be to invite those who've shared feedback with you to keep you in check with any changes you've committed to undertaking. We could all do with seeking and applying feedback like a gamer. Whether it's feedback or feed-forward, not all feedback is created equal. In order to take in the lessons of our own leadership, we need to learn to kick it up a level.

A question from the leading edge:

What's the most valuable piece of feedback you've ever received and how have you fed it forward?

Method

Leadership is the practice of the big-hearted

6

Be four again

'Above all, never stop questioning.'

Albert Einstein

If you've spent any time around a child under the age of six, you know what it's like to be peppered incessantly with questions, from the expertly laddered 'Why?' to the inexhaustible 'How come?' Occasionally it's the more philosophical crackers like 'What happens to me after I die?' Or, as my four-year-old godson James enquired on our way home from his swimming lesson, 'When do we learn to breathe underwater?' It was hard to break that one to him.

Kids are endlessly, relentlessly, (sometimes) brutally curious.

The numbers back it up: one research study concluded that four-year-old girls embody the peak of curiosity, asking 390 questions a day – that's one question every 116 seconds! For parents, often by question number ten, it can be tempting to delegate to Alexa or Siri. But this inquisitiveness disappears too soon. Kids are well ahead of adults (including Siri or Alexa) in understanding that it is not a search for answers that unlocks knowledge, but better questions. Tragically, by the time we hit our teenage years, the insatiable thirst we had for knowledge seems to evaporate. Study after study shows we stop asking questions. In educational research, this corresponds with the age we see children's enthusiasm for learning fall off the proverbial cliff. To paraphrase Maria Montessori, we don't stop asking questions because we lose interest: it's the other way around. We lose interest because we stop asking questions.

Escaping the adult brain

As we shift gears in this chapter from mindset to method, I want to share a story about taking a friend to an escape room for his forty-third birthday. Stupidly (or arrogantly?) I had selected the highest level of difficulty for our escape-room debut and ignored the guidance that suggested we have four to eight problem-solvers to assist in our quest. Over the next two hours, we battled valiantly in a bushranger-themed series of puzzles, codes, logic problems and more. I'm not going to dress this up: we flamed out. Spectacularly. As we sulked afterwards using our free drink token to nurse bruised egos, a six-year-old birthday party got underway. I gestured towards the gaggle of six-year-old girls and asked the host, 'What adjustments do you make for kids?'

He laughed. 'Kids hold the escape record on all of our most difficult rooms!' He looked at me and paused. 'It's not the kids we have to make adjustments for.' There was no escaping my unconscious bias in that moment. He went on to explain that kids ask questions freely, ask for help more readily, experiment without fear and generally don't overcomplicate things. Smiling, he suggested that when we came back, we should recruit a few junior members to our team.

My experience at the escape room isn't an anomaly. In the famed MIT Marshmallow Challenge groups are given twenty sticks of spaghetti, about a metre of tape, about a metre of string and one marshmallow. They then have fifteen minutes to build the largest free-standing tower with the one requirement that the marshmallow has to be at the top of the tower. When comparing the performance of different groups, a study by Tom Wujec found that, for all their training, MBAs perform the worst on average in building marshmallow towers. Engineers perform moderately well (thankfully!), but which group performs the best? Kindergartners! While MBAs wanted to plan their way to an 'optimal outcome' and then execute, kinder kids took a completely different approach. Instead of wasting time trying to establish who was in charge or making a plan, they simply experimented over and over until they found a model that worked. Interestingly, the study found adult performance worsened when incentives were added into the mix: planning time went up and tower height went down – suggesting the more significant the 'consequences' riding on our behaviour, the less likely we are to take risks and experiment. While methodical planning works well in the face of a 'known' problem, in the face of unknown problems, success is contingent on our ability to adopt an experimental methodology.

Questions, play and curiosity are the heart, lungs and brain of the creative organism. And, as renowned education and creativity expert Sir Ken Robinson put it, we have 'killed creativity' by systematically stifling all three essential organs.

Schools and workplaces of the industrial era placed a premium on 'answers' – specifically, the right answers. The source of the gold stars and promotions alike, perfection is prized. We stop asking questions because by the time we reach our teenage years we're acutely attuned to the way society stigmatises mistakes. We become less willing and less able to produce original content, challenge accepted wisdom or offer different opinions for fear of failure and non-acceptance. This system sets us up perfectly to subordinate ourselves to centralised, hierarchical organisational models that reward employees accumulating greater 'process' knowledge.

Leading with curiosity

Companies like Disney represent an alternative view, with Walt himself famously valuing creativity and innovation 'because we're curious, and curiosity keeps leading us down new paths'. The business world rationalised such exceptionalism as the domain of the 'creative companies', instead of seeing the value of curiosity being integral to *every* company. We frequently hear the adage that every company is now a technology company, but I'd argue every company also needs to be a creativity workshop.

The arrival of the notion of the 'knowledge economy', first popularised by management guru Peter Drucker in the 1960s, began to challenge conventional wisdom around skills and leadership. Then, in the early 2000s, when a squad of under-forties entered the Fortune 500 and a new focus on culture saw cult-like tech companies start to dominate the 'Most Engaging Workplaces' lists, the conversation kicked into hyperdrive. These companies started propagating the importance of different skills, such as creativity and collaboration, and touting the benefits of flatter organisational structures that not only permitted but facilitated and encouraged debate. Extraordinary business value was unlocked by the advent of the 'sharing economy'. In the very business models of the Ubers and Airbnbs of the world, curiosity was able to unleash hidden assets.

As the wonderful Sir Ken put it when I spoke to him in 2019, we are now in a world where 'creativity is as important as literacy . . . and human children are bottomless resources of human creativity.' Sir Ken insisted on the need to embrace their endless curiosity for the world, explaining, 'Flexible people and organisations are the ones who still see with a child's eye. They're not jaded, they're constantly stimulated by the world around us.' He also made the point that we need to make sure we're not only retaining our own child-like curiosity longer as adults, but that we're raising children in a way that fosters it. When I first interviewed Ken in 2018, he made the point that children in Western countries spend less than an hour outside each day; prisoners spend two. As Sir Ken put it, 'Our children are doing time.' Further, he said by the age of seven the average child now will have spent two years on screens and one year on their own. His prescription: 'We need to be more conscious, at home and at work, of cultivating environments in which creativity flourishes'.

According to Ian Leslie, author of the book *Curious*, curiosity is actually 'more of a state than a trait'. We all have the potential to be curious, given the right conditions. Leslie notes that curiosity seems to emerge when we are exposed to new information and find ourselves wanting to know more. If we desire to be a more curious leader, then we need to endeavour to get 'out of the bubble' when possible: seek out new influences, ideas and experiences that will help fire up the desire to learn more and dig deeper. Innovators are renowned for intentionally seeking out new stimuli to disrupt their traditional thought patterns. Apple's famous typeface was inspired by a calligraphy class that Steve Jobs attended. And the designer behind the iPhone, Tony Fadell, intentionally hires young creatives so that he's getting the benefit of brains that are yet to be habituated to company, industry or society 'think'. Companies from Marriott through to arts organisations such as Melbourne's Malthouse Theatre have set up 'shadow boards' with Gen Y and Z members to harness this sort of unbridled thinking and get closer to these demographics. And prolific entrepreneur Sir Richard Branson told me that he still, at age seventy and with more than 400 companies under his belt, takes a notebook with him everywhere and challenges himself to find learning in every interaction and every encounter.

Ask the question

Anne Mulcahy, CEO of Xerox and the leader responsible for successfully navigating her organisation through the Global Financial Crisis, describes herself as 'Master of the *I don't know*'. Recounting her approach, Mulcahy said the worst thing you can do is get 'smart person's disease': an affliction that manifests in a desire to give off the impression you have all the answers. Unanswered questions aren't threats; they're catalysts and challenges. The temporary 'feel good' that appearing to be all-knowing might give us is deeply corrosive to team culture. Anne says it was her willingness to be vulnerable and make not knowing 'safe' that allowed her organisation to build a culture of questioning everything they did. A culture, she argues, they wouldn't have gotten through the GFC without.

The commercial value of the right question asked at the right time can be illustrated and quantified by the cost of not asking the right question. For example, in 1995, financial trader Nick Leeson began making riskier and riskier trades, until his losses reached $1.3 billion – around twice the market capitalisation of his employer, Barings Bank. The bank collapsed and Leeson was jailed. The culture at the 200-plus-year-old bank meant that senior managers who were aware of Leeson's approach to risk and knew he was supervising his own trades were unable to speak up. This cost of livelihoods and reputational damage to bank employees around the world could have been avoided by someone, somewhere, asking the question.

It is not feasible to think we can entirely eliminate all problems, but they can be reduced substantially in both quantity and value by fostering a culture and personal practice that encourages inquisitiveness and question-asking.

The art of play

Hand in hand with the notion of being a four-year-old is the idea of embracing unstructured play. When we stop playing, we lose curiosity, humour, perspective and the ability to question. While play is a natural state for children, it's far less so for adults dealing with the pressures and stresses of life. And when we do play, our brains interrupt us, telling us that we're wasting time engaging in an 'unproductive' activity or something that lacks purposefulness. We believe there is no value in play.

Such thinking runs counter to the research. Recent findings in neuroscience suggest that 'play promotes mental flexibility, including adaptive practices such as discovering multiple ways to achieve a desired result . . . Play facilitates expressive language and divergent thinking.' Play is also our most direct route into what Mihaly Csikszentmihalyi termed 'flow': a state of consciousness where we are deeply immersed in the present and feel at our best.

Test yourself. When you make time to read, do you pick up a non-fiction book or a fiction book? I am notoriously guilty of the former, so no judgement! When you engage with kids, do you pull them across to your world and have them do something useful and informative? Or do you get down on the floor and wriggle your way into their imagined world?

INSEAD's Manfred F. R. Kets de Vries argues that the proclivity to play remains an essential part of our make-up throughout our life and that we should make more considerable efforts to retain play as a mode of learning and the source of creative production. He suggests there are four critical components to play that make it so powerful.

Me-time

Me-time speaks to the freedom of play. We decide whether to engage and can direct our own actions during play.

Make-believe

Play sits where cognitive development and social experience intersect, allowing leaps of imagination that are fundamental to the creative development process.

Mastery

Interactive play lets us experiment and gain a sense of mastery over our environment, which gives us a sense of competence and may expand our sphere of competence.

Meaning

Play is critical for us in exploring our identities and the roles we might wish to take up – that is, we both create and find meaning through play.

As adults, we continue to value routine in a world that no longer values routine thinking. We find it hard to accept the unexpected even as our operating environment becomes less and less predictable. And we may no longer recall that some of the best moments in life have been entirely spontaneous.

Play, for many of us, is reduced to having a drink at the end of the week, or indulging in a fitness hobby. Our creativity is cultivated in one or two directions only; perhaps we take photographs or knit. This is the adult paradox: we only play at playing.

Leadership requires that we unlearn how to be so serious. Unless we're engaging in 'serious play'!

Serious play

It's easy to think play only has application to 'alternative' companies, that it couldn't drive value in a traditional business or that it couldn't work at scale. Enter Ross Smith.

Ross is renowned for making play part of the culture at Microsoft. He helped create nearly every version of the company's Windows and Office products that appeared after 1995. A recipient of the Harvard Business Review/McKinsey M-Prize for Management Innovation, Ross holds five patents and is a big proponent of play at work.

In 2003, Ross's Windows Defect Prevention team noticed a fall-off in employee participation for stress testing. The more people who participate, the higher the quality of the test results. Ross's team asked themselves: how do we motivate participation? Their hypothesis was that incorporating a simple game (Hangman) would drive engagement. It proved correct: employee involvement shot up 400 per cent overnight.

Inspired by this early win, Ross launched 42Projects. The initiative encourages employees to expand their thinking into other areas or opportunities when they are less busy. For example, 42Projects team members might play 'productivity games' that encourage new behaviours and gather feedback from people across the company, or participate in projects relevant to their education or past experiences rather than their current role at the organisation. Allowing employees freedom and trust promotes job satisfaction and organisational health.

The success and engagement of Ross' team led to them collaborating with other parts of the business. While testing Windows 7, foreign language–speaking employees were invited to play a game that involved assessing the linguistic quality of the product across 100 different languages and thousands of dialects. More than 4500 employees participated, completing over 500,000 tasks and contributing to a high-quality Windows 7 release.

Ross's team then partnered with the company's IT organisation to get feedback on Microsoft Lync in 2010. This led to the development of Communicate Hope, a disaster relief scheme and one of the largest 'productivity' games ever launched within Microsoft. The key to its success, or of any game that involves asking for help, is getting people 'excited about taking time to participate', according to Ross. 'That's where the motivational potential of games is a key,' he says.

Microsoft's journey with games helped the company to unlock what early childhood educators have long known and what workplace play proponents have been trying to remind us: game play is key to learning and building trust, and trust is key to inspiring innovation.

We need to bring play back.

Who can afford time to play?

One of the major pushbacks against 'play' is that there isn't time enough for the critical work, let alone for something so seemingly unproductive. I always find this a fascinating defence because it implies we're highly productive at present. But according to research, we spend on average 144 minutes a day on social media and about three hours and thirty-five minutes watching television. In total, that's six hours and thirty-five minutes swallowed up by digital consumption. As Drucker highlighted with reference to our 'busy work': 'I have yet to see a knowledge worker, *regardless of rank or station*, who could not consign something like a quarter of the demands on his time to the wastepaper basket without anybody's noticing their disappearance.'

What if, instead of thinking 'my work's too urgent to have time to play', I suggest to you that your work is too important to *not* have time to play? Play is, in fact, serious business. If unleashing our inner child has a serious return on investment attached to it, how do we reconnect with that child? Curiosity is a disposition, not a destination. New world leaders must start to cultivate it as a pre-requisite skill.

Questionable intent

If you don't have an eighteen-month-old niece who gives you a regular excuse to play games of all varieties, there are a number of simple ways of infusing curiosity and play into your day.

Set yourself a daily question goal

Set your intent to ask at least one question in every interaction you're in daily or to hit a total number of questions per day. Keeping a tangible tally can help give visibility on how you're tracking: write a number on your calendar for how many you ask each day or tally them up in an app on your phone.

Have a 'questation'

Try having a conversation where you're only allowed to ask questions. Be upfront with the person you're engaged with about the fact you're eager to understand more about them or a topic and would like to have a twenty–thirty-minute conversation where you only ask questions. Be curious with yourself throughout – how difficult was it to not offer your opinion?

Do a one-minute learning log

At the end of each day take sixty seconds to record the most interesting thing you discovered in response to a question you asked.

Build a kids' brain trust

Whether formally or informally, invite the curiosity of kids into your world. Develop a 'reverse mentoring' relationship where you ask for their opinion on products and experiences.

Next time I head to the escape room, I'm taking a bunch of kids. As adults, we seem to spend so much of our time trying to escape from our lives, we have forgotten how to really 'be' in them. Let's take the seriousness out of answering questions by remembering the pleasure (and power) of asking them.

A question from the leading edge:

When was the last time you played?

7
Manage energy not time

'We think, mistakenly, that success is the result of the amount of time we put in instead of the quality of time we put in.'

Arianna Huffington

If you've worked through the 1980s, 1990s or 2000s, odds are at some point you've been subjected to 'time management' training. Often accompanied by some horrendously complicated workbook that looked like the love child of a Microsoft Excel spreadsheet and a Gantt chart, you probably learnt to schedule your hours, write to-do lists and do a time audit. If it happened to be taught by a guy named Tim, who had a pull-up banner that read 'if you fail to plan then you plan to fail', then I really feel for you (and FYI our time management recovery support group meets the last Thursday of the month at 6 pm).

One of the most game-changing shifts I've made in my life was to stop managing time.

You may have constructed a relatively comprehensive picture of me by now as ambitious with an obsession for goal setting, no off button and a continually overfilled plate. Well you'd be right . . . or at least you would have been up until about seven years ago. Being that way inclined, I lapped up time management advice like it was 'nectar of the gods'. A method of becoming even more effective? Sign me up!

For a while, the Koolaid worked. Like a methodological Red Bull, it helped me to push through to some phenomenal results . . . but also like Red Bull, it should *never* have become the mainstay of my diet because in doing so, it blocked out signals I should have been listening to and using to recalibrate.

And then the wheels came off.

Have you ever been going so hard, ticking all the boxes, burning through all the goals, only to shatter into pieces as soon as you get to take a few days off? It's no wonder really that, like a puppet with the strings cut, as soon as our adrenaline supply shifts from hyper back down to human, we break. According to Dawn O'Neil AM, former CEO of LifeLine and Beyond Blue (whom you met back in Chapter 4), there are three telltale stages of burnout: mental exhaustion; negativity towards one's work and reduced efficacy. Dawn says, 'It's so much better to catch a burnout spiral at the exhaustion stage, rather than continue through and have to remake ourselves entirely from scratch.'

I cannot solely lay the blame at the feet of Tim's time management class. Both the post mortem and the long rebuild led me on an inquiry into how I'd managed to burn out and permit my Tigger-esque disposition to be subsumed by depression. It was a journey that taught me to stop managing time and start managing energy instead. I have never looked back.

I first stumbled onto the concept of managing energy in Jim Loehr and Tony Schwartz's brilliant book, *The Power of Full Engagement*. High-performance coaches, Loehr and Schwartz's work was based on twenty-five years of helping the world's best athletes perform more effectively under pressure. In studying athletes, they had become fascinated by what gave the 'edge' to a world number one versus an athlete further down the rankings. They determined that managing energy was the currency of high performance. What they also uncovered was how the ultra-successful were better at channelling their energy towards the achievement of their goals.

The performance demands that any of us typically face in our professional or personal lives dwarf the pressure on elite athletes. We don't train 90 per cent of our time and perform 10 per cent of the time; we don't have an off season for three or four months every year, and we don't have a career span that lasts from five to seven years (unless we burn out). Whether we're full-time parents, full-time managers, a hybrid gig-economy hustler or some fusion of them all, we're expected to perform at our best eight/ten/twelve plus hours a day and then some, with just a handful of weeks off each year. I remember recording a podcast with former Australian Wallabies rugby captain Stephen Moore where he remarked in disbelief at how little conversation in the corporate world there was around sleep, nutrition and exercise given the demands on workers every day. It struck me that we need to start seeing ourselves as professional athletes and borrowing from them what best-practice high performance looks like in terms of optimal energy management.

Two ideas to unlearn

But before we get into energy management, we need to call out two fundamentally unhelpful mental anchors. The first: that idea that 'life is a marathon, not a sprint'. Whoever said that evidently was not working and living in the new millennium. It's absolutely both: it's a marathon made up of lots of shorter sprints. We are dealing with a world that requires us to exist in constant high-intensity interval training: spurts of high effort followed by short periods of downtime before we have to do it all again. Yet I meet CEOs and leadership teams all the time who are struggling to manage 'change fatigue' and yearning for things to 'slow down' because they desperately need to come up for air. As Loehr and Schwartz say, 'We race through our lives without pausing to consider who we really want to be or where we really want to go. We're wired up, but we're melting down.'

The only method for being match fit for this world is learning to cultivate productive downtime and to manage our energy efforts to get the highest return possible.

The second unhelpful phrase we need to ban is 'I'm too busy'. Somewhere along the way, we stopped responding to people's inquiries about how we were feeling with a description of our mood and instead chose to describe the state of our calendar. We started wearing busyness as a badge of honour, and then a shield of excuses for why we can't try something new or spend time doing things we love. I've been there, done that, believe me. But none of us wants to be that 'busy' person. Not for your family, not for your colleagues and not for yourself.

I bought an accountability coffee mug that reads: 'You have as many hours in the day as Beyoncé'. It reminds me that hoping that managing time will give us more time is a psychological trap. We all get 86,400 seconds in a day and 525,600 minutes in a (non-leap) year, so the secret sauce really boils down to how we choose to use them.

By reconnecting with ourselves physically, mentally, emotionally and spiritually, we can manage our energy. We all know that our energy levels change throughout the day; you may even know the term for this: 'circadian rhythm'. As researcher Christopher Barnes observes, 'This natural – and hardwired – ebb and flow in our ability to feel alert or sleepy has important implications.' There's a large body of research that suggests most of us follow a standard energy arc on a given day. A few hours into the day we hit our peak, we sit there for a brief moment, and then things begin to taper off at lunch, bottoming out at around 3 pm. After this dip, alertness generally increases again until around 6 pm, when it reaches its second peak. From then, our alertness generally declines steadily, reaching its lowest point around half past three in the morning.

The caveat to this general energetic arc is that genetically, some people's circadian rhythm tend towards earlier peaks and troughs (morning people, aka 'larks'), while others tend towards later peaks and troughs (the classic night owls). We also experience changes throughout our lifetimes; we are generally larks as children, then become owls as adolescents and then change back to being larks again as we move toward older age. What's important is knowing whether we're a lark, an owl or a different type of creature, and factoring that into the way we plan our days and weeks and manage expectations and deadlines.

Audit your energy

First things first: what's your own, unique natural rhythm?

When I was first posed that question, I think I pulled the equivalent facial expression of a terrier trying to get peanut butter off the roof of its mouth. Energy rhythms, really? Do I look like I'm wearing hemp pants? I was so used to forcing my energy to fit my work schedule, I'd completely disconnected to how it naturally flowed. I was conditioned to a routine of forcing myself to get up at stupid o'clock, packing my day with as many meetings as possible and consuming too much coffee so I could do all my actual work late into the evening. Out of curiosity, I spent a week not changing anything in my schedule and just becoming aware. What times of the day was I reaching for caffeine because I was flatlining? When was I bouncing off the wall? I realised I, Tigger-like early in the morning, seemed to max out my focus every ninety to 120 minutes, when my body begged for a brief reprieve, and hit a mega wall in the mid-afternoon.

Then I experimented for a week. What time did my body wake up when I didn't set the alarm? What time did I naturally fall asleep? When I intentionally put something that energised me at what would otherwise be a low point for me energetically, could I re-energise myself? Did I do creative or planning activities better in the mornings or in the evening? I noticed that not only was I naturally a very early riser but I was also much more creative either in the morning or late at night. When possible, I inserted exercise into my day as opposed to putting it at either the start or end because I found it made my mid-afternoon wall disappear.

I was blown away by the difference managing my diary according to energy made, not just to achieving professional success but also in the way I showed up for the relationships in my life. I've also opened up conversations about energy management with people closest to me, so I can be mindful of their natural rhythm and they of mine. It's allowed me to set new routines, like morning reading time with my partner before we start our working day or afternoon walk-and-talks with friends.

I'm not concocting a utopian view of the world that says you're entirely in charge of your own energy. Most of us have bosses, clients, mothers, children and even that knob from the compliance department who need us to dedicate our energy on demand. But I am going to challenge you on the fact that you're more in control of your energy than you think and that you can get significant returns for small tweaks.

I say this with a fair amount of confidence because I was myself challenged by the idea of the significant returns for micro-breaks and small acts of self-care when I came across Dr Jaime Lee's work. Jaime is a medical doctor, and health and performance expert. She worked on the front-line as a surgical resident before joining McKinsey and used her passion for health system reform to work with clients around the world.

As Jaime shared during our interview, she felt compelled to start her company, Health Quotient, because 'how we are working right now, isn't working'. Towards the end of her time in consulting, working with influential leaders across the world, it struck Jaime as she'd glance around meeting rooms at her client and colleagues that 'they just weren't well, but they weren't "unwell" . . . They weren't thriving.' Jaime observes that we've become disconnected and desensitised from our own bodies. 'We're so cerebral but the way we prize intellect has come at a cost: we disregard the intelligence of our body.' We're out of practice at reading the signals our bodies might be giving us. Even when we can tap into our body and how we're feeling, we often override it. Jaime makes the point that our minds are so well trained at overriding our bodies that the act of telling ourselves we're fine 'is inextricably linked with our ego and our sense of identity'.

According to the World Economic Forum, burnout alone is costing the global economy $322 billion annually. A Gallup study found nearly 50 per cent of disengaged workers are experiencing stress, leading to a loss of productivity. But it's vital that we look at these metrics as being more than dollars and percentages. These stats speak to the tangible detrimental effects our way of working has on our bodies. Stress and burnout affect our cholesterol, blood pressure, immune system and cognitive function.

The leading causes of harm, according to Jaime, is our 'addiction to our phones and our addiction to action'. She says we have to understand that these devices are designed to give us dopamine hits (with the 'ping' of a notification or the 'whoosh' of a sent email). They activate our reward centre and keep us coming back for more. 'Suppose you can't suspend needing to reach for your phone when it pings – if you can't comfortably be in silence, then this is an area of your wellbeing you need to turn your attention to.'

The other key issue, Jaime says, is sleep. Sleep has become a much more prominent topic in business and personal development circles in the past few years, but Jaime says her data suggests most people are still suffering from poor sleep routines and poor sleep habits. Practising an optimal sleep routine means not looking at screens in the hour before bed. But just as important is how we wake up. Banning phones from the bedroom and investing in an alarm clock is recommended. Don't let yourself check your device while you're still half asleep. 'It takes about thirty–seventy minutes for your body to wake up, so doing gentle exercise, stretching, having a shower or meditating can all help set you up for the day.'

To help deal with this, Jaime is a proponent of micro recovery, which she describes as activating our off switch and circuit-breaking our stress response so our body can undergo periods of recovery. One of her simple suggestions is to regularly stop and take ten deep breaths. Even better, count the time you breathe in for and aim to double your exhale time by comparison. Jaime explained to me, 'When you have a long, slow exhale, you activate your vagus nerve which is in charge of the parasympathetic nerve system . . . it's the body's relaxation system. When you breathe out slowly, you are sending a profound signal to your body saying, "We are safe, you can relax."'

You could also try going out for a five-minute walk in nature without your phone or putting a song on that you can sing along or dance to, just for those few minutes it's playing.

Small interventions like these can play a surprisingly significant part in helping you avoid the spiral of burnout. But as Jamie tells me, 'Micro recovery isn't just a tool for surviving, it's just as much about thriving.' So often we go outside ourselves to look for the balm, the cure, the help. I know I have been guilty of this. But our human systems are incredibly well resourced with all the answers if we just come back to ourselves. Little hacks like silence, stillness and sleep can actually super charge our ability and make a world of difference to wellbeing.

Our practical schedule needs to be built energetically

A few years ago, a buddy of mine launched an ambitious project called 'How's The World Feeling?' As a founder of Spur, a social enterprise focused on mental health, Lee Crockford's goal was to run the world's largest mental health survey and create the most extensive open-source data set of emotions. In October 2016, more than 10,000 people took part in a week-long survey where they were asked to answer three basic wellbeing questions. Participants would respond to questions when prompted throughout the day: how are you feeling (selecting from happy, sad, powerful, peaceful, anxious or angry); how intensely are you feeling that emotion (on a scale of 1–5); what are you primarily doing right now (working, exercising, etc.) and what is your relationship to any people around you (are you alone, around people but not interacting, actively interacting, etc.). The experiment was never intended to be hard science, but the results give pause to consider our own patterns and potentially rethink our schedule. For example, positive emotions tended to rise between 6 am and 8 am and then dramatically nosedive at 9 am, just in time for the typical start of the working day. And the worst day of the week? You guessed it: Monday! And yet how do 90 per cent of companies start a Monday morning? With a team meeting to get everyone focused for the week. Could it perhaps be more optimal to put that meeting immediately before or after lunch when most people are at their natural energy high-point of the day?

After you've done your energy audit, think about what you know energises you. For me it's exercise, cooking – specifically baking or making dinner for my better half – or being in deep conversations with meaningful people (an important distinction: I find inane small talk or people who like to talk about other people to be what my mentor Layne describes as 'energy vampires'). When I plan my week, those building blocks go in first. I don't let 'perfect' be the enemy of 'good'. I don't find one hour a day to exercise every day of the week, but I do find time every day to exercise – whether it's the incidental exercise of walking while I'm on a call or the 12-minute exercise sets I do using an app called Streaks. When I feel the temptation to push it aside because my inbox is overflowing or there's something else I should be doing, I remind myself that I'm a better person for the fact I've made that time to exercise or connect deeply with someone. The focus and energy I'll bring to the next meeting, my inbox or to those reports I've got to write is notably of a higher quality.

Keep track of what drains you and try to put what I term 'boundaries' or 'buffers' around it. Stephen Covey, in his seminal work *The 7 Habits of Highly Effective People*, introduced the notion of 'urgent' versus 'important' and made the point that we are exceptionally good at confusing the two. Particularly when texts, tweets and TikToks (not to mention emails!) ping on our phone all day long. Covey argues we lose about 40 per cent of our productivity every time we switch tasks or something distracts our focus, so those notifications are placing a huge energy impost on you! Think about locking yourself out of social media using apps like Flipd or FocusMe and batching the times you reply to emails rather than allowing them to infiltrate your whole day. I clear my inbox twice a day in my low energy states and *never* check my email first thing in the morning, because, for me, it's the easiest way to confuse urgent with important.

We can't avoid everything that drains us. Those Excel spreadsheets won't populate themselves, and those expenses and receipts won't automatically reconcile. But we can be mindful of not giving over high-energy states (optimal for creativity and engagement) to tasks that don't deserve it. We can also time-bind these tasks (put 45 minutes on the clock and do a blitz) or buffer them with activities we know will re-energise us out the other side.

Start small and establish some MVHs

Habits are hard to disrupt, and they're a topic we're going to frequently revisit throughout *The Leading Edge* because they're the building blocks of bridging gaps. We tend to search for (and over-believe in) the single 'surge' of effort and underestimate the power of consistent steps. An early mentor of mine, Steve Anderson, used to say, 'Success is about doing the fundamentals well consistently.' It's a mantra that has helped me a lot with resetting my habits.

James Clear, the author of *Atomic Habits*, one of the best books out there on the subject, talks about the concept of building minimum viable habits (MVHs). In establishing my new routines or doing something that's positive for my energy, I don't immediately try to 'surge' to my ideal state; I start with MVHs. At the moment, I'm focused on bringing more mindfulness into my days and weeks. I failed miserably when my MVH was 'twenty minutes of meditation every day'. Instead, I started with 1 minute of deep breathing once a day, without missing a day. When that becomes a routine, I'll up it to one minute twice a day and then try to increase my time to multiple minutes, multiple times a day.

The brain appreciates it when we can chunk routines down into a series of small, attainable habits – it gets to take a break! And that's our chance to slide behavioural change in. The beauty of MVHs is that humans tend to want to be consistent. We like ticking off the list, showing we've made progress. The Streaks app is a powerful tool that challenges its users: 'Don't break the chain, or your streak will reset to zero days.'

Think of an energy habit
Think of a habit you know will inject energy into your day or week but that you've struggled to make space and time for.

What would the MVH be?
If you start and it feels too big, or you're not able to build it into your day consistently, instead of getting demotivated, deconstruct it further. What's a smaller building block?

Scale not size
Retrain your focus to being about your reps, not on the size of the weight you're lifting, and you'll be blown away by how much more quickly you start getting results.

If I ever meet Tim from time management again, I might give him a new pull-up banner: 'If you plan your energy, you energise your plan.'

A question from the leading edge:

What is the time of the day where you feel most alive and how do you use it?

8

Get comfortable being uncomfortable

'You don't get to have a meaningful career or raise a family or leave the world a better place without stress and discomfort. Discomfort is the price of admission to a meaningful life.'

Susan David

Nobody has taught me more about fear, courage and high performance than Andy Walshe. He is the master of hacking human and creative potential. Andy spent years as the director of human performance at Red Bull and is one of my absolute favourite humans. I've often wondered whether his friendliness and sense of fun are the reason he gets such high-profile people to say 'yes' to doing all sorts of ridiculously uncomfortable things.

During his time at Red Bull, he was performance manager for Red Bull Stratos, leading the performance plan for Felix Baumgartner's record-breaking jump to Earth from the stratosphere in 2012. Yep, that is every bit as crazy/extraordinary as it sounds – google it, it's mind-blowing. The project set three world records, including proving that humans could travel at the speed of sound without any engine power.

Dealing with fear is going to be a crucial skill on your leadership journey, so strap yourself in and let's ride out some methods for finding your courage in these situations.

The uncommon challenge

Andy tells me that before you embark on getting uncomfortable, you've got to get clear on one thing: what's the purpose? After all, you need a pretty strong motivating force to push you through something tough. 'Getting uncomfortable, principally, is a process of accelerating self-awareness. When you are challenged, particularly in a unique way, you default to who you are pretty quickly.' Andy says this accelerated self-awareness process allows you to get clear on what you love, what you hate, what scares you and what causes you to thrive. Once you're clear on that, you can create a map for self-improvement based on this foundation.

Andy believes nature is our greatest teacher because the natural environment is full of uncertainty. As we grow in our role as a leader, we've often spent countless hours in one environment. The people who really reach 'their edge' as Andy terms it, are those who are prepared to put themselves in uncommon environments.

'People want to portray a version of themselves, which is obviously their best side, nothing wrong with that. But the reality is, when we actually put you in an uncommon space in an uncommon way, we can strip away that façade very quickly.'

Andy will take footballers and send them into Cirque du Soleil, make surfers try their hand at stand-up comedy, send some of the world's most famous artists out diving with Navy SEALs. He's also put people in extreme isolation. You name it, Andy's done it – or it's probably in the pipeline. He's hosted events for corporates that started with everyone having to jump from a third-storey rooftop into an airbag to enter the venue: the more out of your usual environment, the better. But the key isn't just to make people feel challenged, it's then learning the techniques to manage themselves in a high-stress state so when they go back to 'business as usual' they're even more comfortable.

According to Andy one of the most important things we can develop in ourselves is 'how to take a risk, how to manage risk, and how to assess risk'. As humans, this is something we do every day. Life is a risk. Love is a risk. Working meaningfully will always involve risk. But Andy says we often don't build the support we need around taking risks. Our environment predicates courage. Risk requires a team who will have your back and understand that you potentially will fall short of what you've set out to achieve.

If you're prepared to take on the challenge of stepping into uncommon and uncomfortable environments, Andy recommends three key strategies.

Be kind to yourself and reframe

When you're staring rising anxiety and stress in the face, reframe the whole thing from 'this is a threat' to 'this is a challenge'. Andy says when we fall, we need to make it simpler and go again. Be kind to yourself and say, 'Okay, I now know this and can improve next time.' And, 'Just don't stop trying.'

Practise responding versus reacting

Humans have an innate capability, in the absence of information, to fill in the blanks with a worst-case scenario. Andy says distinguishing between assessment versus assumption is critical. 'The assumption is the thing that really crushes humans. It's an ancient, physiological mechanism, but doesn't serve us in the new millennia.' When we feel threatened we react to interpreted threats rather than responding to real-time information. Responding means inserting a second to think and consider versus knee-jerking. I find it helpful to either take a couple of deep breaths or count to three in my head to give myself time to process.

Invest in it

Andy reflects that the difference between sport, the military and business is that in the former two, 'You train all the time, so it's like 98 per cent training and 2 per cent execution.' In business settings, people fail to grow because they never train. It's an interesting observation. Always being in execution mode is a fundamental problem. 'If you want to get world-class performance, you have to train. If you want to realise gains, you have to put in the development time.'

I share Andy's view that the importance of doing this work is only intensifying as we enter the age of augmentation and symbiosis with machines. As creativity becomes increasingly important in the quest for what is 'uniquely human', learning to cope with discomfort and thrive in uncertainty is going to be an increasingly valuable and essential trait.

The year of fear

You've no doubt seen or heard the phrase, 'Life begins at the edge of your comfort zone.' For those who are bold enough, I want to suggest to you that there is serious power in this phrase that is overused but an incredibly under-practised idea. When was the last time we really ventured outside the familiarity of routine, the network of people who appreciate us, and used or relied on skills other than the ones we're relatively confident in?

I've delivered keynotes and workshops to hundreds of thousands of people over the last ten years, and I watch the resonance of the concept but the incredibly low uptake of applying it. I've had emails and messages from hundreds of people who've used this idea to reframe the way they're approaching their life and have had some extraordinary breakthroughs . . . but they're a tiny percentage of those in the audience.

To ask for such courage from you, I want to share my journey with fear. Late in 2014, as part of my rebuild from 'the Crash of 2013' (aka my personal Great Depression), I was reading a lot of personal development literature and I came across this line from Tim Ferriss that hit me like a ton of bricks: 'what we fear doing most is usually what we most need to do'.

I feel like each of us has that one person in our life who, when you call them with a crazy idea, says, 'Awesome, I'm in.' That person for me is my best friend, Charlie – my partner in crazy experiments since 2009. I called Charlie, shared the quote with him and said, 'I think we need to guinea pig this idea . . . How about every day for the next twelve months we do something we're afraid of?' And Charlie said, 'Awesome, I'm in.'

Therein began 365 days of fear. In other words, our 'Year of Fear'. There were some basic rules:

1. We had to do something we were afraid of every day and fears had to be logged in an app (we used one called Make Me) by midnight.

2. If at any point either of us didn't complete a fear, my sports-obsessed self would lose sport for a week (no watching and no playing) and my caffeine connoisseur of a best friend would have to go a week without coffee.

3. We had to add a third rule at the end of about ten days of logging fears: you weren't allowed to use language that diminished the fear. We noticed a pattern where our entries into the app would start with, 'I know this might sound stupid but' or, 'I know this might seem silly . . .' and then we'd go on to describe the thing that we're afraid of. We banned that language. This was an honesty commitment. If Charlie logged something as a fear, I knew it took real courage from him to do that and vice versa. Taking this challenge on was hard enough without layering judgement on top.

When we started our challenge, we didn't realise it, but we had built a great feature into our design: accountability to someone we cared about and respected. Charlie and I went 365 days unbroken, and it wasn't because of the threat of losing sport or coffee . . . there was no way on Earth I was going to let my best friend do something fearful and vulnerable and not meet him in it, every single day. If I'd been doing this on my own, I never would have stuck with it.

Ironically, it took us about three months to get up the courage to tell people about our challenge, largely because we assumed they'd think we had a few screws loose or, worse, we worried that they'd ask us what sort of things we were afraid of, which felt far too vulnerable a thing to discuss beyond the two of us at the time! It struck me as curious throughout the experiment, and in the years of sharing the journey since, that we have such a fascination with others' vulnerability and yet such a determined need to prevent the world from seeing our own. Anyway, when we finally did share the story, everyone asked the same question: *How do you have enough things you're afraid of?*

This question initially stumped us; we felt like we had a never-ending list! Was there something wrong with us? But after a few months of experimenting and discussing the topic, we hit on where that question came from: we've desensitised ourselves to fear. Or Hollywood has. When I say 'fear', I invite you to pay attention to what images or thoughts flood your mind. Snakes? Spiders? Dangling from absurd heights? Being taken by a Great White?

Don't get me wrong. These are all legitimate (and understandable!) fears. But they're likely not the fears that keep us trapped in our comfort zone every day. I would argue it's these fears – let's call them daily discomforts – that are the single most significant barrier between us getting from where we are right now to achieving our goals. Not only do these fears show up every day in situations and circumstances that matter (at work, in our relationships with family and everywhere else) but most of us have become masterful at suppressing, ignoring or rationalising away the need to confront them.

This was one of the most profound lessons I learnt during the year of fear. When I reflect on the year and what I did there are definitely a few 'big' fears I took on, from quitting my job and starting my own company, to signing up for an Ironman 100 days out. I even tried my hand at stand-up comedy . . . But that's not the story of the year. The real achievement was confronting the much more subtle fears that represented a far bigger psychological challenge for me: learning to say 'no' to opportunities and handle my fear that they'd never come around again; having the courage to end relationships that were unhealthy for me; and saying 'yes' to myself and to my ideas. I also permitted myself to be a beginner and try things for the first time, to ask for help and say 'I don't know': sometimes two of the most terrifying things we can do and yet, as I came to find, unbelievably liberating.

It's also inaccurate for me to describe those 'big bucket' fears in a singular sense. Leaving my job and starting a new business wasn't one fear because it wasn't one decision in one moment. In reality, these comprised hundreds of smaller fears because I didn't confront imposter syndrome or struggle to be a beginner or ask for help only once: I had to do it over and over again. The fear didn't dissipate in one effort, so overcoming the fear required the sustained courage to develop a practice of overcoming these micro-fears. Encouragingly though, as we discovered on our year-long experiment, every time we face our fears and give them a shove in the opposite direction, our comfort zone gradually expands to take in entirely new territory – as though we're accumulating new land in a game of Risk. The circumstances and situations we now feel comfortable with and capable in expand.

Let me give you three big ideas and three strategies from our Year of Fear:

Idea 1: The single most important habit you can build today is to get comfortable being uncomfortable

Why? Because change is the only constant, and the velocity isn't slowing down. Ambiguity, uncertainty, transformation and disruption are not temporary phenomena; they are the operating environment for our generation of leaders. These are the match conditions we need to be preparing and developing strategies to deal with. While our comfort zone skills and capabilities are everything that has gotten us to where we are today, they won't get us to where we want to go tomorrow, if we're leading from the edge.

Idea 2: You have to re-sensitise to fear

Hollywood has desensitised us to fear. To take on the challenge of getting comfortable being uncomfortable, we have to re-sensitise to our daily ups and downs. I recommend doing this by taking yourself to a favourite spot where you can have 30 minutes to yourself. Take a piece of paper and a pen with you and draw yourself a chunky doughnut on the page. Label the doughnut hole 'comfort zone' and the chunky doughnut part 'courage zone'. (Feel free to take a doughnut with you if you need it for research purposes to get your sketch accurate . . . can't hurt.) Start with your comfort zone: what are all the skills and circumstances that are totally in your wheelhouse? Are you a finance ninja? A Gantt chart guru? Are you the person everyone in the office goes to when they need help? Name and own those strengths, because we're not abandoning on them, we're building on them. Plus, getting clear on our solid foundations will help inspire the courage to build to a higher vantage point.

Now we turn to the courage zone. Write down some skills, situations or circumstances that you know would be beneficial to have in your wheelhouse but right now feel uncomfortable with. The leaders I work with tend to articulate three categories for these.

- **Hard:** for example, being able to dissect a P&L; speak in front of a crowd; understand and 'speak' technology. These are skills that, more often than not, we know are core to the job description of our aspirational career or to what's 'next'.
- **Soft:** for example, giving constructive feedback or performance appraisals; holding people accountable or calling out poor behaviour; dealing with conflict. These courage-zone behaviours often directly confront our need to be liked.
- **Personal:** for example, apologising; telling people we care about them; admitting we were wrong; being vulnerable. The most profound stories of growth and triumph that I experienced in my Year of Fear, and those who have shared their stories with me as they've taken on the challenges subsequently, have come from

people prepared to push into this category. These personal fears can ripple into every facet of our life and are therefore perhaps the most powerful lever for transformation.

If you're struggling to think of courage-zone behaviours, be a dispassionate observer of yourself for a week. Watch when you pull yourself back, watch for flushed cheeks, sweaty palms, going to the kitchen for another coffee or becoming distracted with washing. These are often the signs we need to re-sensitise to.

Once you've listed a few fears, pick one or two that you believe would have the greatest impact to materially transform your life right now if you dealt with them. When we get through the fear strategies below, apply the framework to these fears.

Idea 3: Acknowledge the red line of resistance

If our fears were easy to conquer, we would have already done it. They're really not. The point is, they're important enough for us to feel the fear and do the frightening thing anyway. To help ourselves, we've got to catch the ways in which we stop ourselves. The inner circle of your doughnut is like a force field, and often we are unconsciously butting up against it. We continually get in the way of our own aspirations with our habits. We can't unleash creativity if we're fearful of being vulnerable and sharing new ideas. We can't be entrepreneurial if we won't take a risk on our ideas or if we demand results by tomorrow. We're also not going to make progress if we let ourselves think about all the reasons 'why not' before we give ourselves permission to try. I share all of these because they're all red lines of resistance that have held me back from achieving what I've been aiming at. Naming what's stopping you is half the battle, then you need to think about how you chip away at the red line. For me, during the Year of Fear, I had self-talk phrases I used as I was approaching doing the thing I was afraid of. I started changing the people I surrounded myself with: I spent time around more creatives and entrepreneurs. Relative to their vulnerability and preparedness to back themselves, my efforts felt positively timid! And that emboldened me to dangle my toe in the water and have a go.

Now for some strategies

Have a purpose

As we saw in Chapter 1, knowing your why is crucial. At that moment where it's a choice between what's easy and what's not, our why needs to be so strong as to compel us to opt out of comfort. Before you start any attempt at tackling fear, name your why as clearly and passionately as you can. You want it to be written in a way that ignites courage in your belly when you read it.

Don't long jump; take baby steps

We need to see tackling fear as akin to building muscle in the gym. Do not try to start by benching 500 kilograms. It's unlikely to end well, and you'll probably never re-enter the gym. We need to set ourselves up for success, so look at the courage-zone behaviour you've circled and think about how you can break it down into steps. If it's public speaking, think about how you could start by perhaps asking a question in front of a large group of people, then maybe at an event you might put your hand up to facilitate a conversation. Whatever you do, don't jump straight to debuting a keynote in front of 400 people with no notes.

Practise fear setting

Charlie and I leant heavily on the cousin of 'goal-setting' during our 365-day challenge – 'fear-setting'. Not only was this a way of calming our emotions about doing the fearful thing but it also served as a strategy for crossing the red line of resistance.

- Step one of fear-setting is to write out in elaborate detail what you believe will happen if you do the 'thing' you're afraid of. You will be blown away by how creative, apocalyptic and dramatic our imaginations can be!

- Step two is coming up with strategies for reducing the likelihood your fear will come true. Could you practise that tough conversation with a trusted colleague before you go and have it for real? Brainstorm different ways of building the confidence with which you're stepping into your courage zone.
- Step three sees us get clear on what we'll do if the thing we're afraid of does happen. If we're up speaking in public and lose our place, do we simply take a breath and recentre? Do we take power away from the fear by naming and sharing it with our audience? Do we make a joke? The more prepared we are, the more likely we can navigate our fight-or-flight response and steer the situation in the direction we want.

We need to view the courage zone process as a continual cycle. The goal here is to reduce the psychological hurdle to 'doing'. When you feel like you've made the ground you were hoping to in crossing a red line of resistance, revisit your sketch and pick another aspect of the courage zone to restart the process. Importantly, never let 'perfect' be the enemy of good.

Every time I write my goals or embark on a reflection process I draw that doughnut and I nominate which habit needs to be my focus in order to achieve my goals. I then think about the mini courage-zone milestones I'm committing to reaching so that I can make that fear fuel for my engine'. And generally, once a year, just to keep ourselves match fit, my crazy best friend and I do a fear sprint. We challenge you to join us.

> ### A question from the leading edge:
> When did you last back yourself to lead at the edge of your comfort zone?

9

Do the work required to hold an opinion

'Opinions are like arse-holes, in that everyone has one. There is great wisdom in this . . . but I would add that opinions differ significantly from arse-holes, in that yours should be constantly and thoroughly examined.'

Tim Minchin

We're in an age where opinion has been weaponised at the expense of truth. Masquerading as fact, opinions are deployed not to invite constructive conversation or debate but to score political or other points. Arguably that has never been better on display than with the 2020 US presidential election. Talking to friends from both sides of the political divide felt like talking to two different worlds separated by a vast chasm so desperately needing to be bridged by understanding.

Today we are expected to have a view on *everything*. In the event that you don't, you can rely on 143 million of your global friends to share their opinions with you every day on social media. A simple 'like' of someone else's opinion translates algorithmically as reflecting your own, and so the echo begins. We risk the knowledge economy becoming the opinion economy – an inflated currency in our polarised world.

In part, this gets to the heart of human sociology and anthropology; we are innately meaning makers. We are continually synthesising thousands of data points in order to make approximately 35,000 remotely conscious decisions a day. The Information Age really ramps up the degree of difficulty: In the last two years alone, 90 per cent of the world's data has been created. Every day, 306.4 billion emails land in our inboxes, and 500 million tweets light up our phones, if not our synapses; In 2020, we created 1.7 MB of data every second for every one of the more than 7.5 billion people in the world.

Information overload has many alternative names: infoxication, infobesity, data smog. 'We are wired to remember and use the information our eyes and ears receive,' says neuropsychologist Kenneth Freundlich of Morris Psychological Group.

> But our working memory – the mental workspace that retains information long enough for us to manipulate it or use it – can hold fewer than ten items at a time. Being constantly bombarded with far more information than we can process works to the detriment of our memory, our concentration and ultimately our ability to produce timely results and make good decisions.

According to David Kirsch in the University of California's Cognitive Psychology Department, overload also triggers anxiety, hence the phrase 'information anxiety'. The unfortunate antidote? Swiftly formed opinions.

Opinions are a dime a dozen. They're also more often than not unhelpful. They distract us from the real work of having to make meaning in a way that we can take to the bank. Well-thought-out opinions lead to conclusions and decisions that others can rely on. Well-researched opinions can change the dial on what we are prepared to put resources behind and be held accountable for. In other words, well-formed opinions can give you a leadership edge.

Anyone can have an opinion. Not everyone has a rigorous, robust and considered opinion.

The importance of good opinions

Opinions are linked directly to democratic ideals. As Evelyn Beatrice Hall said in 1906, 'I disapprove of what you say, but I will defend to the death your right to say it.' (What? You thought the French philosopher Voltaire said that? So did I. But that's the thing about opinions versus researched facts: you find out that this famous quote was actually created by one of his biographers, to describe Voltaire's attitude!) Beyond freedom of speech, there are a growing list of reasons we should consider cultivating this skill.

We're in a knowledge economy

People are hiring and firing based on our ability to add intellectual value, not to regurgitate facts. Anything that is definable and repeatable is capable of being automated, so the real value-creation of the next generation of workers and leaders comes from intellectual dynamism. In the 2020 World Economic Forum's list of the top ten future skills, five of the ten relate directly to being able to interpret, interrogate and initiate based on new information. Critical thinking, judgement, decision-making and cognitive flexibility all crack a mention. If you want to invest in your personal stock portfolio, these are the traits that are going to dramatically rise in value.

We're in the age of misinformation

Distinguishing between fact and fiction has never been harder or more crucial. To unpick complexity using key information and pick up on misinformation using a discipline of fact finding is now critical. Leaders must be clear on their source of truth, or risk peddling lies. We exist within echo chambers, unless we consciously bust ourselves out of them. It's on us to swim against the tide of algorithms, cookies, likes, shares and network leads that attract curated news angles, product placement and promoted campaigns.

Our opinions represent what we stand for

In order to own our narrative, we need to own our opinions. To do this credibly, our opinions must be defendable, well evidenced and somewhat original. Whether we reference the credibility of our opinions using statistical evidence, multiple reference points from thought leaders or lived experience, our opinions are only half as strong without accounting for the full story. Opinions need to take in their antithesis in order to be ground worth standing on. They need to hold the counter arguments within the argument. Whether we agree with someone's opinion matters less in our character judgement than whether we agree that the opinion is based on worthy consideration.

Think of your most strongly held opinions, be they environmental, political, spiritual, people-based or morally founded. What are they grounded in? How have you formed them? For example, you might have inherited ideals from your parents or your time at school, others you may have picked up from influential bosses, mentors or books. Which do you feel are truly your own?

Few people better embody the idea of staking your life on your opinions than Maria Ressa, founder of *Rappler*. *Rappler* is a Philippine online news website based in Manila. It started as a Facebook page named MovePH in 2011 and evolved into a complete website in 2012. At the time I corresponded with Ressa's team, she was fresh from having been convicted of 'cyberlibel' and awaiting a sentence for what could be up to six years in prison. The accusations were levelled at Ressa over an article that alleged links between a Filipino businessman and a judge. Amal Clooney, the barrister leading a team of international lawyers representing Ressa, said the court had become 'complicit in a sinister action to silence a journalist for exposing corruption and abuse'. Ressa herself at the post-verdict press conference declared 'Freedom of the press is the foundation of every single right you have as a Filipino citizen. If we can't hold power to account, we can't do anything.'

Rappler has exposed and documented the 'brutal' anti-drugs campaign run by Philippines president, Rodrigo Duterte, which is estimated to have led to thousands of extrajudicial killings. The president, in response, has called *Rappler* 'fake news' and his administration has brought several cases against it.

In an age where truth is hard to find, how do we distinguish fake news from fact?

What makes a 'good' opinion?

Charlie Munger, the long-time business partner of Warren Buffet, is famous for saying, 'I never allow myself to have an opinion on anything that I don't know the other side's argument better than they do.' In fact, he goes further to say that it's bad to have an opinion that you're proud of if you can't state the other side's case better than they can.

That's not how most of us play the opinion game. In an amusing (and insightful) experiment a few years ago, NPR published an article one Tuesday morning on their Facebook page titled 'Why Doesn't America Read Anymore?' It was like crack for patriotic keyboard warriors. Like digital moths to a social media flame, audiences descended on the post, leaving comments passionately rejecting NPR's assertion, defending their own reading record or blaming the demise of the American education and whichever administration they deemed responsible for it. But those who clicked on the article received the message:

> Congratulations, genuine readers, and happy April Fools' Day! We sometimes get the sense that people are commenting on NPR stories that they haven't actually read. If you are reading this, please like this post and do not comment on it. Then let's see what people have to say about this 'story.' Best wishes and have an enjoyable day, Your friends at NPR.

Ironically, their post had been subtitled 'In these times, the story matters more than ever'. Our friends at NPR were testing a hypothesis that a majority of people who engaged with their content online did so without even reading it.

Studies back up our tendency to hold an opinion without doing the work. According to a 2016 study by computer scientists at Columbia University and the French National Institute, 59 per cent of links shared on social media have never actually been clicked. In other words, most people simply retweet news without ever reading it. The average Facebook user clicks on only 7 per cent of the political news stories they see in their feed, meaning they are generally only getting small doses of information through polarising headlines.

When we are short on time and compelled to auto-scroll, how do we consolidate our opinions? One idea is to pick content pillars to support your why. For example, if my why is 'to be the change I want to see in the world', I could shape my feeds to inform me across relevant content pillars: change movements, hope and global inequality. When narrowing our topics though, it is equally important to broaden our sources. Make sure to diversify the content and voices you're taking in and reach out to people who will disagree with you.

Formulating an opinion worth holding requires us to first look outward and explore, before looking inward to challenge our own arguments. In putting together a project on data privacy recently, I secured time with a range of stakeholders who represented vastly different sources of knowledge, experience and objectives. Only then did I form my own view on what the research needed to test. By training ourselves to become impartial judges of our own beliefs, we force ourselves to live in an extended worldview. Here is the easier-said-than-done key to making opinions work for you: become your own toughest critic; suspend your own belief; abandon your best-loved ideals when they fail to stand up to counter arguments. The practice of opinion-making should see us adapt or destroy our ideas, assumptions and stances on a regular basis. This is the work required to hold an opinion and doing it will deliver enormous personal and professional dividends.

Mental models for making critical sense

To begin with, we need to 'do the work'. By that, I mean do the reading and the listening. We may need to seek out as many arguments on the topic in question as possible and think through the assumptions and interests that sit beneath them. Who benefits from the statement in question? How reliable is the source? What are the ulterior motives of the publisher? It's time to dial up your critical thinking. It helps if we have some frameworks to use to evaluate new information. This is where mental models come in.

Many people use informal models, either in their head or in writing, but making these more formal is helpful for improving their clarity and usefulness. Whether we realise it or not, models are at work everywhere, and are often described as a practical approach to wisdom. Most of us have probably never had more exposure to modelling than we did during the COVID pandemic when our news feeds were full of epidemiological forecasts and economic modelling of what the pandemic would mean for unemployment and GDP. Models help us to synthesise information and communicate. They also require us to develop a logical structure or coherence, which supports us to make better decisions and improve our understanding of our own decision-making processes. This, in turn, can allow us to develop repeatable systems and hone processes to improve the accuracy of our forecasts.

If you happen to have gone through a schooling system built on rote-learning and regurgitation (i.e. most of us), mental models are quite a different idea. If rote learning is just hitting a tennis ball against the wall (you get back what you give out, repeatedly), mental models are like unleashing yourself on a jungle gym, with ball pits, a trapeze and an array of apparatus at your disposal.

Sounds like a more enjoyable way of jumping through hoops to me!

In a famous speech in the 1990s, Charlie Munger summed up mental models by saying, 'Well, the first rule is that you can't really know anything if you just remember isolated facts and try and bang 'em back. If the facts don't hang together on a latticework of theory, you don't have them in a usable form.'

In the information age, knowledge is no longer power. Rather, applied knowledge is power. More and more, businesses are requiring us to be adaptable with the mental models we bring to the workplace.

The first thing to remember is that there is no such thing as the 'ultimate model'. Models are contextual to the field of observation, study or application. The point, well articulated by the founder of the online knowledge-sharing community Farnam Street, Shane Parrish, is that 'the quality of our thinking is proportional to the models in our head and their usefulness in the situation at hand. The more models you have – the bigger your toolbox – the more likely you are to have the right models to see reality.'

What mental models do you rely on, and are you aware of when and how you use them to make sense of the world around you? Here are some I bet you have going on in the background:

- Supply and demand: understanding the flow of economics
- Maslow's hierarchy of needs: understanding what people will pay attention to
- Reciprocity: understanding the power of giving is the power of receiving
- Margin of safety: understanding the pressure a system can withstand without breaking

Mental models are everywhere, including in your own mind. The trick is to use them readily, change them often and overlay them as needed. Try this:

- List the top five problems keeping you up at night.

- Work out whether you are applying various mental models to these challenges in order to understand them.
- Actively search for an alternative mental model to apply.
- Can you find a solution that holds up to multiple mental model applications?

How do we test our views?

Before we jump into the specifics, I want to borrow from comedian Tim Minchin's stellar commencement address that I opened the chapter with once more:

> We must think critically, and not just about the ideas of others. Be hard on your beliefs. Take them out onto the verandah and beat them with a cricket bat. Be intellectually rigorous. Identify your biases, your prejudices, your privilege. Most of society's arguments are kept alive by a failure to acknowledge nuance.

This evokes such a powerful visual for me as to what it means to do the work required to hold an opinion. The work isn't done once we've developed a set of mental models; we need to continue to shape, question and challenge those models, updating as necessary. We have to check our own biases and blind spots. Each of us has them; they're part of our brain finding shortcuts to make decisions, an adaptation (or hangover, depending on the circumstance) from our Paleolithic origins. Having biases doesn't make us bad but failing to acknowledge them can lead to bad decision-making. As Farnam Street describes it, having an understanding of your limits, incentives and weaknesses goes a long way towards helping you understand your own proclivities towards information. One of the most powerful biases we need to catch is confirmation bias: our tendency to selectively perceive information in favour of facts and insights that confirm our initial hunch, often to the exclusion of all else.

What do you think of Trump?

This loaded question has recently divided a nation and a large portion of the world. But how many of us have sought out the opposing viewpoint? One of the challenging parts of engaging with counter opinions is contending with 'cognitive dissonance', the discomfort that comes with having two conflicting views, opinions or beliefs. When we confront the idea that we're wrong we typically react defensively. As Tina Soika describes, cognitive dissonance 'is most powerful when it is about our self-image: if we find ourselves doing things that are not consistent with who we think we are, that in itself creates dissonance. It can make us feel inadequate or foolish.'

When our beliefs and our required actions don't line up, cognitive dissonance will often stall the decision-making process and lead to inaction. We shut down or double down. We'll say things like 'I'm entitled to my opinion', 'that's what I believe, okay?!', or 'just because you think differently from me doesn't mean I'm wrong.' Often these phrases are retorts used to shelter beliefs we should have abandoned. Activist and founder of the #MeToo movement, Tarana Burke, talks about the need to be able to hold the tension between two truths or to acknowledge the existence of multiple truths. This gets to Minchin's point about acknowledging nuance, but we have to fight ourselves to stay open enough to appreciate it.

I find spoken word poetry one of the most exposed and exquisite domains in which the work of holding your opinions up to the light is being done. While spoken word has a rich history, from ancient Greece to the civil rights movements and anonymous bards to the US Youth Poet Laureate Amanda Gorman, spoken word poetry took on a heightened prominence in the 1980s when 'slam poetry' competitions emerged, where random members of the audience are asked to judge short recitals by poets.

Some of the most superbly expressed ideas and powerful imagery I've ever encountered have come in slam poetry form. Anis Mojgani, a New Orleans slam poet of African American and Iranian heritage, is my personal favourite. His poem 'Shake the Dust' gives me goose-bumps; his work is deservedly described as 'fiercely hopeful word arias'. Scores of brilliant slam poems have been written as part of the Black Lives Matter movement.

One of the things I find compelling about this medium, even if you never read it in front of the crowd but use it as a training exercise as you craft and refine your own opinion, is that it is neither adversarial (as debate is) nor is it an esoteric sermon from the mount. Great slam poetry makes you feel the ideas, and the best will leave you with food for thought long after sound has stopped reverberating through the microphone. Try it on for size and see how it pushes you to support your ideas.

As Rabbi Ben Hecht described in the *Huffington Post*, 'Having strong opinions is necessary to positively affect the world – but that is only truly possible if those opinions also reflect the reality of the spectrum of thought. The valuable, strong opinion is not the one without any questions or doubts but the one which reflects this honest complexity of multidimensional reality and human limitation. It is the opinion predicated on the recognition of variance inherent in the full recognition of the range of values.'

Sometimes I will pick a topic, let's say Black Lives Matter, and I'll scatter my factual truths as dots on the page – a mind map of sorts. I will challenge myself to draw 'logic lines' between the dots, and in doing so, unearth my assumptions, beliefs and non-factual values. It is in these spaces between held truths that we find room for the alternate narratives that elucidate our opinions. It doesn't mean we have to let go of our opinions, but rather that we might need to expand on them.

We also must recognise that sometimes 'I don't know' is the bravest thing we can say. When we find ourselves in a conversation on a topic beyond our knowledge, there are many ways to engage intelligently from a place of not knowing. For example: 'That's interesting, I'd never considered that perspective before', or 'What led you to know so much about this topic?' When people can see you actively listening to their opinions, you will not only learn what they think, but why they think it . . . and that enables you to critically form your own opinion.

There is extraordinary power in admitting we don't know, in signalling that we're willing to learn and in asking for help. There's so much shame wrongfully associated with 'I don't know' and yet some of the most powerful, vivid moments of my leadership journey to date were bearing witness to powerful leaders deploying that phrase with major decisions on the line. The key is allowing 'I don't know' to be the beginning, not the end, of the conversation. Admitting we don't know is like being chafed by an ill-fitting wetsuit for the hour-long swim leg of an Ironman – you'll do anything to finish and take it off. That discomfort can be a powerful catalyst for our curiosity and development.

Give it a go!

- Pick something you have a strong opinion about and intentionally seek out someone on the other side of the coin. Ask questions. See if you can reframe their argument back to them. Can you take on Charlie Munger's challenge of reciting the other side's argument better than they can?
- Use the 'five whys': when you think about an opinion you hold can you give five robust reasons why you believe it to be true or hold that opinion? When you find yourself defaulting to reasons like 'because' or 'I just do', hit the research and strengthen your opinion.
- Enrol in a poetry slam. Think about how to bring your views to life with the power of spoken word.

A question from the leading edge:

Think about an opinion you hold strongly. How well can you defend it against those who disagree?

10
Start before you're ready

'Start where you are. Do what you can. Use what you have.'

Arthur Ashe

I've never been 'Ready'. Not when I chaired the G20 at age twenty-four. Not when I did an Ironman at twenty-five. Not when I was asked to interview President Obama and certainly not when Penguin Random House asked me to write a book! To be honest, I'm convinced 'ready' isn't really a thing.

We have not evolved to be 'ready', because the world is constantly evolving!

In my head, 'Ready' is a Pleasantville-esque town where the ducks line up, everything is entirely in order and things happen as though gracefully choreographed. In reality, I firmly believe 'Ready' is a mirage. It's an alluring yet illusory place that's always just a little further along from where we are right now. Because the mirage sparkles and shines in a way that the ground under our feet doesn't, we delay or defer taking action. As Wayne Gretzky famously said, 'You'll miss every shot you never take.'

Core to embracing this idea of starting before we're ready is realising that 90 per cent of success is simply showing up, in the fullest way, and letting the action unfold. Which, as a recovering perfectionist, has taken me the better part of a decade to get comfortable with. We have to learn to trust our instincts, judgements and capabilities. In my early twenties, I was obsessed with the idea of 'plans' – you needed to have a plan for your life, for how you were going to get from A to B, for how that next opportunity was going to come good. And if you deviated from the plan, you'd obliterate your chances. But then when I started interviewing leaders and I asked them about this mythical, meticulous plan I was convinced everyone had, I couldn't find anyone who'd corroborate my theory. They all told me they never had a plan or, if they had had one, that the script of their life had deviated so dramatically from said plan that they only found themselves when they had the confidence to get truly lost! Gradually (I wish I could pretend it was overnight but it probably took me 500 points of counter evidence to abandon this particular opinion), I loosened my grip on the idea of being 'ready'. I changed my mantra to 'ready to have a go'. Now this is the state I constantly sit in.

The idea of starting before we're ready is not an excuse for half-arsing our work and this chapter should be held in tension with 'preparation discipline'. While the examples following are by and large entrepreneurial, please don't be mistaken in thinking that the notion of starting before you're ready applies purely to launching a new business or product. This applies to pushing for promotions, putting your hand up for new responsibilities and being prepared to say 'yes' or to be the catalyst for introducing things that excite you into your scope of responsibility at work.

Being ready to have a go

The founder of legendary start-up accelerator Y Combinator, Paul Graham, encourages change-makers to 'Live in the future, then build what's missing.' No doubt this method helped him launch the likes of Airbnb, Dropbox, Reddit and hundreds of other companies, by creating from a state of future possibility rather than current restraints. Starting before you're ready picks up on that essence; it means stretching and then going to work to get up to speed. Here we're talking about two things: trying multiple ideas and not getting in your own way.

Cycling up our ideas and experimentation velocity

Entrepreneurs I work with often talk about the fact that innovation is less about the tireless quest for the 'one idea' as it is about finding the ten thousand ideas that *don't* work as quickly as possible.

Get out of our own way

I'm talking in particular to people who would much rather take the risk of overbaking something by twenty minutes than they would let it out of the oven even one minute under 'done'. If you're one of these people, or a recovering one like me, suspend your scepticism for just a minute because there are some nuggets of gold in lean methodology and design thinking for each and every one of us, in any given context – intrapreneurs and entrepreneurs alike.

Prototyping

Bringing an idea to life doesn't have to be complicated or expensive. Australia's non-profit Adara Group works in maternal, newborn and child healthcare in remote parts of Uganda, and remote community development in Nepal. And I mean remote – twenty-five days' walk from the nearest Nepali road. They also run a knowledge-sharing pillar of work to amplify impact. Like many places around the world, the Ugandan region they work in has a high level of respiratory distress syndrome in premature newborns; some 65 per cent of newborns struggle with what is the most common cause of disease and distress in babies born more than six weeks prematurely. In developed countries, continuous positive airway pressure (CPAP) and other solutions are available to make sure newborns get breathing support. But too often in low-resource settings, without electricity supplies, let alone the necessary equipment, respiratory distress syndrome is a death sentence.

Unperturbed by the relative lack of resources and mission-driven to keep kids alive, as a key part of Adara's work in newborn health, she works in partnership with Kiwoko Hospital and research partners PATH, the University of Washington and Seattle Children's Hospital. Whereas a standard CPAP machine could cost anywhere between US$800 and US$8000 and relied on a continuous electricity supply, PATH developed an inexpensive 'safe bubble' CPAP kit that does not rely on an electrical power source. It includes an ingenious fixed-rate air blender that blends room air with oxygen, allowing staff to deliver safer, more appropriate levels of oxygen to newborns when needed. The proportion of oxygen and room air is critical – too little oxygen means there is not enough oxygen in the cells and tissues of the body, but too much oxygen can be toxic, resulting in blindless and lung and brain damage. The device is expected to cost less than $US20. PATH is the export innovator and Adara is the expert implementer.

Audette Exel, Adara's founder, is a truly extraordinary woman. To me she is the embodiment of the essence of the Ralph Waldo Emerson quote, 'Do not go where the path may lead, go instead where there is no path and leave a trail.' Her breadcrumb trail of sector-crossing and model-pioneering innovation is remarkable. She also has one of the biggest hearts of anyone I know. She's guided me through break-ups and career decisions aplenty and there are few people on the planet that I have the deep-seated respect and adoration for in the way I do for Audette.

Audette's story is one of social activism and feminism. Audette was sure she would be a human rights activist. But when she broke her knee jumping in the Australian Parachute Championships (as one does!) Audette ended up having to finish a law degree at the University of Melbourne instead. She describes hobbling into a university full of kids who drove nice cars. Having been a commercial cleaner for five years as she worked her way through university, and coming from a left-wing activist family, Audette realised she knew nothing about money and power, and decided she ought to. After her law degree, she took a sharp right-hand turn and went into the world of corporate law and finance. At one point, Audette was managing director of one of Bermuda's three banks, one of the youngest women in the world to have run a publicly traded bank, and also acted as chair of the Bermuda stock exchange. She tells me in our interview: 'I was still an activist young woman but an activist young woman who realised she could use the tools of power and capital to effect change.'

In 1998, Audette established Adara in order to deliver the highest quality health and education services to some of the most vulnerable people in the most remote places on the planet. In setting it up, Audette deliberately messed with the social-enterprise business model. She says, 'I am not a woman of wealth. Never have been, never will be. It's not something that interests me. So I figured that I could change the model. Models, models, models! I've always been playing with models.'

What Audette did was go to a bunch of bankers and ask them to use their mastery for purpose – by doing one deal a year where they hand their fees earned over to the disadvantaged. Adara now co-leads deals with multiple volunteer stakeholders including: the chairman of Goldman Sachs; the Executive Chairs of Barrenjoey Capital Partners; the head of investment banking at Citigroup; the head of Equity Capital Markets at Herbert Smith Freehills; and former heads of JPMorgan, UBS and others. All serve as Adara's authorised representatives on their financial services licence. As new world leaders are we thinking proactively enough about return beyond the construct of financial models?

Audette then hired development specialists and asked them to collaborate on evidence-based best practice for service delivery to the most vulnerable groups in the world's toughest places.

Critically they didn't have to worry about where the money was going to come from (their banking colleagues would take care of that) so their exclusive focus was best-practice solutions.

Speaking about the development of the CPAP technology, Audette stresses that prototypes should only command as much time, effort and investment as are needed to generate useful feedback and evolve an idea. In this instance, they not only wanted their prototyping cycle to be cheap (they still need to make every dollar stretch as far as possible) but also for their solution to be viable: the end product had to cost less than $50.

As the Adara team practised and as the literature stresses, the goal of prototyping isn't to finish. It's to learn about the strengths and weaknesses of the idea and to identify new directions and tweaks that further prototypes might take. It's also worth noting proto-typing isn't confined to products; it works for services too. While prototypes of a service innovation will not be physical, they must still be tangible. This is often why it's suggested that you think about filming or 'capturing' a service prototyping in some way in order to be able to meaningfully take stock of the learning. Starting before you're ready requires us to have faith in ourselves, faith in the process and faith that the problem we are trying to solve requires a solution. To learn by doing is the ultimate call to action. You will be surprised how many like-minded change-makers sense your urgency and step in to lend a hand.

Make it handmade first

One of my favourite conversations about 'starting up' was with General Assembly co-founder Matthew Brimer. 'Brimer', as he is commonly referred to among friends and colleagues in the start-up world, is a serial entrepreneur, community builder, venture investor and a general instigator of mischief. He was inspired to start General Assembly after witnessing less than impressive attempts to take learning 'digital' during his time as a sociology undergrad at Yale and later seeing the need for a community epicenter for technology and design in NYC. What began as a single co-working space in 2011 has since grown into a global education company serving individuals and companies alike, with campuses in nearly twenty cities across four continents and tens of thousands of graduates worldwide. Brimer and his fellow co-founders sold the company for $413 million in 2018. Meanwhile, Brimer had already jumped into his next venture – co-founding Daybreaker, a global community and lifestyle brand producing conscious and wellness-oriented experiences around the world – with a specialty in joy-inducing (and completely sober) early-morning dance parties. He also launched General Assembly's philanthropic arm, Opportunity Fund, so that anyone willing to work hard and follow their passions can have a meaningful career pursuing work they love. Most recently he co-founded a community-powered venture capital fund (playfully known as simply 'The Fund'), pooling expertise and capital from successful entrepreneurs to invest in the next generation of mission-driven founders in major start-up hubs around the world. And he's already cooking up a new venture that is still under wraps!

Brimer's honesty is incredibly refreshing. When he spoke about GA's humble beginnings he reflected, 'Contrary to popular belief, most entrepreneurs don't know what they're doing when they're first getting started.' He told me it wasn't until several years into the GA journey that they became a global online education company. At this point, Brimer and the team began to understand their actual value was in the learning community and career-oriented curriculum they were building, and their focus moved to fewer professors and more practitioners. Brimer says, 'There are lots of evolutions of the founding idea along the way, and you just have to try new stuff all the time, and then keep doing more of what works and less of what doesn't.' Though that might sound obvious, so often we can become blinkered by how we want something to play out rather than how it actually does.

My personal favourite feature of GA's foundations was the stated work value, 'The first time is always handmade.' As Brimer explains, 'For us, that means when you're first trying something or getting a new initiative off the ground, it's actually a good thing for it to be totally manual and handmade and imperfect and not automated. As long as you can get the job done, even if it's humans rather than software doing most of the heavy lifting behind the scenes, that's fine. If your product works and people are enjoying it and finding it useful, you can figure out how to automate it later.'

In Brimer's view, 'It's far better to build something that people are obsessed with – even if it's clunky – than to overbuild something people are indifferent about.' Make your vision in handmade form first, and work out whether customers love it or not before you pour your blood, sweat, and tears into realising every little feature. Just stay focused on the love!

Don't be the Segway

It's worth noting that no amount of time or money will make a round peg of an idea fit through a square hole. By rapid prototyping early, and then testing the value of our idea through creating what MBA courses call a 'minimum viable product', we can avoid wasting time, money and other resourcing.

Alternatively, we can do what Segway did. For those unfamiliar with this 'vehicle', the Segway is undeniably a technological marvel. It has better balance than a human and leaves a car's fuel efficiency for dead. If you believed the investor and company hype, it was going to be bigger than the internet. The company poured $100 million into research and development, and expected to be selling one a minute – 10,000 a week – in its first year. The $5000 Segway was birthed into the world with all the bells and whistles of a Silicon Valley product launch, and yet in the six years after launching, Segway sold just 30,000 units, suggesting an average of more than two months per sale.

Why? Social sentiment sank the Segway. They weren't approved for transportation on roads everywhere, limiting their usefulness. They were awkward to ride and, at more than 45 kilograms, they were heavy to move around when not being ridden. Looking through online critiques, customers describe the aesthetics of the device as akin to an expensive vacuum cleaner or a mobile speaker podium, it turns out not many people wanted one.

Segway also highlights the pitfall of developing and testing an idea under a veil of secrecy. One account of its development noted, 'Employees kept the shades drawn, and in some cases, they sealed the blinds with tape, lest someone try to peek through the narrow gap between the blind and window frame. They hid the Segways in plywood crates before transporting them.'

But working this way kept Segway from figuring out what people might want or need in a scooter. As one earlier engineer remarked, 'How do you do product testing if you can't go outside?'

It turns out what holds up under the neon glow of an engineering lab doesn't do so well in the harsh light of day. The faster you test your ideas with real people, the better.

Run your own race

At this point, I want to talk to my female readers for a quick minute because all of the literature tells us that women find it particularly challenging to start before they're ready. Hang around, though, guys – it's worth you being aware of this phenomenon too, because making any progress on diversity and inclusion requires men, women and non-binary people pulling in the same direction.

In a *Harvard Business Review* article by Tara Sophie Mohr, which sparked a global conversation around what has now been termed 'The Confidence Gap', she cites an internal Hewlett Packard study that found that men will apply for a job when they meet 60 per cent of the criteria. In contrast, women will only apply when they meet 100 per cent. Mohr was sceptical that the differential in application rates centred solely on confidence, so she dug further. Mohr found two compelling gender differences. A big reason women didn't apply was not wanting to face failure. Almost one in four surveyed said their top reason for not going after the job was: 'I didn't think they would hire me since I didn't meet the qualifications and I didn't want to put myself out there if I was likely to fail.' Only 13 per cent of men said this. The other discovery was that women were nearly two times more likely than men to 'play by the rules', justifying not applying as being a result of 'following the guidelines'.

While we may all subscribe to our own window of the gender spectrum, the truth of the confidence gap goes beyond male or female findings. The question is around owning our self-worth. It's easy to see ourselves as 'not-enough' when we are sitting in a place of inaction. We have no momentum, no wind beneath our wings. When we are starting from the ground, considering flying, we are rooted to the spot, thinking how risky the flight path looks. This is the confidence gap. It only grows with over-thinking. But when we've taken off, however clumsily, all we're worried about is flapping our wings, staying up in the air. It's much harder to talk ourselves down when we are rocketing forward in action. I wonder if the confidence gap isn't the distance between thinking and doing. Internationally renowned leadership coach Eva Young is quoted as saying, 'To think too long about doing a thing often becomes its undoing.' So, what do we need to do to get started?

The five-stage design thinking model

What's that idea you've had simmering on the backburner for so long? You know, that flash of brilliance you've been waiting for to be 'ready' to explore? What would be the equivalent of getting yourself to try it? As the saying goes at the go-to design thinking company IDEO, 'If a picture is worth a thousand words, then a prototype is worth a thousand meetings.'

The five-stage design thinking model was originally proposed by the Hasso Plattner Institute of Design at Stanford. It is widely available and continually used by individuals and firms to improve how they develop their products. If you haven't come across it before, try testing it out in whatever area you're working or trying to create change.

1 Empathise
Learn about the audience for whom you are designing to better understand the problem and test your assumptions.

2 Define
Pull together all the information generated in the Empathise step to construct a point of view that is based on users' needs and insights.

3 Ideate
Brainstorm and come up with creative solutions. Start 'logically' and then create the space to allow for alternative solutions to problems.

4 Prototype
Build a representation of one or more of your ideas to show to others.

5 Test
Return to your original user group and test your ideas for feedback.

I do not find starting before I'm ready easy or pleasant (I was the kid who took three years to come to terms with failing her driving test for Pete's sake!) but I find it imperative. I've learnt that the higher the velocity I try ideas with, the earlier I seek the feedback of others in the process and the more I surround myself with people who are on a similar journey, the easier it's becoming. The idea of *The Leading Edge* began with an idea scribbled down for Mindsets, Methods and Mastery on the back of the proverbial napkin. I then worked my idea into deliberate conversations with my network of emerging leaders to find out what they were missing. I went back through the thousands of interviews I'd had with inspiring leaders to map the uncommon threads of leadership compared to published literature. Next, you guessed it, I made the time and space to allow stream of consciousness to take over and tried not to freak out when 180,000 words lay somewhat unfiltered in front of me! I then worked with my team to cut the manuscript by half and tighten up the priority themes, before testing with a bunch of diverse, honest and smart readers. As you can see, I have followed the five-stage design thinking model in order to write *The Leading Edge*. Now you're holding it in your hands.

I'm so glad I started.

> ### *A question from the leading edge:*
>
> If money and time were not a constraint, what would you start right now?

Mastery

Leadership is as accessible as hard work

11

Unlearn, learn and relearn

'The illiterate of the 21st century will not be those who cannot read and write, but those who cannot learn, unlearn, and relearn.'

Alvin Toffler

More than 2000 years ago, the seed of a civilisation sprang into being on seven hills in central Europe. That 'civilisation start-up' would go on to scale and sustain itself for over 500 years as one of the most significant economic and cultural powers the Earth had ever seen. At its peak, the Roman empire occupied more than 5 million square kilometres and was home to approximately 20 per cent of the world's population. Lionised for its leadership and innovation, scholars have pored over this period of history looking for the 'secret sauce' to its mastery: was it Caesar? Was it the ability to triumph in successive battles? Was it their rules and laws?

In fact, as philosopher Baron de Montesquieu explained, the Roman empire's success could in large part be traced to its willingness to always give up its practices for better ones. The Romans' Julian calendar was not the first calendar, but the most influential in European history. Romans took naturally occurring cement and processed it as fast-drying liquid to build their arches and columns. Roman architecture itself was copied from the Greeks and embellished. Examples of

Roman adaptations abound. But there is perhaps no better example of achieving mastery than through the cycle of 'learning, unlearning and relearning' demonstrated by the Romans.

With future-fit mindsets and methods at our disposal, we are headed towards mastering leadership and becoming a catalyst for change in the world. But mastery is not a static state. To be masterful, your movements become fast and fluid. Essentially, you already know what's going to happen next, and your sensibility is such that if something seems slightly remiss, you're experienced enough to know how to correct it. What does mastery look like in an uncertain, ever-changing, increasingly complex world? Is masterful leadership perhaps no longer about having the answers, but asking the questions?

Interestingly, it was when the Romans were at the height of power that they lost their learning rhythm, their cadence of give and take, learning and unlearning, and became stagnant in their own success. (The word 'decadence' derives from 'decay'.) But unlearning can be confronting and many who have reached a level of success don't realise their own dire need for unlearning until a sense of decay has already set in. This is the paradox of success and a lesson to us all on our leadership journeys.

Skills mismatch

'Skills mismatch' wasn't a phrase I was overly familiar with until I found myself trying to shape employment policy in 2014. As the recently appointed chair of the Youth Summit for the G20, hosted that year in Australia, I was charged with representing the voice of 1.5 billion young people across the G20 nations. In deciding which issues to raise with world leaders on behalf of this diverse array of young people we asked ourselves: what is the common challenge? As it turns out, overwhelmingly, it was getting a job. While I could point out extreme outliers (Spain hit 64 per cent youth unemployment that year), across every G20 nation youth unemployment was three to four times the headline national unemployment rates. In addition, a steady stream of reports foreshadowed the automation of work to mean that, within the next decade, about 40 per cent of jobs were set to disappear.

In the multitude of conversations I had that year with G20 leaders, employment ministers and labour experts, the conversation frequently came back to 'skills mismatch' – a term economists were using to describe the pronounced global disconnect between the jobs available and the skills possessed by job-hunters. Clearly we needed a massive overhaul of our education systems and learning frameworks. But I just remember thinking, 'Jeez, I'm going to grow old while this bureaucracy grapples with "solving" youth unemployment.'

I intend no disrespect to well-meaning public servants and policy-makers. The experience with the G20 made me so passionate about the importance of systems reform that it inspired my undertaking the master's degree of public policy to improve my ability to participate constructively. But, because the system by its very nature cannot move as dynamically as the world does, or as quickly as we as individuals can, I saw firsthand how difficult it was to get agreement on measures, to massage language, to manage a multitude of stakeholders with competing priorities. I sat there at the G20 table, surrounded by masterful leaders, feeling that we were already so far behind. It made me realise lifelong learning is imperative – and that in the age of hyper career–mobility the buck stops with each and every one of us.

I've discovered that learning actually has three important facets to it. At any given time, we need to be asking ourselves:

- What am I working on **unlearning** that no longer serves me?
- What am I working on **learning** to expand and develop myself further?
- What am I working on **relearning** because it's important to me once more?

It's just like riding a (backwards) bike

You'll have heard the phrase, 'Oh, it's just like riding a bike.' We are generally describing a skill that, once learnt, can never be forgotten. It also reveals just how ridiculously challenging unlearning is: how do you rewire things that are hardwired?

To consider that we need look no further than the lessons offered by Destin Sandlin's backwards bike. In 2016, Sandlin, an engineer and the founder of Smarter Every Day, took a regular bicycle into his workshop and flipped the handlebars around. So instead of turning the handlebars right to turn right and left for left, the two were reversed. Destin's experiment was aimed at getting to the heart of how difficult it is to unlearn things that are so entrenched they've taken up permanent residency in our brain and our muscle memory.

Most days, we shuffle through the world on autopilot. We're creatures of muscle memory and rote habit, relying on predictions because our brains are too slow to keep up with our bodies. Our brain receives feedback about what we're doing but that takes about eighty to 100 milliseconds. As a shortcut, the better we get at doing something, the more we start making predictions.

Which is why a backwards bike so brilliantly upends our entire internal model. In a video well worth looking up on YouTube, Destin shares how it took him *eight months* to learn how to ride the bike, and describes the tipping point where the new neural pathways kicked in and riding the bike the 'wrong' way became mentally 'right'. This is why unlearning is hard: we're trying to erase history at the same time, unlike when we're learning something new.

Naturally, I was intrigued, so I got a handy friend of mine to help me backwards my bike. And off I went . . . as unsteadily as a toddler taking first steps. It's hard to articulate how simultaneously awkward and frustrating an experience it is but I got to the point where riding the backwards bike, while still frustrating, also felt oddly exhilarating. It felt like rekindling what it must have been like when I was five and learnt to ride for the first time. There are few times in my life I can say that I genuinely felt like I could feel my brain working to connect new neural pathways. The other was when I tried to teach myself the piano.

Interestingly, after conquering the backwards bike himself, Destin gave it to his six-year-old son, promising him if he met the challenge he would come on a trip to Australia to meet an astronaut hero. His son managed to learn to ride the bike in two weeks. (I'm tempted to recruit Destin's son for our next escape room mission!)

Backwards just might be forwards when it comes to unlearning.

Unlearning

I want to start with unlearning because I think it's the hardest component of the learning cycle. Whether we're mucking around with a new feature on our iPhone or wrapping our head around new lingo that's infiltrating our lexicon ('cancel culture', 'post-truth', 'youthquake' and 'vape' have all been added to the Oxford dictionary recently), at some basic level, we're always unlearning. It might just be one of the most powerful habits we can get intentional about. Whether it's unlearning our assumptions, our prejudices or our self-sabotaging habits, as Peter Drucker famously said, 'We spend a lot of time teaching leaders what to do. We don't spend enough time teaching leaders what to stop.'

In our goal-orientated, forward-focused world, we learn from an early age to demonstrate a commitment to positive actions. We get good marks and endorsement for completing work on time. When we enter the workforce, those early social triggers are reinforced; everything in an organisation is designed to demonstrate a commitment to outcomes. We rarely get credit for ceasing to do something, yet, with the current rate of skills obsolescence, unlearning is essential.

To learn the mastery of leadership today, we need to unlearn hierarchy, unlearn stereotypical measures of strength and unlearn how we quantify value. All of these things have radically changed in the past couple of decades. For example, what has the working from home movement forced by COVID-19 shown us about the construct of presenteeism? We know that the assumed correlation between productivity and sitting twelve hours at the desk outside the CEO's office is superficial if not artificial but, as pandemic distancing restrictions ease, we see managers return to old systems of recognition and reward, almost with a sigh of relief, and employees return to their desks in rigid office attire, with a sigh of remorse. Have we unlearnt old assumptions in order to learn new ways of being? Or have we upended our world to shuffle back to business as usual on autopilot?

Unlearning is an active state. We cannot overlay learning and relearning until we clear the slate of unhelpful neural pathways. Active unlearning is most often visible when we celebrate *not* doing something.

In one travel company I know, every time they make a sale, the person responsible gets to 'ring the bell' in the office and everyone stands, applauds and cheers. It's a bit of harmless fun designed to recognise employee effort, celebrate success and boost morale. But what if we flipped it? If the sales consultant that day had their back up against the wall with a hard bargainer and realised that to do the deal would mean losing the company money, should they say 'no' and walk? Why couldn't there be a quick ring of the office bell for doing that?

Avoiding mistakes as a leader is one of those unseen, unheralded achievements to which society devotes little time or thought. It gets no attention, but it can be as critical as everything else we do put together. As you evaluate your own performance, consider what you may need to unlearn. It may feel like your own undoing, but I promise it will make space for greatness.

Choose to evolve

Atlassian, the Australian 'unicorn' software company that was started with $10,000 worth of credit card debt, has made unlearning into something of an art. Atlassian's work futurist and head of R&D, Dom Price, characterises unlearning as making a choice between relevance and obsolescence. 'For us,' he tells me, 'this is about staying open to understanding the future of work. How are we open to unlearning our old habits, and then how [are] we open to trying something new?'

Unlearning is a habit Dom practises personally, and credits Atlassian founders Scott Farquar and Mike Canon-Brookes as role models. It's also become a company philosophy and offering. Atlassian believes in the idea of unlearning so strongly they've built an internet browser plugin called 'Daily Unlearnings' that prompts you to reflect on the productivity of your behaviour and make small tweaks throughout the day. I also love Dom's suggestion for how to try unlearning. He says: look back at your quarter, year or current role and pick three things you are committing to stopping. Then ask yourself:

- What did I love about the last quarter?
- What did I loathe?
- What did I long for?
- And what did I learn?

For the things he longs for, Dom only gives himself permission to start them if he stops other things. 'So I have to take the loathed, and I have to stop them, and that's my permission to add in the longed for,' he says. The harder part is actually learning to lift the bar even higher and stop things that *do* work but that aren't going to increase your effectiveness. As Dom says, 'The hard thing in doing that is I stop something that has surety, because I know it worked last quarter, and I replace it with something without surety that is an experiment that's highly likely to fail. But, if I don't embrace that exploration, I will never learn anything new.'

Learning

Once we've freed some space through unlearning, we have the capacity to turn our focus to the new skills and capabilities we want to acquire. I don't mean you have to pursue any kind of formal qualification, return to a classroom setting or become the world champion in whatever you've chosen to turn your attention to (though power to you if you choose to do any of that). What I want to focus on here is skills for the *rapid acquisition of capability*. We need a rapid learning regime that is designed for the dynamic world we have to be able to succeed in, a world that demands we continually evolve and grow.

There are two major mental barriers to learning:

- Most of us violently resist having a go at anything we feel we'll be bad at, don't understand or might embarrass ourselves in.
- We are daunted by the intimidation factor of the idea that 'it takes 10,000 hours to master a skill' (popularised by Malcolm Gladwell in his book *Outliers*).

Let's take the second barrier first. One of my major inspirations in this topic area is the best-selling author Josh Kaufman. In Josh's best-seller, *The First 20 Hours: How to Learn Anything Fast*, he debunks Malcolm Gladwell's thesis that it takes 10,000 hours to learn a new skill. Josh explains that while the 10,000-hour rule holds up to research, it is focused on the mastery required to reach the top of an ultra-competitive field (for example, to become a professional golfer). But usually our goal is not to compete at a world-class level: you're more likely to want to pick up a skill to achieve a certain outcome. The goal is to perform well enough to produce a result that is meaningful to you, to enjoy the process and to perhaps rediscover a love of learning. (I'm currently learning how to draw, in part to improve my embarrassing form in Pictionary but largely because I believe it'll change how I create presentations, for example. I like to think my stick figures are progressing nicely . . .)

Kaufman's research shows that if the goal is to learn a skill in a way that allows you to perform well enough for your own purposes, you can usually achieve it with around twenty hours of deliberate practice using four steps. To summarise:

1 Deconstruct the skill
Break down the parts and find the most important things to practise first. What are the building blocks you need to start with?

2 Self-correct
Use reference materials to learn enough so that you know when you make a mistake and can, therefore, correct yourself.

3 Remove barriers to learning
Identify and remove anything that distracts you from focusing on the skill you want to learn.

4 Practise at least 20 hours
Ideally over a relatively condensed period of time – it doesn't need to be a week but don't let it turn into twelve months. This way you compound your learning.

Ditch the line 'practice makes perfect'. Focus instead on 'practice makes possible'. And celebrate your incremental progress. For those thinking about taking their leadership to the next level some skills worth considering spending twenty hours on include storytelling, financial acumen, problem solving, deepening your cross-cultural awareness, learning a language of relevance to your work or doing the work to hold an opinion.

Relearning
Relearning is the forgotten cousin of learning and unlearning. As defined in *Psychological Science*, 'Relearning is more than a method of testing memory; it is an integral part of learning and can be viewed as an iterative process in which we learn, forget and then

relearn as many times as necessary to achieve a specified level of retention.'

Scientists at the Max Planck Institute of Neurobiology have shown that the cell contacts our brain forms when we learn something are retained even when we don't need them anymore. These temporarily inactivated contacts allow us to learn something again more quickly than the first time, even if we think we've forgotten it. In one experiment, they temporarily blocked one eye of their participant group and monitored the response of the brain's nerve cells. 'After approximately five days, the nerve cells had rearranged themselves so as to receive and process information from the other eye – the brain had resigned itself to having only one eye at its disposal.' What surprised researchers the most was that the majority of adaptations that had developed in response to being made one-eyed remained even after the 'block' was removed. As project leader Mark Hübener explained, 'Since an experience may occur again at a later point in time, the brain apparently opts to save a few appendages for a rainy day.'

This insight is crucial to our understanding of learning and memory. It explains why after so many years 'out of action' we can still zoom our way down the ski slopes or ride the crest of a wave . . . or get back on the bike and ride. What have you allowed to lie dormant that's worth dragging out, dusting off and putting to work again? Perhaps you were a forensic questioner as a kid but you've stopped probing. Or you used to be a really talented artist but it's been years since you made the time and space to unleash your creativity. Skills we learnt but have let lie low aren't lost; we can (and should) build them back up where they're relevant to our current endeavours.

The oldest millennial I know

I can't think of a better poster person for lifelong learning than my friend, and the oldest Millennial I know, Everald Compton. Everald describes himself as a 'young Aussie in his eighties'. He founded National Seniors Australia in 1976. He served on its board of directors for thirty-five years, twenty-five of them as chairman. He then took up a new role as chairman of the federal government's Advisory Panel on Positive Ageing. He is currently chairman of Longevity Alliance Australia which is based at the University of Queensland where he is an adjunct professor. He's also one of the most prolific tweeters I follow and will proudly tell you he's been married to Helen for sixty-one years and counting.

Everald and I met when we shared the stage for an intergenerational panel discussion on Australia's future in 2015. His warm commitment to his 'why', his openness to new ideas and insatiable curiosity immediately had my heart. When I interviewed him for this book he began by telling me about his latest five-year plan, which he has every intention of replacing with a new five-year plan when he turns ninety-four, because he's 'never going to retire'. Everald comes to every conversation with a playful eye for overthrowing assumptions. He constantly tries on new mental models and discards them readily. I am enthralled by the malleability of his mind.

According to Everald, we need to stop talking about ageing and start talking about vitality: how we live happy, long lives. He says we miss the point when we talk about physical health. 'Everyone needs to be exercising their brain too and there's two ways you've got to do it: you've got to continue to absorb knowledge and you've got to create. In other words, you can't just read, you've got to write.'

For his part, Everald reads five books at a time. He spends two-and-a-half hours a day reading and then he makes a point of writing a presentation for government, for universities or to publish to stimulate broader discussion. He'll do four or five drafts before he shares it. Everald also volunteers as a mentor at the local primary school; he's currently helping a ten-year-old launch a pet care business. He's quick to point out he never got a formal degree or officially certified in anything. 'I've just gotten out there and grabbed the learning I needed. There's a rich treasure trove of resources and opportunities out there if you're just prepared to go hunting.'

It strikes me that Everald's almost flippantly natural use of leadership mindsets and methods discussed in *The Leading Edge* so far may shine a light on what mastery in the new world looks like. Talk about playing an infinite game!

I ask him if there's a message he'd like to share and he says, 'There is no such thing as being past your use-by date.' And then he hangs up our Zoom call to get back to writing his next book. Five-year plans wait for no-one!

> ### *A question from the leading edge:*
>
> When was the last time you did something for the first time?

12

Go for
goals

'The person on top of the mountain didn't fall there.'

Vince Lombardi

Say the word 'goals' and most people turn their minds either immediately to sport or the old SMART goal-setting acronym. Instead,
I think of goals as dreams pulled down to Earth. They are weighty
in our hands but weightless in their connection to our North Star.
That's my measure of the validity of goals; whether they feel real
enough to imagine attaining, but elusive enough to move us closer
to our guiding light.

I like to play a game with some of my audiences. We begin with
everyone standing and I ask people to sit down only when they can
affirm the following questions:

- Do you have goals? (About 30 per cent drop off here.)
- Are they written down? (About 50 per cent drop off here.)
- Are they somewhere you see them every day? (We're down to
  fewer than ten people by now.)
- Have you shared them with someone who can support your
  pursuit of them and hold you accountable?

I then invite the audience to applaud the handful of people who are
still standing. Because irrespective of how many hundreds might
have stood initially, according to how I was taught to set goals, these
are the only people who are doing it effectively.

If you want to master your leadership capability, the statistics make a strong argument for nailing this skill and making a habit of it. If you write down your goals – even better write down some action steps as well – and share them with someone who will hold you accountable, then you are significantly more likely to achieve them. I got hooked on this relationship. As my former roommates and partners will attest, goals and I became bedfellows – arguably a little too much, as there was a period in my early twenties where I decided to blu-tack my goals to the ceiling above my bed so they were the last thing I saw before I went to sleep at night and the first thing I saw when I woke up. Hardcore, I know. In my defence, all the ceiling goals got achieved (though I think that habit was probably part of the reason I was flying solo in that bed for a lot of that year!).

Jokes aside, I can't find a championship-winning team, a record-breaking athlete, an influential leader or a pioneer of change who mastered their craft without setting some goals. As management consultant Stephen Barnes puts it, failing to set goals 'is like turning up at the airport without a ticket': you're not going anywhere.

Setting your mind to the task

If you're determined, not even fear can stop you. When I interviewed Jessica Watson, who sailed solo in an extraordinary and dangerous voyage around the world at age sixteen, she told me, 'I was a terrified, timid little girl who then decided I wanted to sail around the world.' It happened in that order: the young Australian didn't find her courage on the water and *then* decide to sail around the world. She confirms, 'I decided that I was going to have to overcome my fear and in deciding not to be that person, I decided to sail around the world.'

Jess is quite something. At 165 centimetres, she is capable of achieving things ten times her size and then some. I've long admired her ambition, determination and work ethic. One of the things I find fascinating is that despite having sailed her pink yacht more than

19,000 nautical miles around the world, she describes herself as being reasonably conservative and 'not adventurous at all'. An interesting self-description for someone whose exploits have seen her named as one of the fifty greatest explorers in Australian history alongside the likes of Douglas Mawson, Matthew Flinders and Charles Kingsford Smith. But Jess is quick to stress that the volume of risk management and contingency planning that went into achieving her goal would rival many military operations plans!

'I'm a conscientious, cautious person. I'm the last person to jump off the end of a jetty or anything like that.' Jess says she examined every dimension of the voyage and details involved and challenged herself to ask, 'Is it actually that dangerous?' With every stage of the planning process undertaken, Jess was mentally de-risking her mission step by step. While the whole thing sounds incredibly daunting – being entirely alone in the middle of the ocean, facing huge waves (even writing it is daunting, to be honest!) – she gave herself confidence by taking precautions. For example, selecting a boat that was going to be incredibly resilient against the conditions she'd face. Jess said her self-belief grew by the way she managed what was within her sphere of control. In her mind, 'If we do all of these things and if I understand all these things, I'm actually not in such a dangerous position.'

The learning curve for Jess was steep, as is often the case when attempting an audacious goal. But she's quick to stress that you shouldn't let that overwhelm you and that you should never under-estimate what can be readily learnt from resources at your fingertips. Not to mention how willing people are to offer their advice and experience if you reach out. Jess says having had conversations with people who'd experienced some of the unique challenges she'd face on her journey, like 210 days in isolation, were pivotal to helping her develop the strategies to succeed. One of the people Jess reached out to for advice (who happened to be an explorer himself) ended up buying her the boat she needed!

'Even today, it's nerve-racking for me to ask someone for advice. You think, "Why should they? Why would they want to help?" But I continue to do it because I've proven to myself over and over again that it's just extraordinary where those conversations can lead.'

For Jess, the isolation and the power of the sea were far less of a worry than her concern that she might be stopped from trying to achieve her dream. There was *significant* public opposition to her quest, with some pundits and commentators going as far as to question the sanity and competence of her parents for letting her do it. Yachting experts spoke out against the trip, as did the Australian Childhood Foundation. But Jess, and those in her corner, were steadfast about her ability to conquer the challenge and meticulousness of the training and preparation that had been undertaken.

It's worth mentioning here that we all need to be aware of goal-sceptics. Carry the scepticism of others lightly (if you carry it at all) and make sure you triangulate their opinions with the feedback and input of other trusted sources.

On her journey, Jess had to keep calm through waves of up to 12 metres, in which her yacht, the *Pink Lady*, was knocked sideways many times. She discovered that the key to mental strength was to break big goals down. Drawing on insights from the many adventurers and elite sportspeople she's learnt from, Jess explains that the same approach is equally effective when it comes to tackling seemingly impossible and audacious goals. Her sage, tried-and-tested advice is to chunk goals down into bite-sized portions that focus on 'what's important now'. In her case it was what lay in the next few kilometres. Ask yourself, *What do I need to do to make this next domino tip?* Don't lose sight of the overarching goal but invest your energy and focus into that next nudge. When you join up all those nudges, it can take you almost 20,000 nautical miles across the globe – the power of goal-setting in action.

The mastery of purposeful goals

I've come to believe that goals, like any framework or formula, will be what you make of them. Part of that 'work' is in applying the goal-setting process. For example, there's a *reason* people say to write goals down. Psychology professor Gail Matthews, at the Dominican University in California, led the first definitive study on goal-setting with nearly 270 participants. The results showed that we achieve 50 per cent more goals if we write them down. A simple thing to do for a much greater chance of success!

There's also a *reason* to place goals somewhere you see them every day. As we talked about in Chapter 7, Stephen Covey talks about the temptation of the 'urgent' at the expense of what's 'important'. If your goals are not top of mind, they'll quickly become bottom of the priority list. They won't get the time and attention they deserve and, you guessed it, they won't happen. Make them your phone wallpaper, put them on a post-it note next to your computer, write them on a piece of paper that you carry in your wallet. You do you; just make sure the 'you' you're striving for is always your light on the hill.

There's a *reason* to share goals with others, too. Our chances of actually achieving our goals are dramatically increased when we share them. We gain clarity on what it will take to accomplish them when we see another person's reaction to hearing them. We increase accountability because speaking it makes it real . . . and we *hate* losing face, so we engage a powerful motivational driver in the process.

Personal goals are most often a team effort of some sort. No goal can ever be met without self-motivation on your part but, unfortunately, motivation does not always materialise on call. Sometimes we can supply our own internal motivation but frequently, during the most challenging parts of the journey, we need external support to stoke the fire. There's a reason that everything from Alcoholics Anonymous to Weight Watchers to fitness communities like Strava focus on peer and community models – they work. Gail Matthews's study found that participants who regularly reported their progress to a friend achieved more goals compared to participants who kept their goals to themselves or just shared them once. Positive social peer pressure is powerful. It's also good to be strategic about who we pick: recent research out of Ohio State University finds that people tend to be more committed to their goals after sharing them with someone felt to be of higher status or whose opinions garner respect.

Here are four questions to think about as you determine who you'll share your goals with.

Do I trust them?
Often our most meaningful goals are our most vulnerable – so to share our biggest dreams and aspirations requires trust.

Do I care about their opinion?
This is often what rules our siblings out; we love them, but we've spent decades ignoring their suggestions on what we should wear or whether the person we're dating is any good. You want to be dedicated and unwilling to give up on your goal, which is more likely when you share that goal with someone you look up to or don't want to lose face with.

Can they help me step towards my goal?
Whether it's offering emotional support, tactical advice, providing a much-needed pep-talk or being able to call us on our BS, we need the people we share with to be positive contributors to our goal pathway, not detractors or passengers.

Can they (and will I) commit to regular accountability?
If they're a friend we only speak to once a year or whose plate is so full they just won't have bandwidth to be able to support us right here right now, then we probably need to re-evaluate.

I introduced you to my best friend Charlie in Chapter 8, recounting our Year of Fear. It turns out we hold the record on the Make Me app for the longest consecutive days of logged behaviour change. I can assure you the only reason that's the case is because we unconsciously built accountability into our challenge design.

Phase it in

Here's the unbelievably obvious but all too often underestimated key to goal-setting: goals need to motivate you. They need to light fire in your belly. Goals need to make you jump out of bed in the morning. *Your* goals need to bust *you* out of whatever limitations restrict you.

When Lisa King left her executive marketing role to start Eat My Lunch out of the kitchen of her home in Auckland, it was because she couldn't fathom that one in four Kiwi kids live in poverty and many don't have lunch every day. Her belly-fire was lit. She was jumping out of bed and her determined goal was to make it possible that when we buy our own lunch every day, we could feed a kid who wouldn't otherwise get to eat lunch. A one-for-one model, Lisa's original goal was simply to 'try it'. As she told me, 'We all have amazing ideas, but in the reality of jobs and mortgages and kids, and life, you think it's never going to work.' How can we take our motivation and not let it go to waste? Lisa's advice: 'I say "just try it", "just do it" – you never know what's going to happen.'

What happened to Lisa was that demand quickly outstripped what her home kitchen could produce, so she changed gears and scaled up her vision and goals to became a social enterprise that could allow all New Zealanders to own a part of Eat My Lunch. Lisa, like countless trailblazers I've met, defined her moon-shot goal and chunked the audacious mission down into goals that still stretch, but are more manageable.

The most effective way to break big goals up into smaller ones is to align long-term, medium-term, and short-term goals into an overarching strategy. As soon as Lisa had the moon-shot within her sights, and could articulate to her stakeholders the way she would set about achieving her series of goals, the business snowballed. Eat My Lunch has provided more than 1.5 million meals to New Zealand school kids (and counting) and the Eat My Lunch School Survey has shown an 87 per cent improvement in concentration in class, a 62 per cent improvement in attendance and a 69 per cent improvement in behaviour – all testament to the power of Lisa's forward motivation and ability to reverse engineer.

Here's a three-step approach to build a 'goaled' star strategy.

Shoot for the moon

What's the moon-shot goal? What would your dream be if there were absolutely no limitations? Allow yourself to think really big here. This goal should be a couple of years in the distance, at least.

Scan the horizon

Next, think about what horizons you want to break it down into, to move towards your goal. They may be annual, may be half-yearly, or perhaps you have stages you need to accomplish that make more sense. Earmark what those horizon milestones and accomplishments are.

Step out on the journey

Finally, think about your short-term goals. These are goals that you can achieve more readily. They will be actionable tasks that you can start doing tomorrow and immediately create some 'domino-effect' momentum.

When I think about this phased approach to goal-setting, I think about a quote from historian E. L. Doctorow (which okay, if I'm totally honest, I stumbled on as a teenager in a *Sisterhood of the Traveling Pants* novel). He said, 'Writing is like driving a car at night. You can see only as far as your headlights, but you can make the whole trip that way.' I've found that framing incredibly helpful many times over in the years since; you know where you're going, even if you can't see it at that very moment. And you don't need to.

Creating effective goals

While I've used goal-setting for many of my professional achievements over the years, in writing this chapter, I've reflected on how goals can help master direction in our personal lives too. Anyone can steer the ship when the sea is calm; when the waves pick up, it's a different matter. And nothing makes the water more turbulent than the personal stuff. This is where some of the hardest decisions and choices of our lives rest and, in those moments, we want to give ourselves every tool possible to help ourselves navigate it.

When I consider the most painful moments in my life, ending a relationship that I knew wasn't good for me is up there. I really didn't want to disrespect or hurt my partner so I wrote down my feelings and got clear about what needed to happen and why. I tested where my head and heart were at with people I trusted: could I still make this work or was it time to call it? I visualised different future scenarios and checked in with what felt right in my gut. 'I need to leave' came bubbling up. I focused on my horizon. I wanted to feel congruent with the best version of myself again – this became the 'why' that was powerful enough to help me overcome all the doubt and fear. I got really honest with myself about the conversations that would need to be had and broke it down into steps. I gave myself a clear time frame. Most importantly, as much as I was tempted to throw the plan aside due to tears, pain, doubts and the harsh reality of splitting up two interwoven lives, I stayed focused on what I knew was the end result I needed. Totally unconsciously, I'd applied all the principles and processes of goal-setting.

At a time when I felt as though I was being tossed around the emotional high seas, unsure of which direction to swim (or whether I still even knew how), these frameworks were my life raft.

Whether it's for personal goals, professional goals or anything in between, shine your headlights into the dark night and edge your foot onto the gas. Here are some ways to get started.

Make your goals first person, present tense and time-specific

For example, 'On 30 January 2022, I have built an AI-assisted learning platform.' To set compelling goals, we need to create a sense of ownership and enliven our identity. Using 'I have' or 'I am' invites our imagination to conjure a clear image of that future self.

Ensure you can track your progress

Goals where you don't know how you're tracking until D-day rolls around make life difficult. We need to have a way of continually recalibrating our approach based on the feedback our progress is offering. Rather than writing 'created a learning tool', have a definition of what success looks like that you can track progress against, like looking at a word count progress tally at the end of every week.

Weigh up specifics against closing doors

This point applies particularly to promotion-based goals. I've seen a lot of people become incredibly demotivated when a particular goal doesn't happen. When we set goals, it's essential to evaluate what degree of specificity is helpful and what is harmful. Could we frame it: in 2022, the platform is named 'next best thing' in *Harvard Business Review*?

Be clear on your level of ambition

A mentor of mine who spent many years working at Google relayed to me the story of her first performance review. She'd come from a background in large-scale consumables where you were score-carded to within a millimetre of your life. Hence, she was sweating profusely as she headed into her first Google performance review after only having hit 85 per cent of her annual targets. Immediately on the back foot and apologising, she was quickly stopped and told by her manager that if she hit any more than 65 per cent of her targets then she really hadn't been ambitious enough when setting them in the first place. Not what she was expecting! Now in an environment where she was being encouraged to be significantly more ambitious than the culture she'd been in previously, she could level up. Google didn't want incremental, assured goals; they wanted serious stretch ones. How does your environment affect your goal-setting?

There's no right or wrong in setting goals; there's what works for you. I set goals at the start of every year and I typically take a Goldilocks approach: I'll have a set of highly invested goals I think I'll be able to do fairly easily; some that are a stretch but on a good day I could land and some that are moon-shot numbers but that I want to have a crack at. When I was younger I used to pride myself on the number of goals I had for any given year (the spreadsheets are actually mortifyingly embarrassing; I apologise to the mentors I inflicted them on), as I've gotten wiser I've recalibrated, creating sets of attainable, stretch and moon-shot goals in the key aspects of my life: family, work, health, community.

Remember, we are writing a goal that fires us up, so what sets you alight is up to you.

> ### *A question from the leading edge:*
>
> When you say your goal out loud, does it spark your heart, head and imagination?

13

Prepare with discipline

'The will to succeed means nothing without the will to prepare.'

Juma Ikangaa, record-breaking Tanzanian marathon runner

In 2012, I found myself the world's youngest president of a Rotary Club – and feeling paralysed. As a 22-year-old, I wasn't from the typical demographic of Rotary members, but I'd been drawn to the organisation through work I'd been doing in Kenya, where they'd provided some of the seed capital for the micro-finance project I was working on. When I'd returned, I presented our results at a Rotary meeting in Perth and was asked, 'Why aren't you a Rotarian?'

I looked around the room and it didn't look like I belonged in Rotary. But then they played a video that talked about Rotary's work at the forefront of eradicating polio from the planet, providing sanitation around the world and so many other phenomenally good things. It finished with a statistic: of Rotary's 1.2 million members, only 12 per cent were women, and only 2 per cent were youth. I remember feeling like an alarm bell was going off in my head. What I'd learnt about this organisation's work in every pocket of disadvantage on the planet showed me we needed them around. I put my hand up to get involved and about eighteen months later, there I was as president.

My goal was to lead a transformation of Rotary that would attract young people – or at least do so on a micro 'club-level' in our little pocket of the world, and, I hoped, catalyse broader conversation for change within Rotary globally. To this day, it remains one of the hardest change projects I've ever undertaken. I was oblivious to the politics that surrounded my appointment and as such, was completely ill-prepared for the cultural challenges and conflict I was going to have to contend with.

Feeling lost and totally unsure what to do, I went out looking for someone I could learn from. I specifically wanted someone who'd been able to drive reform within traditional, conservative organisations. I needed someone who could help me develop better strategies and approaches for my leadership.

A mentor connected me with Lieutenant General David Morrison AO, who was chief of the Australian Army at the time. General Morrison shot to public awareness when a video he recorded went viral on YouTube in 2012. It was off the back of a scandal that had led to an independent review of the Australian Army by the federal sex discrimination commissioner. In it, Morrison told soldiers that if they had issues about serving with women, they should leave. 'They [female soldiers] are vital to us maintaining our capability now and into the future,' he said. 'If that does not suit you then get out. You may find another employer where your attitude and behaviour is acceptable, but I doubt it.'

The video was symbolic of a much broader agenda of cultural transformation and increased diversity that General Morrison was undertaking through the army. This struck a chord with me, and when I asked General Morrison if he'd be willing to share his insights with me, he invited me for lunch. It turns out he felt just as eager to learn from me as did I from him! Over the years since, the conversations I've had with this exceptional leader have provided me with decision-making guidance and life lessons that I continually find myself reflecting on – and actioning.

Insights from military manoeuvres

In 2015, my conversations with General Morrison expanded into the opportunity for me to spend time out with the Australian Army in remote north Queensland. During one of their most extensive combat exercises, I was an eyewitness to a (very real-feeling) simulated battle. I've long admired and read about military leadership, decision-making and strategy, but to see the process in action took that appreciation to another level.

During my time observing the training drill, there were two particularly significant takeaways the leaders impressed upon me:

Prepare so you can adapt – plan for no plan

There's something about extensive preparation and planning that doesn't seem congruent with the way we naturally think about adaptiveness. How can innovating on our feet or following an instinctive gut reaction be predicated on planning? But the army shows that the ability to adapt is a direct *result* of thorough preparation. 'The plan only lasts as far as the start of the battle,' one of the captains informed me as he talked me through the extensive, multi-week planning process that precedes an operational drill. 'We are rigorous in our preparation, and in our anticipation of the enemy's tactics so that we can be adaptive moment to moment.'

Weeks before the first tent peg is put in the battlefield, HQ leaders are prepping by asking themselves fundamental questions: What do I need to do? What resources have I got to do it with? What are the enemy (or competition) trying to do? What resources are *they* trying to achieve it with? Through this inquisition process, the leaders can begin to foresee the enemy's strategies, and understand what the telltale signs will look like for any particular course of action when they're actually going head to head.

Whether you call it red teaming, war-gaming or stress-testing, planning to have no plan should be part of every leader's source code. Why? Because this gives us a chance to hack our own strategy before an irretrievable amount of money, time or material resources have been invested. Red teaming is a relatively simple process you can do around a table with some of your supporters, before 100 per cent committing to your moon-shot goal. It's basically fast iteration scenario testing. The process of making a plan and encouraging counterfactual arguments reveals not only weakness but new opportunities for innovation and growth. The practice also reinforces healthy feedback relationships, clear goal-setting and chunking, and increases the discipline you feel for owning successful outcomes in the face of uncertainty.

No-one can be constantly prepared

Preparation is entirely contextual and one aspect of that context is timing. Soldiers have three twelve-month phases they rotate through: readying, ready and reset. This rhythm balances the fact that while no-one can sustain high performance all the time, the requirement to protect national security means sufficient personnel must be ready to be called into action at any time. With this rotation, they have a brigade readying for battle, a brigade prepared for immediate deployment and another resting off the back of their operational duties. The three phases have very different intensities, expectations and roles – a practice steeped in the theory of high performance. The critical insight: no-one can sustain peak performance indefinitely, and to ensure we achieve the results we're after, we need to manage our energy, workload and duties accordingly. Think back to Chapter 7 and what our exploration of managing energy revealed. What part of the day, week, month or year works with your rhythm and peak energy levels to do the disciplined groundwork of upskilling, goal-setting, and scenario-planning? In addition to preparation, we also need to build in evaluation. I mentioned earlier that I tend to take a week at the beginning of each year to lay my goal-setting work. In that week I rigorously test my assumptions, aspirations, reasons and alignment with my support crew. I write everything down so that

it is solid, structured and sharable. When I feel like the plan lights
me up, I put weekly check-in alerts in my diary. I schedule regular
collaboration sessions with people who inspire me. I work out what
resources I need to throw at my stretch goals, and I make sure to
reserve them on a timely basis. And with all that in place . . . I'm free
to throw it all out the window and adapt to opportunity!

Does this sound exhausting? In a way, this groundwork frees up
my creativity and opens up opportunity throughout the year. I feel
that one week of disciplined planning and an hour of time each
Sunday morning to assess how I'm travelling take a lot less mental
load than waking up most nights worrying about where I should be
headed.

Prepare for performance conditions
Mind boxing

Harinder Singh, also known as Sifu, is a speaker, author, high-
performance coach and bonified Ninja warrior. He is the go-to for
the tough guys and gals in the police, the military, special forces and
secret services around the world, in part because he comes from a
long line of tai chi masters. They are also probably impressed by the
fact that he is responsible for spreading Bruce Lee's martial arts and
philosophical legacy. But if hot chocolate could be translated into
a sound, it would be Sifu's voice. He's a fascinating and seemingly
paradoxical blend of Zen mixed with brutally tough. Figuring that
SWAT teams wouldn't put up with much BS, I thought I might
have finally found someone who could bring mindfulness to life for
me in Sifu.

When I spoke to Sifu about the work he does training people
for high-intensity, zero-margin-for-error working environments, he
emphasised that it was all about developing techniques in advance
to perform under stress in the moment. And the key to performing under stress is the conservation of energy because when fear and
anxiety hit, they cause a psychological and physiological response that

restricts our body. We tighten up. 'Now you're in a state of energy drain,' Sifu tells me. 'When stress hits you, you resort to having only 10 per cent of your capabilities available. So, you fall to that percentage.' Sifu points out the major flaw in training ourselves to get bigger, stronger or faster, without working on our capacity to perform under stress: we're still always going to drop to 10 per cent of our capabilities.

This is interesting because our traditional notion of training for high-pressure situations is, more often than not, to make ourselves execute under pressure over and over again – the theory being that we build muscle memory. Rather differently, Sifu advocates mastering 'mind-boxing': learning how to fight with our thoughts so we can remain centred in the situation we find ourselves in and therefore able to access far more than 10 per cent of our capabilities. He is quick to stress that this approach has stood the test of time, having been passed down, unbroken, through hundreds of years of Wu Dang monks and Samurai teachings. These are people who were expert at staying in the moment when the moment arrived.

Sifu talks me through the process of mind-boxing:

Start very simply. Just become aware of the inhale, and become aware of the exhale. Then thoughts will come: *Why am I doing this? Oh my god, I've got to pay the bills, I've got to pick up the kids. I have a presentation due.* That's the enemy. So now the fight starts. Step by step, become aware of when you're thinking and visualise yourself giving the thought a sharp round-house kick. Bring yourself back into the moment. This moment may be a couple of seconds, even a few minutes before the next thought comes. But you're present. Now you've just got to catch the next one. And then you start to string together these moments of presence, one breath, one moment at a time, and then it starts to build. What's incredible is that your mind is a fantastic tool, it's a muscle – you've got to think of it that way. And it then learns how to mind-box all on its own.

We do still have to train in order to have the skills we'll need to overcome the challenge itself, Sifu reminds me. But by equipping ourselves with this tool for mental presence and clarity, we'll be significantly more prepared to meet any eventuality that arises.

Visualisation and focusing the mind

Alisa Camplin is a pocket-rocket of a human being. She should be in a Berocca ad for the amount she can cram into any given day or year. Alisa initially shot to prominence as a freestyle aerial skier; she was Australia's first-ever woman to win a gold medal in the Winter Olympics, in Salt Lake City in 2002. And she credits visualisation with helping her bring home the gold.

Alisa's Olympic dream lead-up was more like a nightmare. Six weeks before the Games, she had an accident in training that saw her fracture both her ankles.

Now, fracturing both ankles is inconvenient at the best of times but even more so when you need to hurtle down a ramp at up to 65 kilometres per hour, launch off a ski jump flying three storeys into the air (while doing several flips and twists) and then stick a landing on the steep side of a mountain.

Alisa was completely shattered by the news. After eight years of pursuing her ultimate goal, she felt thwarted at the final hurdle. She credits a strong bond with her sports psychologist who encouraged her not to mentally and emotionally throw in the towel, but to take a different approach to preparation. That approach was to ready herself for competition entirely in her head, while confined to her bed.

Under normal conditions, Alisa could do thirty to forty aerial practice jumps on water per day, maybe sixty during a trampoline session and fifteen out on the snow. Without the ability to do any of this, Alisa needed to find a less conventional way to maintain her competitive edge. She decided to try visualising jumps – effectively train her muscle memory in her mind – because from the perspective of neuroscience, the brain can't really differentiate between a real or imagined experience. As Alisa put it in our interview, 'If you visualise them first (jumps in different situations), when they do eventuate in real life, it's like you've been there before, and you've practised how you're going to respond, and so you're emotionally calmer, more practical, readier. And that might mean that you have an advantage over your competitors.'

Embracing mindfulness and visualisation did not come naturally. A driven A-type with an indefatigable work ethic, Alisa was used to training incredibly hard to achieve goals. You can take it from her when she stresses that the only way to get the benefit of visualisation is to really believe you'll derive value from it. The moment it 'clicked' for Alisa is when she realised she could not only out-jump her competitors in her head, she could also mentally prepare for all sorts of different scenarios. From that point, like with everything she does, she committed herself 100 per cent.

'It was all about making it realistic and high quality. I could actually practise repeating my jumps more accurately and with improved technique.' She would squeeze her tummy as she was visualising coming down the ski run, feel herself stand up tall for the jump and squeeze her thighs so it felt like she was pushing against the ramp as she launched into the air. Alisa also found the visualisations became stronger and more effective with the more senses she could awaken, so she tried to evoke not just her sight and feeling but hearing and emotions too.

Visualisation has long been a part of elite sports and high performance. Al Oerter, a four-time Olympic discus champion, and the tennis star Billie Jean King were among those using it in the 1960s. Performance strategist Matt Mayberry provides further examples: 'Boxing legend Muhammad Ali was stressing the importance of seeing himself victorious long before the actual fight. As a struggling young actor, Jim Carrey used to picture himself being the greatest actor in the world. Michael Jordan always took the last shot in his mind before he ever took one in real life.'

The truth is, if you're unable to picture yourself achieving your goal, you probably won't. Critically, the more vivid an image you can conjure, the more effective it will be.

If you're up for it, start thinking about your personal goals. Spend ten to fifteen minutes picturing yourself achieving each one, in as much detail as possible: where are you, how old are you, who else is there with you? What will you do once you reach your goal? How do you feel? What impact will this have on your life? Once you have this image crystal clear in your mind, make visualising your goals part of your daily or weekly practice and it will help to move you forwards with more velocity.

Don't skip the self-talk

Self-talk goes hand-in-hand with visualisation. I've gone from being a hardened sceptic to an evangelist on this topic; yep, I knocked it 'til I tried it. The theory is that we say 300 to 1000 words to ourselves every minute (even if you're introverted externally, you're a chatterbox internally!) so we want those words to be positive and self-encouraging. And yet, more often than not, we say things to ourselves that we would never say to our best mate.

The application of positivity all comes down to what researchers call 'explanatory style.' Eric Barker has explained this well.

When bad things happen, what story do you tell yourself? There are three essential elements here. Let's call them the 3 Ps: permanence, pervasiveness and whether it's personal.

Pessimists tell themselves that bad events:
1. Will last a long time, or forever. ('I'll *never* get this done.')
2. Are universal. ('You can't trust *any* of those people.')
3. Are their fault. ('I'm *terrible* at this.')

Optimists, well, they see it the exact opposite:

1. Bad things are temporary. ('That happens *occasionally*, but it's no big deal.')
2. Bad things have a specific cause and aren't universal. ('When the *weather* is better that won't be a problem.')
3. It's not their fault. ('I'm good at this but *today wasn't my lucky day*.')

When talking to ourselves, we need to lean heavily toward optimism. This might be easier said than done. Start by catching negative self-talk and giving is a Sifu-style round-house kick. Use affirmations to put yourself in an optimal mental state. And when preparing for something that matters, make sure your optimism leans towards realism: *I can do it, and I will do it better if I give myself time to prepare.*

While I have a naturally Tigger-ish disposition, I've still found it can be helpful to etch little positivity reminders in places where I'll see them frequently. I've written self-talk and motivational quotes on my mirror in whiteboard marker and intentionally set my background on my phone. I change up the quotes regularly according to what it is that's resonating for me or, as the case may be, that I need to make resonate. I also use the momentum plugin so my internet browser flashes up a motivational quote (and beautiful scenery) every time I open it. All these little prompts help to nudge me into that mindset of feeling capable of achieving what I wish to.

Make the time and take the time

Preparation for anything significant will take time; dedicated, focused time. Speaking to people who've mastered the craft you're seeking to conquer or who operate at a high level in your chosen pursuit can help give you a gauge of the time you'll need to devote to preparing. For example, my Ironman coach told me if I wanted to conquer the 226.31-kilometre monster I'd need to be doing about twelve hours of training in week one but that would build to more like twenty-two hours. Then you can manage your expectations and schedule accordingly.

One thing we may need to factor in is procrastination. Some people power through their preparation and reward themselves with time leading up to the deadline. Others roll their preparation around in their mind while the clock ticks down, and only get cracking when they have one minute less than what they need to actually master the task. Preparation should be both messy and meticulous. Let's consider that the up-front super-organised type may be motivated to complete their preparation as a box-ticking means to success. The procrastinator, on the other hand may be putting off a fear of not being able to execute. Either way, we need to back ourselves by making the time, and taking the time. Making the time involves scheduling, making lists, ticking off progress, managing productivity. Taking the time involves brainstorming, marinating ideas, breaking with best-laid plans, and being curious. The non-negotiable is getting sh*t done.

As my high school volleyball coach used to always say, 'Hard work beats talent when talent doesn't work hard.' When it comes to the fundamentals of repeatable success, there are few pillars more important than preparation. While most people are focused on performance, preparation is the quiet achiever. And preparation is possibly the most achievable superpower going around.

A question from the leading edge:

How are you preparing for tomorrow, today?

14

Work 'on' and 'in'

'Sometimes we have to step back to see that we're moving forward in the right direction.'

Anon.

When you're juggling conference calls, social media and an overflowing inbox, it can be hard to make time for what's actually important. In fact, it can be hard to even maintain perspective on what is important.

While ticking a hundred-and-one tasks off your to-do list each week may give you a great sense of accomplishment, activity doesn't always equal real achievement. If the individual tasks aren't actively in line with and supporting the strategy we've set to achieve our goals, then we're likely falling into the trap of activity for self-validation's sake. Sometimes, as if to give us an extra kick in the guts, we're acutely aware we're 'stuck' in this trap, which doubles down on our feeling of stasis and frustration.

When I worked in large organisations, I couldn't help but notice how easily I was consumed by their 'operating rhythms' – company-wide habits that dictated how time is managed. Every organisation has them: the Monday morning kick-off meetings, the Friday 'week in review' wrap-ups, the continual cycle of one-on-ones with direct reports. Plus, I worked in open-plan offices, so people could 'pop in' to chat at any point. There never seemed to be time for anything other than what was immediately in front of you.

It is a cop out to blame our environment as the reason we never have time. I've worked for myself for years now, which effectively means I'm in control of everything – for better and worse! And yet, I routinely find myself thinking that I don't have enough time to work *on* my business, instead of just *in* it.

Research says I'm not alone. A study by Rich Howarth, CEO of the Strategic Thinking Institute, reported that 96 per cent of 500 surveyed leaders said time was a hurdle in being able to think strategically about their work. It was cited as the number one reason for 'lacking strategic performance.'

Surely there's got to be a better way?

To start with, we can establish greater awareness of what's important to us and then create accountability around where we're spending our time and energy. The Eisenhower Matrix, a simple two-by-two diagram with 'urgent' on one axis and 'important' on the other, a concept introduced in Chapter 7. The critical distinction: urgent activities require immediate attention, whereas important ones contribute to your mission, values and goals, and require discipline. Quadrant two, which is 'non-urgent and important', often includes things like relationship-building, recognising new opportunities, planning and prevention. I use this tool every Sunday to categorise the work I need to do in the week ahead and to create accountability about where I'm devoting my time and energy.

Another tool is the time audit. Record your schedule for two weeks and review where you spent your productive hours. How much time are you spending on non-critical urgent things as opposed to important things? What additional value could you be realising by making a shift? And don't speculate: investigate! Look at the screentime app on your phone and discover how many minutes you spent in the vortex of social media. Just make sure you don't fall into the trap of 'performing' while you're being watched!

Don't *judge* your baseline, just establish one so you've got a clear place to work from. If you're not good at accounting for your time, you could even try paying yourself based on what you log as productive time. Any additional funds from your salary or client invoices get donated to charity. This will sharpen up your intentionality around a time audit, even if you are naturally charitable!

As we saw in Chapter 7, shifting the allocation of the hours available to us in the day to more strategic tasks requires us to master a different relationship with time. I find 'working on' works best when we're in peak energy state or feeling creative, once you've tracked where in a week those natural peaks are for you, think about how you ring-fence some time-on.

Beware the toll of your switching costs

Multi-tasking is a myth. And no matter how much I reeeeeally want to believe in its mythology, every study out there shows that attempting more than one task at once means a significant decline in productivity, especially if the tasks are complex (even if you're a woman).

But if you've ever fought with Google maps while driving or tried to subtly reply to an email under the table, while simultaneously attempting to engage in a team meeting (sucks when you're thrown a question and you've only been half-listening, doesn't it?), you know this already. Our brains are designed for a single focus. Even when we think we're managing multi-tasking, as far as our brains are concerned, we're just switching between tasks.

Constant multi-tasking just tires out our brains and reduces our ability to think. Psychologists have compared how long it takes for people to get everything done, including how difficult tasks are or whether or not we are familiar with them, so that they can measure the cost in time for switching tasks. It was found that even when people had to switch completely predictably between two tasks every two or four trials, they were still slower when switching than when repeating. Increasing the time between trials to prepare people for the switch helped but did not entirely eliminate the cost of switching.

Multi-tasking, or disrupted attention, 'produces shallower thinking, reduces creativity, increases errors and lowers our ability to block irrelevant information,' says Dr Sandra Bond Chapman, founder and chief director of the Center for BrainHealth at the University of Texas at Dallas. As Renuka Rayasam has described Chapman's findings: 'Because the brain was not built to multitask, over time it can lead to heightened levels of stress and depression and lower overall intellectual capacity.'

What's interesting is how much the advent of the technological age has exacerbated the multi-tasking problem. In the Industrial Age, we 'left' work at the factory, at least to enough of an extent that the myth of work/life distinction was manageable. Nowadays, our email pings, Zoom calls happen at all hours and we're working to deadlines in different time zones; work and life are increasingly fused. Technology is rewiring our brains to be addicted to disruption.

Smartphones are making us dumb. Seriously dumb. Our ability to think decreases – and not just a little – when our smartphone is within reach. Researchers had people do a series of tests that looked at their brains' ability to hold and process data (aka what everyone needs to be able to do in a meeting . . . why have one otherwise?). All participants turned their phones to silent mode. Some were asked to put their phones face-down on the desk; others in their pocket or bag; and another group had to leave their phones in another room. The result? People whose phones were in another room significantly outperformed people with their phones on the desk, and did a bit better than those who put their phones in a pocket or bag. Even when we're not letting them actively disrupt us, phones have been linked to unconscious brain drain.

Recent psychological studies have shown that the human brain can become addicted to information just as readily as it can get

addicted to recreational drugs. What's interesting is the role anticipation plays in kicking our dopamine loop into gear – and dopamine
feels good. But according to Sharon Begley, author of *Can't Just Stop:
An investigation of compulsions*, our understanding of dopamine is
still evolving. We used to think dopamine produced pleasure, and
it was the feeling of pleasure we became addicted to. What's come
to light in the last few years is that the dopamine circuitry actually
predicts how much you will like something and how much pleasure
it will give you. It then calculates how much reality fulfils or falls
short of the prediction. The emerging idea is that 'when reality
falls short, we feel a dopamine plunge. That feels bad, so we keep
trying to do something that will make reality live up to expectations. That, to me, fits in with compulsions.' As we all know, the
constant scroll really isn't that satisfying. It's simply a dopamine
fuel–pleasure–reward circuit that we hot-wire ourselves into.

Since learning about this, I've taken to the habit of leaving my
phone off one day a week and it's blown me away how good I feel
for it. Friends who still want to use their camera have committed
to keeping their phone on airplane mode for the weekend. The
grounded sensation of not being instantly available really helps
focus our minds on the present, and on the important as opposed
to the urgent. Plus, despite the stories I'd told myself, the world has
yet to end on any day that I've done it. So far, so (SO) good.

Play a little experiment:

- Let the buzz run flat. Resist the impulse to pick up and attend
  to your phone every time it buzzes. Did you find it hard or easy?
- Swap push for pull. Can you uncouple yourself from push notifications and stop your email having the licence to interrupt you at
  any point? If you can, your concentration, flow and productivity
  will deliver you a far greater reward.
- Tally it up. Keep a tab (or check the phone usage stats that your
  device auto-accumulates) as to how many times you interacted
  with your phone this week. Consider whether every time you

picked your device up, it felt worth taking a 40 per cent hit to productivity? Ask yourself whether it was worth on every occasion being distracted in a manner that then required additional energy to refocus on what you had momentarily chosen to divert from.

The trap of marginal thinking

Another major motivation for thinking about how we work 'on' our life and not just 'in' it is to protect our most important relationships from becoming the collateral damage of distracted decision-making.

In his bestselling book *How Will You Measure Your Life?* the late Clayton Christensen demonstrates the 'trap of marginal thinking'. He proposes the idea that '100% of the time is better than 98%'. Christensen's premise is that many of us have convinced ourselves that we are able to break our own personal rules 'just this once' – and the results can be catastrophic.

He paints the scenario through a marginal thinking frame, bringing to life an executive who decides to stay at work for the evening versus returning home for dinner with their family 'just this once' – because at the margin, getting the 'to do' list cleared seems to deliver greater reward. But, as Christensen says, 'If you give in to "just this once", based on a marginal-cost analysis, you'll regret where you end up.' In the case of this executive, two years of 'just this once' led to finding himself divorced. Trying to contend with the urgent demands work was placing on his time, he'd lost perspective on what mattered most. His behaviour hadn't been tracking to his personal priorities; it had been diverted to putting out company fires.

Christensen also looks at why the world's most successful companies, which are well established financially and have smart, hardworking staff, are often disrupted by start-ups – in theory, that should never happen. As bestselling author and *Harvard Business Review* contributor Michael Simmons puts it, 'The reason why successful companies fail is that they invest in things that provide the most immediate and tangible evidence of achievement. And the reason why they have such a short time horizon is that they are run by people like you and I [people focused on achievement].' Companies are only able to be as future-focused, strategic and long-lasting as the individuals who operate them. If we're not careful, it's easy for the busyness of the day-to-day to subsume us to the point where we lose sight of our bigger 'why'.

The lesson Christensen's book taught me is best encapsulated in this quote: 'It's easier to hold to your principles 100 per cent of the time than it is to hold to them 98 per cent of the time. The boundary – your personal moral line – is powerful because you don't cross it; if you have justified doing it once, there's nothing to stop you doing it again.' When we commit 100 per cent to something, we don't involve the energy-sapping willpower we require when we navigate the grey area of 'should we/shouldn't we' every time the scenario comes up. When you make a commitment to how you're going to invest your time in order to best serve the different areas of your life, be zealous in sticking to it. Like the bad taste left in your mouth when you default back to fast-food, or use angry words with loved ones, a preference of healthy choices will become second nature quicker than you might expect.

When I interviewed former Australian Prime Minister Julia Gillard early in 2021, she spoke about the dire need for today's leaders to carve out time to do the deep thinking. She urged young leaders to understand the pressure they are under to make precise decisions with partial information, changeable objectives and indefinite timelines in today's operating environment. She was adamant that the trust within a team must allow a leader to say, 'I don't know yet,' and that leaders must win themselves the space to think clearly and 'use it wisely'.

Blue sky day

Daniel Flynn is one of Australia's most successful young social entre-preneurs. Well before he'd hit thirty, Dan was a managing director of the social enterprise Thankyou. Dan originally started Thankyou when he was nineteen as a bottled water company, after discovering that nearly 900 million people are without fresh water on the planet. Thankyou now manufactures and sells a range of products from handwash to nappies, with profits used to provide clean drinking water, health and hygiene projects and short-term food aid (the company has donated more than $17 million so far). In fact in 2020 they stopped making their original product (bottled water) entirely because they said it was a 'dumb product that shouldn't exist' – a reference to the extraordinary environmental footprint created by bottling something we can get out of the tap, plastic-free.

Dan is married to one of his co-founders, Justine, and describes himself as very passionate about what he does. Their relationship is beautiful to behold but it hasn't been an easy ride. Both Dan and Justine have spoken publicly about the difficulty of managing burnout and shouldering the responsibilities of leading and serving as chief visionaries for their rapidly growing social enterprise. They've been co-pilots of one hell of a rocket ship over the last decade, and they've started a family as well.

When I spoke to Dan for my podcast, he described a discipline he's built into his routine to enable him to continue to maintain perspective: a 'blue sky day' is what he calls it. 'You just kind of go and look at the blue sky. The idea is that you just pull up, clear everything, and think. It's amazing what thoughts come when you've got space. I have a blue-sky day built into my diary every fortnight. Every fortnight for one day in the week, I am offline, out, no meetings.'

Dan uses this blue sky day to journey to places where he knows he'll find nourishment and inspiration. For him, the best settings are somewhere near water or in the bush. Then he gets his notepad out and writes and journals and draws whatever comes to him. He intentionally leaves tech behind. 'For me, it's actually a really deeply reflective time. It probably helps ground me as a leader . . . some of the greatest ideas I've had have dropped on these days. They are times for me to reflect, for me to write.'

Dan finds it funny how often people ask whether his blue sky practice is valuable beyond his religion and faith. 'I'm like, oh my gosh, absolutely. The act of clearing your day, creating space . . . too many of us get caught up working in what we do but not *on* what we do. So for me, this blue sky day is my opportunity to work on what we do. I'm thinking about structure, strategy, where are we heading.'

Whether it's a blue sky day or a regular retreat, Fortune 500 business coach Ora Shtull has some advice worth following. 'Many people start with blank calendars and relinquish total control by allowing others to fill them up with meetings. They end up with a packed schedule of other people's priorities – not their own.' Work out what is important for you and reserve time for that before other people are allowed to influence the shape of your day and week. This might take some negotiating and rearranging with others; prioritise and navigate accordingly. You likely won't be able to get everything you want but push for what matters most. It can help if you frame it to colleagues, friends and everyone else as being about putting yourself in the best state possible to show up for them. You will likely find that your new schedule will not fit everything you had in your old one. For working out what has to go, I like Shtull's 4D test: 'What can you delete? What can you delay? What can you delegate? What can you diminish?'

Building 'on' in

Alex Bodman is the global executive creative director for music streaming juggernaut Spotify. Alex joined as the first global creative director for the streaming service in 2015 and has since built an in-house creative team of more than thirty people, who've played a major role in helping the platform grow to a subscriber base of 130 million and an active user base of 286 million. It doesn't surprise me that Alex has been incredibly successful, and that people have flocked to work for him. He's a great guy, doing some really cutting-edge work.

When I interviewed Alex, we spoke at length about the challenges of the creative industry: the high rates of burnout; the intense personalisation of the work that can make placing boundaries challenging; the relentless expectation to be creative. Alex commented that he observed early that the people who managed to build influential, lifelong careers seemed to have a balance. 'There's the work, and then there's them. They know not everything is going to work out, not everything will be loved, but they've managed to hold on to a passion to push and to advocate – which is crucial because if you lose that fire, then it's kinda pointless. You're never going to convince anyone of your idea.'

Alex started aiming to hire 'people who know how to sleep at night, whether the day went their way or not'. He also focuses very intentionally on team dynamic when hiring. 'The team you build is so important,' he explains. 'Not just because you'll be giving feedback on their work, but for me, it's important because they should be inspiring you and there should be a sort of mutual energy that you get from working with them. This is the reason why I, and so many of my fellow creative directors, are getting more and more obsessed with diversity. Different viewpoints and ways of going about things give everyone energy.'

Alex also leads his team in a way that, in many respects, is counter-cultural to the industry. 'If you're working in New York agencies you're used to twelve-hour days; you're used to weekends being a luxury. You're used to a grind and for a period, you can run purely on the adrenaline.' But Alex suggests that what the industry is essentially doing with this culture is taking a bunch of very talented, driven people in their twenties and thirties and putting them in a pressure-cooker environment (that has to be counter to long-term creative growth).

'I model the behaviour of leaving the office at 5.30 pm to see my kids, and sure, if I have to jump online later and tidy up a few things I will, but my expectation is we should pretty much have our work done by then.' According to Alex, the advertising industry typically runs on sixty- to seventy-plus-hour weeks, which means staff can slip into a bit of an echo chamber without the right inputs. 'I want my team at the gallery opening. I want my team out, having dinner with friends and having interesting conversations. I want them feeling nourished and interested in and connected to culture. That's how I know they'll flourish most creatively.'

As for me, I am constantly playing with ways to get 'on' both my business and my craft of speaking and moderating. There are staples: quarterly days out to set goals and reflect on my values and habits; routinely taking myself into uncomfortable and lateral learning environments and having rich conversations with different people because it's what stimulates my thinking most effectively. Attending live performance – particularly theatre, stand-up comedy, slam poetry and 'The Moth' storytelling nights – also transports me creatively. And when I really need to get 'on', I put on my shoes and I just run – for however long feels good.

I resonate with what Dan says about heading out without necessarily having a purpose and then finding it all ends up being purposeful anyway. It's a bit like this line I've always loved: 'When the student is ready, the teacher appears.' When the space is created, the ideas and solutions appear. Make sure you create the space.

A question from the leading edge:

When did you last disconnect in order to reconnect with your bigger picture?

15

Build your tribe

'The values of the world we inhabit and the people we surround ourselves with have a profound effect on who we are.'

Malcolm Gladwell

Living in these individualistic times, it's easy to feel that to get something done, you've got to do it alone. It's also really easy to feel lonely as a leader. But I firmly believe if it takes a village to raise a child then it takes an army to raise a leader. And it takes a diverse army to raise a great leader.

The paradox of the modern age is that we've never been more connected, yet we've never felt more isolated. We're plugged into a multitude of social media networks that connect us to people 24/7, but these connections float suspended on a superficial level. We have reduced emotion to emojis. We present a hyperbolic version of ourselves. We hit 'like' to stay relevant, comment to express our extremes and share to make sure we're part of the action.

Is this how we need to lead movements? Mastering a message and motivating supporters requires us to be purposeful about the closest relationships in our lives. Social networks can be helpful the same way networking at an event can be, but it is not where leaders are born. We need to work on our relationships as part of self-leadership before we can move on to creating change within and beyond our sphere.

To start with, let's bring our focus to our core network – not the peripheral hundreds or thousands of people we're connected to online. How many real relationships can we actually maintain?

According to British anthropologist Robin Dunbar, the 'magic number' is 150; a figure now known as Dunbar's number. He became convinced that there was a ratio between brain sizes and group sizes through his studies of non-human primates. Through his studies, Robin concluded that the size of the neocortex – the part of the brain associated with cognition and language – is linked to the size of a cohesive social group. He and his colleagues found remarkable consistency around the number 150.

When my exquisitely introverted partner was reading the draft of this chapter, she exclaimed that the idea of having 150 relationships was probably about 140 too many! But according to the theory, the tightest circle has just five people: our loved ones. That's followed by successive rings of fifteen (our extended family; good friends), fifty (friends), 150 (meaningful contacts), 500 (acquaintances) and 1500 (people you can recognise). People move in and out of these circles, but the idea is that space has to be carved out for any new entrant.

Save space for your Ss

I believe there are four types of relationships worth cultivating and regularly accessing:

Sages

We all have that person in our lives who's our loving truth-teller. They're our wise sounding boards. The ones we call when we need advice. The people who aren't afraid to tell us the brutal truth but do it in a way where you know they come from the best possible place, with the best possible intentions.

Supporters

We all need a cheer squad. Whether they're serving as the source of a pep talk before we go take a courageous leap or giving us encouragement during the tough moments, we need people who can help us reset. I often refer to these people as my 'circuit-breakers'. They can always help me find the silver lining and they always make me believe in myself.

Sponsors

These are the people who open doors and back you into them. They're the ones who serve as references and referees. One of the things I've come to understand over time is an extraordinary number of key conversations about you (with regards to promotions or new opportunities) happen in rooms you're not even in. Sponsors are the people in those moments who advocate for you. Sponsors have to be earned; they need to see your value and your values in action to back you in.

Sparring partners

Who helps you poke the intellectual eyes out of your ideas? Sparring partners are capable of playing your devil's advocate. These people help you raise your bar higher, understand risks and prepare for the haters. They help you become fit for purpose – your purpose.

Do you have all four? If not, grab a piece of paper, pull out your phone and make a list of people who you think could play those roles.

One of the best ways to cultivate each of these four relationships for yourself is to flip the table and focus on who you can play these roles for. Being an open and curious mentor often winds up with you learning just as much as your mentee.

Fuelling your connections

I first came to question how we leverage our relationships strategically at a leadership program in Los Angeles. One of the speakers got up and asked, 'How long does it take to learn from a lifetime of experience?' I was sitting in the auditorium at UCLA as a wide-eyed nineteen-year-old, on my first trip to the US, with 500 young people from around the world.

'Coffee,' the speaker, an entrepreneur by the name of Virgil (gotta be wise, right?), answered his own question. All it takes is to ask someone out for coffee.

Though I can't really explain with any rhyme or reason why this concept hit me like a thunderbolt, it did. That night I pulled out my journal and made a commitment to myself that I would reach out to at least one person a week whom I admired, whose impact I respected or wanted to understand the effectiveness of, and ask if I could take them to coffee. These people would not be within my fifteen extended family members, my fifty friends or even my 150 meaningful contacts. I would reach out through the ripples to my 500 acquaintances and 1500 loose contacts and learn what I could from my extended tribe.

Virgil's point about coffee was building on an idea that was baked into the heart of the leadership program: don't create mediocrity, copy genius. There are natural laws of human behaviour that govern decision-making, motivation, and results. Successful people, companies and communities leave a trail of breadcrumbs for us to follow. Why not discover what these natural laws of success reveal and apply them, instead of trying to make it all up as you go?

In more than a decade of applying that habit I've been fortunate to never receive a 'no'. It certainly doesn't mean every conversation has been a winner. I've also had to wait and politely follow up, in one instance for more than eighteen months (that woman is now one of my most trusted confidantes and mentors). But there is no habit I've practised more regularly or that has made more of a contribution to my growth and development as a person and as a leader than this one.

Many of these coffee dates have morphed into mentoring relationships, and even my own podcast series, #coffeepods. But I want to emphasise something really important here: I didn't go seeking mentors; I went seeking learning.

Let's interrogate the word 'mentoring' for a moment. Mentoring is the topic I get asked about most regularly at the end of my keynotes. 'How do I find a mentor?' 'What makes a good mentor?' 'How do I ask someone to be my mentor?' I also see how overwhelmed people are by the idea. I think it auto-generates some sense of rigidity, like someone forgot to give us a manual for the secret handshakes to get let into that elite mentoring club. I think it also triggers people who optimistically embraced their company's ill-fated attempt to assign everyone a random mentor and got a dud.

Ditch the notions of obligation and formality. Take the pressure off and literally think of this as a coffee experiment: how much can you learn from someone's life experience over a long black (or an americano for my US buddies)?

Kicking off your coffees

Of course, once someone has agreed to your coffee date, you need to know how to make the most of your time. Here are my tips for embracing the opportunity to seek learning:

Know what learning you're seeking and why

Before contacting anyone, be able to articulate this both to the people you're asking to help you find that learning or to the person you're going to ask. This requires doing some self-reflection relative to the goals you've set for yourself: what knowledge gaps are you seeking to fill or what advice are you eager to get? What can this person you're seeking learning from specifically help you to solve? I prefer to mentally prepare my questions but others (like my partner) prefer to have them written out. Having been on the other side of a number of these conversations now I assure you that whatever your method, preparation always impresses.

Identify who matches the learning you seek

Many great sources of advice and insight are right under our noses. Look to your circles of relationships. Do you already know the person and you've just never cultivated that sort of learning relationship with them? Does someone in your closest five or fifteen know a perfect fit?

Get a warm intro or write a warm intro

In the event that you don't know the potential mentor firsthand, ask to be introduced by a mutual contact. LinkedIn can be a really useful tool for mapping a path to the learning you seek through the network you already have. Make sure, whether you're writing the intro or asking someone else to do it for you, that you make your 'why' clear. For example, that you're eager to pursue a similar career path to them and would love their advice on how they've navigated getting to where they are. Or perhaps you're facing a similar strategic challenge to one that's in front of them and would love to hear about how they approached it and whether they'd be prepared to be a sounding board for your ideas. People have an overwhelming willingness to make time for people where they can see a clear benefit in doing so. That can range from an ability to help them solve a problem through to investing in someone they feel will pay it forward down the line.

It's on you to wait, to flex and to follow up

The hustle is always on the seeker. And here's one of life's secrets: next to no-one has good follow-up game when they don't get the response they want in the first instance. It's understandable to feel put off if you get ignored but politely following up demonstrates commitment. Wait a reasonable amount of time – say a week or two – before you do it and if that gets doughnuts consider another approach six to twelve months down the line, if having that knowledge exchange remains important to you at that point in time. I estimate 5 per cent of the people who reach out to me seeking time actually follow up when there's a delay. That's one of my filters for whom I make time for and it's something Virgil taught me. He made those of us who wanted to be mentored by him read five leadership books, handwrite book reports describing what we'd learnt and how we were going to apply it (chapter by chapter) and then mail them to him. In more than twenty years of putting that offer in front of 500+ eager, motivated and successful young leaders, Virgil says he could count on two hands those that did the work. Do the work.

Gauge your connection and respect their time

I am meticulous about showing up early and ending these coffee meetings on time. I always think it's important you offer to pay, though sometimes your guest will insist on picking up the tab. Sometimes I leave these coffee conversations and think 'wow, what incredible learning' and I feel like I've managed to garner everything I wanted out of the conversation. Other times, I feel like I've barely gotten through a fifth of the questions I'd hoped to ask and we just had the sort of bounce and rapport that suggested this connection could be a more ongoing one. At that point it's worth asking if a second coffee in another month or two would be possible.

Say thank you

This sounds so 101 but probably the thing I marvel at the most when it comes to networking and mentoring is how much better we can all get at saying 'thanks'. And I'm not just talking about expressing your gratitude to the person who made the time to share their views with you (I hope that's a given!). I'm also talking about circling back to the person who made the introduction for you and letting them know how it went and what you got out of it. The second part is as important as the first. Whatever learning you just experienced was courtesy of the person who made it possible, so make sure they know you appreciate it. I know I can speak from personal experience when I say that when I'm thanked for facilitating a connection,

I'm ten times more likely to help that person out the next time they ask for help than I would be otherwise.

Apply before you reapply

Do not, under any circumstance, reach out and ask for more time if you haven't gone and applied or actioned all of the advice or suggestions that you committed to undertake when you last spoke. If a curve ball gets thrown at you or new information comes to hand that fundamentally changes the situation, that's different. Same goes for if you've had a total change of heart or redirection. But otherwise, put your learning to work. Ensure that your next conversation can be compounding on the first, that you have done the heavy lifting to now be playing at the next level.

Healthy boundaries

For all its amazing benefits, I experienced in my twenties a couple of ripper examples of tricky mentoring situations, ones where I got completely thrown under the bus by people whom I genuinely thought had my best interests at heart. On one occasion, I had a 'mentor' ardently suggest I apply for a role on a particular advisory board, only to overhear her denigrate my qualifications for the role the very next day while in the women's bathroom at a conference. In another instance a different mentor offered me a role, which we then had numerous conversations about and verbally contracted. But then, after I'd quit another role in order to take up this one, they reneged because 'to be honest we never really had the intention of taking the organisation in that direction'. That was a winner. I've also been told to avoid (or go into business with) particular people, change certain behaviours and characteristics (I've been told I am both too confident and too shy – go figure!), and even that dating certain people wasn't advisable for my career. All of the aforementioned advice had some pretty questionable motives or some clear personal baggage attached to it or both.

I had to hold the advice lightly, assess it objectively and let it go.

When I was diagnosed with depression and was doing the post-mortem analysis of 'how on earth did I get here?', one of my big revelations was that part of it centred on the people I had been giving my time, effort and energy to. I was investing too much in people who had no intention of reinvesting in me. These weren't 'bad' people; they just weren't people, situations and circumstances that were good for me. One of the most profound learnings I've had over the years since is that it's often not the loud criticism made by people who dislike (or even hate) us that shakes us from our knowing. More often than not it can be the quiet scrutiny of the people we love most. Putting boundaries in place here are some of the toughest conversations we'll ever find ourselves in. No-one ever taught me about 'healthy relationships' or having these sorts of tough, interpersonal conversations growing up.

We want people to like us, and we assume that setting boundaries will upset others and push them away. In reality, setting boundaries enables us to be more compassionate, empathetic and present. Clear boundaries often strengthen relationships by enabling communication and reducing resentment. Setting boundaries isn't always easy, but it begins with knowing your own limits, and being comfortable saying no. To this end, boundaries can be physical, material, mental or emotional. Every person who has mastered leadership has had to master boundaries. There is no other way to make the space required for ourselves.

Psychologist and coach Dana Gionta says having healthy boundaries is as simple as 'knowing and understanding what your limits are.' She identifies a few steps to establish personal boundaries that are worth considering, adopting or adapting.

Tune into your feelings and learn your limits
Consider what you can tolerate or what makes you feel uncomfortable or stressed. Resentment is a huge red flag that your boundaries

are being crossed. It can come from being taken advantage of or not appreciated by someone imposing their views on us, or is a sign we're pushing ourselves beyond our own limits because we feel guilty, or overwhelmed by the weight of expectation.

Be direct and assertive

Sometimes you will need to be explicit in establishing and maintaining your boundaries, especially with people who may not understand them. It is not your job to explain *why* you need a particular boundary, but you *do* need to make your boundaries known. I've found it helpful to prepare phrases before I'm in 'boundary'-type conversations. For example, when I'm asked to undertake a role that I don't have capacity for I'll say something like, 'I like to be able to throw myself fully into everything I do and unfortunately my plate is too full at the moment to be able to do this opportunity justice.' It's true and it helps make it easier to say 'no', something I still find difficult on the best of days.

Give yourself permission

Giving yourself permission requires a healthy dose of self-awareness and a radical amount of self-love. When you set boundaries, you may fear another person's response, you may feel guilty and you may doubt your decision. If people don't respect your boundaries, that's a warning sign that they're someone you need to back away from quietly and calmly . . . like Grandpa always told me to do with a snake!

Consider your past and present

Your childhood, family dynamics and social circles will all influence how you go about setting and preserving boundaries. Consider the identity markers you internalise around relationship expectations and obligations and then consider if they need to be reset.

Make self-care a priority

Self-care probably needs a rebrand because for some reason the packaging indicates it's a luxury! When our own needs are taken care of, we have the energy, peace of mind and capacity to be more present with others. It makes us a better partner, parent, friend, worker, mentor and everything in between. You don't need to spend money to prioritise self-care, either. Take a great book and snuggle up by a fireplace, get lost in nature, cook yourself a really nourishing meal. Whatever fills your cup, just do it, unapologetically.

Relationships worth cutting

This is a bit of a taboo topic so let me just come out and say it: odds are, there are some people in your life who shouldn't be there. Or at least shouldn't be allowed to play the role they're playing.

What I want to emphasise is that we all have a finite amount of energy, time and bandwidth and it is our choice as to where we allocate that. Life is too short to sacrifice ourselves. We are able to give the best of ourselves to the people and things that matter only when we clear space for them. Be bold enough to walk away from people and things that no longer serve you; it's one of the bravest things you will ever do.

A question from the leading edge:

Who are the five people who enable you to be the
leader the world needs you to be?

Part Two

If leadership starts from within but never moves beyond our individual lives, can we truly call ourselves leaders? I don't believe we can. While leading *ourselves* at the edge of change in Part One asked us to dream big, now leading *others* to the edge of change will challenge us to become the leaders the world needs us to be. This is where the most worthwhile impact begins.

To operate from the leading edge requires us to be bold enough to put a vision out there and to try to rally others around it. In Part Two we will learn how to get buy-in for our vision. We'll test ourselves on what we know about building culture, leveraging diversity, taking risks, publicly giving and receiving feedback, improvising, empowering and building common ground. Part Two coaches us to cultivate the talents and capacities of others, to ask better questions and to shift systems towards progress. It's the pursuit of these challenges that not only makes leadership interesting, but makes it *meaningful*.

Once more, we'll walk through mindset, method and mastery ideas and practices. I hope they embolden you, wherever your exact starting point may be and inspire you not to stop when you're tired but to stop only when you are *done*.

The leading edge of leading others means seeing human potential and putting belief and energy into helping others realise it. It means building powerful teams, collaborations, coalitions and partnerships supported by sound structures and systems. It means not just to speak up and out, but to amplify the possibility of change with substantive action.

Think of these next pages as a dare for collective action.

When one becomes many, anything is possible.

Part Two is about realising that potential.

Mindset

**Care deeply for
humanity
Hold human
idiosyncrasies lightly**

16
Motivate the collective

'There is no greater power for change than a community discovering
what it cares about.'

Margaret J. Wheatley

Achievement of anything purposeful is always a collective effort.
Change is not the story of a lone wolf or an individual architect, but
the tale of a person who created a compelling sense of urgency that
inspired others to pay attention, someone who could create a bridge
between their own personal aspiration and a shared notion of 'us'.
Establishing a common belief creates a collective identity and turns
a moment into a movement, or an idea into an ideology.

But the story of human achievement is rarely told as a
collective tale. Instead our culture of hero-worship lionises the lone-
wolf genius. When we talk of Jobs, Lincoln, Thatcher and Gandhi,
of Einstein, Mandela, Armstrong, Earhart and Goodall, it is true, of
course, that these leaders are luminaries. However, their narratives
of individual achievement create a false illusion that history is made
and shaped by uniquely gifted enigmas. An unhelpful misrepresen-
tation that denies the important role of teams and places change
beyond the reach of 'mere mortals' like you and me.

Today, the world is in crisis on so many fronts. The compounding
problem of the hero narrative means we all too often sit suspended in

a state of wishing and waiting . . . for the messianic leader or inventor to emerge who can take us to the next promised land or revolutionise life as we know it.

What if we *are* the leaders capable of activating the collective? What if the world needs *us* to step up right now?

We cannot afford to wait.

The 'Why' we are all responsible for

I remember staying up late slaving over an assignment on US Secretary of State Condoleezza Rice for my Year 10 English class. As the Secretary to President George W. Bush, and the first African American woman to ever hold the position, Secretary Rice seemed fascinatingly out of place among powerful white men, yet utterly in her element. She always said that to be successful, a person has to know their own DNA. She knew that she loved policy much more than she loved politics – and by sticking to a style of leadership that she believed in, she was able to build a strong personal brand that others could invest in. She would continually avoid framing things in partisan terms, preferring to speak the language of values (like faith, freedom and democracy) that could unite people from both major US political parties and from an array of backgrounds. Rarely do we see leaders form a bridge instead of a divide.

The personal story of Secretary Rice is remarkable. She grew up in racially segregated Alabama during the oppressive Jim Crow era. In our interview, she credits her family, faith and education with helping her achieve the extraordinary heights that she did, saying her parents raised her to believe 'I might not have been able to have a hamburger at Woolworth's lunch counter, but I could be president of the United States if I wanted to be.' Her initial plan was to be a concert pianist, but early into her undergraduate studies, she admitted to her parents she wasn't quite sure what she wanted to do. 'I told them it was my life,' she said. 'They told me it was their money, so find a major.' She pivoted into politics after walking into her first class and finding herself utterly spellbound. Within diplomatic relations, she sensed diplomacy. Within policy setting, she was determined to reset empathy.

Politics aside, the pioneering accomplishments of Secretary Rice inspired me. Her insatiable work ethic, effectiveness as a communicator, her courage to be the 'first' or the 'only' in so many rooms and to never allow that to diminish her voice. If someone had told my Year 10 self that fifteen years later I'd be sitting opposite Secretary Rice in person, with the opportunity to use my own voice, I would have fallen off my chair.

On stage in San Francisco, I asked Secretary Rice about the collective why. How do we take our own belief, the thing we cherish deeply, and give it over to the collective to enable real change?

She recalled being Secretary of State during the 9/11 terrorist attacks, referring to them as 'arguably the hardest moment in the last generation'. When I asked how she was able to lead amid such pain and adversity, she said, 'You can get through difficult times, but it doesn't happen magically.' She continued, 'It comes down to an ability to unite people behind a common vision. A shared sense of purpose.' She claimed she didn't look to Washington or state governments to take responsibility for sparking revolutions but asked herself daily, 'What am *I* doing to take responsibility?' Importantly, Secretary Rice said, this requires us to give people the autonomy to take ownership of their purpose, 'to colour outside the lines', as she puts it. I don't think we've ever needed leaders who purposefully colour outside the lines more.

To Secretary Rice, change starts with having a purposeful vision and empowering people. 'We have to find a way to mobilise human potential . . . The greatest leaders are the ones that can nurture the leadership of others.' That starts by leading in a way that enlivens the why of others. It starts when we allow others to see their purpose in ours and co-create the momentum that leads to change. A collective why has the power to alter how we speak to each other, whether we choose to purchase unethical products, where we decide to work and play. Individual purpose might get us out of bed in the morning but without tapping into a shared 'why' there will be no new dawn.

The importance of collective effort

The fourteenth-century origins of the word 'leader' mean 'to go before as a guide'. But that idea of a guiding force or presence seems highly aspirational compared to many of today's leaders, who seem content to stand silent at the edge of the path and watch us lose our way. Some leaders obsess over problems, constantly telling us what's wrong but failing to inspire us to act differently. Others optimistically assure us that things will work out, encouraging us to be our whole self but not providing the strategic focus to allow us to be resilient to change. And others care so deeply they are paralysed with fear. In observing this current state of leadership around us, we illuminate just how critical it is that we focus on leading in a new, more purposeful and empowering way.

We need to be leaders worth following.

As a ten-year-old, I walked past a homeless man in the street in Perth. Being the shrinking violet that I am, and with my mum busily distracted in a nearby bookstore, I decided to strike up a conversation with him. 'Whatcha doing?' I asked, only to have him reply, 'Trying to earn enough for a roof and a feed.' I couldn't quite wrap my head around his answer. He proceeded to tell me that the $4.10 of silver coins I counted in his hat was a good day and he was doing well. I had about two nanoseconds to take that in before Mum found me and delivered a medal-worthy stranger-danger lecture.

But as I lay in bed that night, while it bucketed with rain, all I could think about was how come I was lucky enough, by lottery of birth, to have a roof over my head and a stomach full of food. The more I thought about it, the more it enraged me: it was profoundly *wrong* that the guy I'd met on the side of the street struggled daily for both. I ruminated over how many people must be in a similar predicament.

The next day before lessons began, I bailed up my school principal telling him what had happened and asking, 'I want to fix it, how do I fix it?' Fortunately, he was the kind of person who didn't shut the door on me but instead engaged in a chat about what helping could look like. We came up with a plan and ran a massive food drive through our primary school, making a donation at the end of semester. I felt like we'd helped, until two years later when I had to do a project on a 'community social issue' and I visited the shelter we'd supported, only to have the manager tell me they were helping twice as many people as they were two years earlier. We'd put a small bandaid on a wound that continued to grow.

I became obsessed with how we can sustainably solve problems at scale. I grew interested in social enterprise and headed to Kenya to work on a microfinance project, raising money to help a small community of twenty-two women in the Korogocho slums outside Nairobi. But as we travelled through kilometres of slums, I struggled to fathom that all our energy was not even scratching the surface of the issue. I realised we needed better tools to lead change effectively. And that 'we' started with 'me'. I apprenticed myself, spending the better part of a decade on a fact-finding mission across the corporate, non-profit and public policy arenas seeking to understand different structures, strategies and capital allocation. But again, as I sat in class at the Harvard Kennedy School, being tutored by intellectual giants and surrounded by brilliant scholars, I was again struck by the feeling that all of our theses, our theories and conclusions will yet again fail to scratch the surface.

We cannot do it without you. And you cannot do it without everyone else.

From 'me' to 'we', through 'why'

Sitting in Secretary Ash Carter's class at Harvard gives you a rare insight into the remarkable mind of the man who was the twenty-fifth United States Secretary of Defense (from 2015 to 2017). What

I learnt is that collective action is a mindset game. In serving as Secretary of Defense, he was responsible for the largest organisation in the world – a workforce of more than three million civilian and military personnel and an annual budget of more than half-a-trillion dollars. Secretary Carter became known for his savvy leadership and for ensuring the Pentagon thought 'outside its five-sided box'.

In a period of changing values in and around congress, Secretary Carter was responsible for significant transformation in the Defense Department. Redefining the entire view of adversaries and allies, partners and private enterprises, Secretary Carter also redefined talent management, opening all combat roles in the military to women – a process that is now a Harvard case study. Secretary Carter is a scientist by both inclination and training (he has a PhD in physics), which brings a calm, considered and methodical approach to the way he evaluates matters that are often more commonly associated with intense emotion and vitriolic political debate.

Secretary Carter stresses that identifying a clear, powerful overarching why that is universal and defensible is key, in this instance preparing America's military as a 'force for the future'. Now, who in the military would object to that aspiration? That to best protect America the military needed to be as fit for purpose as possible? By extension, Secretary Carter argued this endeavour required access to the full pool of available talent (not 50 per cent of it) and the ability to retain talent once they joined. Again, difficult to object to but given the political (and emotive) nature of the topic, there could be no chances taken. From there, Secretary Carter and his team embarked on a phase he terms 'doing the homework', which involved:

- verifying that this was the right decision for the effectiveness of the force
- determining implementation
- ensuring that it was feasible without incurring significant cost
- anticipating likely questions and objections.

In other words: making your 'why' watertight.

Verifying the decision included conducting both sentiment surveys as well as employing teams of researchers to study everything from unit cohesion to physical standards. They wanted to elevate the 'why' (beyond 'women in the army'), not impose it. This 'homework' also helped to identify the key pillars to take into account in the implementation – to make sure the mechanics and blowback around the 'how' didn't bury the 'why'. In this instance, all military services were given the autonomy to develop their own plans on implementation but were required to incorporate seven guiding principles, ranging from 'no quotas' and 'consistent standards', to objective promotion criteria and requiring data-based decision-making when it came to concerns around overseas deployment in certain regions.

Extraordinarily, the change was implemented with almost no criticism or blowback.

Secretary Carter made me appreciate the criticality of shaping a why that is watertight and the importance of messaging, data and stakeholder engagement. We can't assume everyone's why will be grounded in the same mindset, but if we work at finding a way of 'purposing-up', we can scaffold to a higher purpose that allows a broader audience to get on board. From there, we can really make things happen.

Connecting my 'why' to yours: unlikely allies

In 2015, history was made when Ireland became the first country in the world to pass a referendum legalising same-sex marriage. The nation's Catholic identity (78.3 per cent) and the historic stranglehold of religion on Irish public policy made the campaign an unlikely victory, yet more than two-thirds of the Irish population voted to legalise same-sex marriage: 62 per cent. The turnout was high, especially among young voters, which boosted the 'Yes' vote, and the overall turnout of 61 per cent was higher than at the poll to ratify the historic 1998 Good Friday agreement (a significant milestone in the Northern Ireland Peace Process), when 56 per cent of the electorate came out to vote. Forty-two of the republic's forty-three constituencies voted 'Yes' to legalising same-sex marriage, and the urban/rural split that was feared did not eventuate.

How did it come about that Ireland delivered such a resounding 'Yes' to marriage equality?

Tiernan Brady was at the forefront of the campaign, helping to design the strategies that led to the emphatic victory. The Irish political and LGBTQIA+ rights campaigner, who also served as CEO of Australian Marriage Equality when Australia returned its own emphatic 'Yes', has profound lessons about connection and communication, and how to construct a purpose that breaks down cultural and religious divides and inspires action. His strategy was focused on giving people reasons to vote for marriage equality not in spite of their faith but *because* of it.

Finding a collective why is about tapping into our shared humanity. It works for that exact reason: we amplify and draw focus to what we have in common as opposed to trying to weaponise our differences to motivate action. Tiernan explains, 'All too often, instead of trying to understand the majority who we are trying to persuade, we take the position of 'no, you have to understand me first'. And of course, if you're a minority, that's not a very strategically brilliant position to take!' Tiernan has also observed that too often, when thinking about change, we take the narrative of, 'It's about time you stopped being so backwards, people, you're terrible.' As it turns out, people rarely change when told they're wrong or archaic or stupid; more often than not, they just dig their heels in.

Tiernan illustrates the point:

There's nobody in the world that I ever met, who upon being called a homophobe, clutched her pearls and said, 'Well, now that you've told me how ignorant I am, I can't wait to support you!' So instead, we need to understand the values of our nay-sayers. For many in Ireland, it was faith and family. Instead of telling people 'those are bad values', we have to jettison the mould, we have to find a way to say 'actually they are great'.

Tiernan tells a story of door-knocking for marriage equality in Ireland. One of the team was met at the door by a woman in her mid-nineties, who said: 'I've been waiting to talk to you.' The door knocker immediately stiffened, expecting a hateful lecture about being a sinner. Instead, the woman spoke about her brother, who had moved to Melbourne seventy years earlier and had died twenty years ago. He'd moved for no other reason than he was a gay man and he needed somewhere to hide. The woman broke down as she told of her profound shame at how her family had gradually made him invisible. How, for seventy years his sister and their family walked the streets of Galway, and when asked how John was, they'd say, 'Oh, he's fine.' 'Has he met a girl?' they'd ask. 'No, no, no, he hasn't settled yet,' they'd reply. While some minorities suffer verbal and physical abuse, she wondered out loud about what could be worse than being made invisible.

As Tiernan tells the story:

The 95-year old woman sobbed at the door. She went to vote that following Friday, and she voted for her brother who had died twenty years earlier. She voted 'Yes', but she didn't vote for a philosophy. She didn't vote for a law change. She voted for her brother. She cast her ballot. And then she did what she did every morning: she went to Mass.

As this shows, one of the things the Irish campaign did brilliantly was to turn human rights conversations into conversations about *real* human beings. It sounds simple, but it's a rarely deployed strategy. They wanted to stay away from high-level religious doctrine versus civil rights arguments and mud-slinging debates because these diminish the validity of the legitimate and genuine questions people have. When people who disagree with us ask questions, this doesn't make them bad people; it makes them sensible. And the generosity of our answer in taking in their perspective will often define the result.

A collective why is at its most powerful when it's owned, not imposed. The language used to articulate it cannot be foreign, it must be everyday and tailored to the contextual culture.

Tiernan talks at length about how one of their early observations is people's fear of saying the wrong thing or hurting someone's feelings was stifling important questions and conversation. People have an innate curiosity about 'difference' but when we starve that curiosity of the oxygen questions provide, it can turn to fear and discomfort. Tiernan says, 'If we want people to see our lives, we can't expect them to use our language. As they make a journey to seeing our lives, we have to let them use the language and cultural framework they live in.' When we fear asking or answering the questions, we create a barrier to the change we need to happen.

Tiernan recounts another door-knocking story where a woman in Dublin came to the door and said, 'Oh, sure, of course, I'm going to vote for you. It's not your fault you're the way you are.' Now, that might be phenomenally politically incorrect. But actually, that's a joyous moment. That's a moment in which someone who is in their seventies, who has grown up with the institutional language of homophobia, through all the government messaging, the church messaging, to the broader social messaging, has still seen the truth of the need for change and is willing to come on the journey. Tiernan says, 'And instead of us being angry about that we go, "That is what victory looks like."'

To be a leader capable of inspiring collective action, we must find a way to sit with the messy pain and angry frustration to reach the humane forgiveness implicit in connecting our own why to someone else's. For a true north to move the needle, it needs to register on everyone's moral compass.

Anchoring collective purpose

A great example of a leader taking an individual why to a collective why can be found in the story of the CLIF Bar company. If you've been anywhere near the energy bar aisle of a supermarket (particularly in the US) or participated in a marathon or triathlon, you've probably seen or consumed a CLIF Bar. They're the brightly coloured bars with the cartoon rock climber scaling a jagged edge. (The honey oat ones kept me alive during my second Ironman!)

What you may be less familiar with is the story behind the bars. In 1990, Gary Erickson set off on a one-day, 280-kilometre bicycle ride with his friend. He'd packed the only available energy bar at the time, but famished and fatigued, halfway through his long-haul effort, he realised he just couldn't eat another unappetising, sticky, hard-to-digest bar. Right then, he had what he calls 'the epiphany' – he knew what he wanted to create. Because his mother was a terrific baker, he asked her to help find the perfect ingredients and recipe. They worked for a few months until Gary settled on a bar that tasted better than anything that was available on the market and contained nutritious ingredients that would sustain energy. He named their creation CLIF Bar in honour of his father, Clifford, who had introduced him to wilderness adventures and encouraged him to follow his passions in life.

CLIF Bar was formally launched in 1992 and accumulated a cult following within the climbing and cycling community. At first the bars were sold through bike shops, outdoor stores and natural food retailers, but once word began to spread, Gary was able to expand distribution of the bars to include grocery and convenience stories and other retail outlets all over the country.

As the energy bar category grew rapidly throughout the 1990s, so did the pressure for Gary to sell the CLIF bar. Yet in 2001, he and his wife, Kit, decided to stay private. This allowed them to develop an innovative five-bottom-line business model guided by their 'five aspirations': business, brands, people, community and the planet.

In 2010 they offered 20 per cent of the company to their employees through an employee stock ownership program, which led to stronger business performance with staff now financially invested in the purpose of the business, as well as invested in the organisation's mission.

The company diverts 85 per cent of its office waste from local landfills, through reduction, recycling and composting. In 2012, the company's headquarters were awarded the highest standard buildings can earn as a measure of their sustainability. And recognising that food is at the centre of everything it does, the company prioritises using organic ingredients and farming methods. Gary notes proudly: 'We've proven that sustainability is good for business.'

As part of the company's expression of its 'people' aspiration, CLIF Bar 'provides employees with an onsite fitness centre, personal trainers and concierge services such as organic produce delivery. Employees can opt for a flexible work week and are encouraged to participate in volunteer opportunities during the workday. They also enjoy a sabbatical program, sustainability benefits and onsite childcare.' The company has been named the best place to work by *Outside* and *Fortune* magazines.

As Gary said in an interview with *Forbes* when probed about the centrality of purpose to the CLIF Bar company:

> The first 'why' was to make a better energy bar for athletes that focused on performance and taste, something that didn't exist at the time. CLIF Bar defined the expectations of the bar category. But the more profound 'why' came when I decided not to walk off the field. A big-money exit was not why I created CLIF Bar. There was tremendous relief in that defining moment of turning down the buyout.

CLIF's success came down to having a clear why that went beyond delivering a product. Not only did it meet the needs of its target audience (hungry adventurers) but in building a business anchored

in a set of principles, it united and engaged that community –
converting them to be equally principled consumers and advocates.

Getting buy-in to the vision

When I work on a change initiative or a company visioning project,
I'll put the subject in the middle of a whiteboard and then draw the
handy heuristic of Tony Robbins' six human needs out on six spokes:

- Certainty: assurance you can avoid pain and gain pleasure; a
  desire for stability and surety
- Uncertainty/variety: the need for the unknown, change, new stimuli
- Significance: feeling unique, important, special or needed
- Connection/love: a strong feeling of closeness or union with
  someone or something
- Growth: an expansion of capacity, capability or understanding
- Contribution: a sense of service and focus on helping, giving to
  and supporting others

Let's take a vision you would like to get buy-in to. I invite you
to draw up the human-needs wagon wheel and think about how to
frame the story of your why through those six different drivers. How
can we ensure your why is aligned to multiple human needs?

A few years ago I was working with a transformational educational leader who was struggling to overcome the resistance of her
staff to a dramatic shift in the school's curriculum and pedagogy.
Her language was all about the 'education revolution', 'being at
the cutting edge' and 'pioneering the future of education' – which
totally grabs someone like me who's energised by growth but, when
addressing a profession (stereotyping teachers here for a moment)
and a cohort of parents who typically have 'certainty and stability'
somewhere prominent in their drivers, it was leading to enormous
resistance. We worked on changing the messaging, running a narrative that was about how the data supported the need to change; how
the unsafest thing would be to keep education as it is with all that
we know about how the world was changing; and explaining the

'stage gates' of implementation and review that had been built into the process. Slowly, but surely, sentiment started to shift.

We tend to write the narrative we like to hear, but it's not always the one that invites our audience along on a journey. When you're thinking about the why of your change project and who you need to engage to make it happen, you have an opportunity to select a dominant narrative. Are there particular messages you need to target particular leaders or teams or subcultures or a combination of these within your stakeholder group? Some of the time, this may rely on you reading the room and using intuition to put forward the dominant narrative for this occasion. Other times, data will help you prepare. Above all, you must begin to shape a multidimensional story about purpose.

Designing for purpose is more complicated than hitting a single nail on the head. Our framework must not only be built to welcome in diverse people through multiple access points, but also be robust enough to protect the collective from storms of criticism, doubt or backlash if they arise.

A question from the leading edge:

Does the way you share the story of your why encapsulate the why of others?

17

Get adaptable with EQ

'Our ability to manage ourselves and handle relationships "Emotional Intelligence" matters twice as much as IQ.'

Daniel Goleman

There's been an interesting shift for those who've tracked the world's most in-demand skills over the last five years. 'Emotional intelligence' has emerged as a critical skill. This skill didn't make the list when the World Economic Forum forecast their 'top ten skills for 2015', but emerged as number six on the list by 2020. As we find ourselves talking about the increasing automation of technical capabilities, we're seeing a growing conversation about which skills robots can't out-human us on: caring and compassion are taking on a renewed sense of prominence.

The concept of emotional intelligence was first popularised by Daniel Goleman in a book by the same title back in 1995. He argued that EQ, as he called it, was as critical for success as IQ. *Emotional Intelligence* sparked a new conversation around what it meant to be 'smart'. By Goleman's definition, 'Emotional intelligence is the ability to perceive emotions, to access and generate emotions so as to assist thought, to understand emotions and emotional knowledge, and to reflectively regulate emotions so as to promote emotional and intellectual growth.'

Daniel gave structure to five critical components: self-awareness, self-regulation, motivation, empathy and social skills. Emotional intelligence relies on you being able to understand and manage yourself, as well as to understand the emotions and feelings of others (empathy) and finally to influence them (social skills).

You may have already ditched the old golden rule of 'treat others as you would like to be treated' as somewhat emotionally unintelligent. It is actually a far better approach not to assume what's best for you is best for others, and to treat others as *they* would like to be treated.

To music buffs out there, when we talk about EQ in the land of beats and mix-tapes, we are referring to equalising the frequencies of soundwaves so that everything is balanced and clear. Similarly in leading collective change, any goal we're trying to achieve requires everyone to be on the same wavelength. EQ is the leadership tool that can adjust the output for smoother input. Showing empathy both relies on, and enables, listening.

Fine-tuning your EQ in a foreign environment

I was on a week-long, live-in leadership program and on the morning of the second day we'd been bussed off to a nearby university and split into two groups for an activity. My group was briefed to be the 'Alpha'. We *loved* affection and interaction and were all about relationships. In our group's code, failing to adequately greet or converse with a fellow Alpha was a major cultural no-no. We had a card game we played, but it was peripheral to the interaction itself and there was no point-scoring to speak of. We were all about cooperation and non-competition; we weren't big on personal space and we had a very hierarchical structure in our society.

Fully primed, we began mucking around as Alphans before we were told the real run of the morning: our mission, should we choose to accept it, would be to venture down the corridor into a foreign land known as Beta and ascertain Beta's culture. The Beta tribe would also be sending observers and visitors our way. The moment a Betan offended one of our cultural practices, we were to send them packing back down the corridor, which meant, in reverse, the moment we culturally offended Betans we'd be sent packing too.

I was the first observer sent traipsing down the hallway to Beta. Walking in felt about as foreign as it could feel, given I had been on the bus with this group of people only an hour earlier. There were next to no words in Beta, but they did seem to be intensely engaging in some kind of card game. I went to shake the hand of a Betan and *boom*: I was shown the door. Apparently, Betans weren't big on handshakes. Maybe I should have gone for a high-five . . .

Over the course of the next hour, we sent observers down the corridor and they came back with morsels of insights: speculations about who was the chief of their tribe, how they greeted one another, attempts to decipher the language of their interactions (unlike Alphans, Betans spoke broken English at best and very sparsely). Then the activity ended and we were each paired with a Betan to debrief with a series of questions:

- What comes to mind when we think of Betans/Alphans? We thought the Betans were cold, competitive and unwelcoming; they thought we were loud, affectionate and spontaneous.
- How did Betans/Alphans appear when in your culture? Betans said we stuck out like sore thumbs because we were boisterous and asserted ourselves immediately, both physically and vocally; Betans seemed invisible in our culture.
- How did it feel to be in the other culture? Betans felt intimidated by our enthusiasm and how close we stood to them; we felt intimidated by their lack of warmth and our inability to decipher their goings-on.
- How did you cope when in the other culture (i.e., withdraw, get aggressive, etc.)? We had the whole gamut of coping strategies here.

As we spent the next hour unpacking just how incredibly far off base each of our two groups had been at getting to the bottom of what made the other tick, my fifteen-year-old mind was blown.

This wasn't an activity that our program's director had just dreamt up to find a way to occupy a bunch of teenagers for the morning. This was a game called BaFá BaFá, and it had its origins in the US military. Around 1971, the US Navy became very concerned about the culturally insensitive and offensive behaviour of American sailors on leave in foreign ports, and determined to do something to avoid incidents that were threatening relations between the US and its allies. The result was the simulation game BaFá BaFá created by Gary Shirts. Gary intended it to improve participants' EQ by helping them develop cultural competency. Cultural awareness training reveals to participants the impact of culture on the behaviour of people and organisations. Programs like BaFá BaFá are considered to have dramatically improved the culture of the US military over the decades since.

As is so often the case with 'culture shock', when we played the game there wasn't a bad intention among us. How had we gone so wrong? For one thing, our attempt to comprehend the 'other' culture was entirely projected through the paradigm of our own. This is known as 'anchoring', a common psychological bias. Adding to that, we'd taken as truth the observations of our teammate who'd travelled down the corridor to experience the foreign scene before us. Rather than retaining a healthy scepticism and experiencing a new culture for ourselves, we attempted to build on top of our own norms and cultural practices. We hadn't come into the situation attempting to be sensitive to the needs of other. We barrelled our way in, hoping to forge bonds and have a positive impact, but forgetting that true relationships are never forged on one person's terms alone. In failing to be sensitive to the needs of others, we'd completely bypassed the subtlety of how they wanted to be treated.

Good intentions aren't good enough

Working in the women's empowerment space has continually humbled me on the inherent danger of good intentions, and never more so than when I spent some time in Kenya working to establish the microfinance project discussed in Chapter 16. We taught business skills in a giant shipping container on one side of the slums to our twenty-two *mama shujaas* (Swahili for 'superwomen') every afternoon. These women were phenomenal: strong, passionate and joyful – so joyful in fact that towards the end of our time in Kenya we often arrived in the afternoons to a shipping container rocking with beautiful African song and dance. This group of superwomen were also singularly focused on one goal: being able to afford to send their kids to school so they could provide them with a better life. The women we were working with were living on around about 75 cents a day and were trying to feed anywhere from three to eleven kids.

One day we were wandering through from a different part of the slum and stumbled on what looked like a brand-new but totally deserted well. Now, that wouldn't have necessarily struck me as curious except that the women had told us they had to walk an enormous distance to get access to water, making it an activity that often subsumed their entire morning. This well was a stone's throw from the container. I asked, through our interpreter, 'Is that a well?' The answer came back: 'Yes.'

'Is it broken?' I enquired. The reply came back: 'No.'

Confused, I asked, 'So why doesn't anyone drink from this well?' (It might be worth mentioning at this point that a prominent organisation you might have heard of had spent a solid amount of aid money installing that well.) 'Because this is an ancient battleground and there are bad spirits in the ground. We can't drink that water, it's poisoned with bad spirits. We would die.'

Never, if you'd given me one million guesses, would I have hit upon that answer. Unfortunately, neither did the well-meaning aid organisation. If only they'd asked the locals, rather than projecting their own assumptions. A culturally aware, adaptable leader would have placed the well more appropriately and changed the lives of these women and their children positively. Well-meaning intentions do not absolve us of the imperative of adapting our work to ensure those intentions translate into thoughtful and considered actions. Misguided efforts are debatably even worse than no effort at all because we're using up resources (for little to no effect) that could be deployed elsewhere. There's a lot of value in seeking to understand before we seek to be understood.

The defaults we design for and the need for redesign

The first time I understood that some people appreciate silence was when I took a Myers–Briggs personality assessment. After we'd completed the questionnaire, the facilitator asked us to sit in silence for five minutes ... It is no exaggeration to say I was practically climbing up the walls by the end of it! Then she asked, 'How was that experience?' Before I could answer 'like some unusual form of child abuse' a few hands went up and described it as blissful, deeply contemplative and a joy to go inwards amidst the noise of the day. I was incredulous: people enjoyed that?!

At least one-third of the people we know are introverts. I feel lucky that some of my best friends, colleagues and my better half are introverted. They are the ones who typically prefer listening to speaking; who innovate and create but dislike self-promotion or taking credit; who favour working on their own over working in teams. To great introverts – such as Rosa Parks, Chopin, Dr Seuss, Steve Wozniak – we owe many of the most wonderful contributions to society. In her phenomenally bestselling book *Quiet*, Susan Cain argues that we dramatically undervalue introverts and lose a huge amount in doing so. She charts the fascinating rise of the extrovert ideal throughout the twentieth century and explores how deeply it has come to permeate our culture, education and workplaces.

In 2018, I had the opportunity to interview Susan Cain. Susan has a very calm, warm manner, even when she's waiting in the wings to walk on stage in front of 2000 people – something that, despite her world acclaim, she still finds nerve-racking. Susan's passion, and one of the key thrusts of *Quiet,* is how we set up workplaces 'in a way that works for everyone'. Using introversion as the example, she urges us to visualise having an internal battery that represents our neurobiological system. The wiring into that battery is very different for introverts and extroverts. Introverts react more to stimulation, so they feel more alive when there is less going on around them. Extroverts are the opposite. Susan's call to action is this: 'If you want your people creating their best and interacting with each other at their best, you have to situate them in environments where they can choose the amount of stimulation that's coming at them at any given time.'

The 'norm' of most operating environments tends to be the 'norm' of the majority. That may be white people, males, extroverts or whatever other way you want to dissect the status quo. The norm exists as a set of invisible, often unspoken rules that reinforce the power dynamic of the dominant culture. Susan hilariously characterises the nightmare of the open-plan office and group brainstorming sessions, where extroverts descend on the startled introvert 'like flash-storms'. In these settings, as Jon Ronson described in his review of Cain's book, 'the loudest, most socially confident and quickest on their feet win the day, whereas the contemplative and quietly well-informed tend not to get a word in'.

The moral of the story: groupthink favours the dominant extrovert.

Why is this problematic for leadership? Well, when we think of a 'natural-born leader' we tend to think of extroverts or extroverted moments. We conjur images of presidents and prime ministers addressing crowds in their thousands, generals commanding battlefields (be they real or the metaphorical battlefield of the sporting ground) and public demonstrations of strength and confidence. But, in Jim Collins's *Good to Great*, a landmark study of the best-performing companies at the time, all eleven companies had two common characteristics: their people had a fierce sense of will and dedication to the company; and each of the CEOs was described as quiet, unassuming, low-key and softly spoken. These traits do not typify 'leadership', yet all the eleven CEOs who had achieved standout performance were this way inclined.

This revelation encourages us to think not only about how we define leadership, but how we shape agendas, feedback processes, conversations and collaborations to ensure that the squeaky wheel doesn't soak up all the oil. It's a warning to make sure we don't miss out on our entire workforce ascending to the height of their talents purely because we've dismissed people as not a 'natural leader' or haven't designed an environment that caters for all.

When I ask Susan about the relevance of her message in the age of innovation and disruption, she says:

> We're under a kind of collective delusion right now that all ideas emerge from a very collective and gregarious process. Of course, we definitely want the exchange of ideas, and we want the collaborative moments for sure. But we desperately need to bring back moments and spaces for deep thinking and deep flow and deep work. And a lot of that happens in private . . . Because you cannot do really deep creative work without solitude, you just can't do it.

In an age of increasing stimulation and shorter attention spans, Susan says we need to be disciplined and deliberative about deep work. She cites examples like Jeff Bezos and Amazon where, prior to board meetings, people spend weeks working on a single six-page memo for discussion; when everybody shows up, they sit there quietly for the first half an hour and read the memo and think about their response. Only then do they start the conversation. If this sounds a touch extreme, Susan also suggests things like having meeting-free Tuesdays. 'It might be the introverts who are emotionally hungry for it, but all of us need the space, whether we're extroverts or introverts.'

One of the ways of putting EQ to work is being attuned to the needs of the people around us and creating the conditions for them to thrive. In a world that more often than not comes with a factory setting of 'extrovert', this particularly means being alive to the needs of introverts. The COVID-19 lockdown here in Australia gave us all a chance to experience a quieter world. Start by opening up a conversation about what's working (and not working) about the way you currently lead. Then together make a commitment to trial at least one idea to reset the preset.

The five love languages

I wish these had a better name. In fact, I've wished this so many times over that I've almost written to creator Gary Chapman begging him to run a new print edition under a different title. Too radical maybe, but I'm convinced that, as incredibly successful as this concept has been (the book has sold *millions* of copies), there are so many people who would reap its rich benefit if it was applied to the business setting.

One night at a conference I was attending, a couple came in and presented on their relationship. They spoke about love languages, minimisers and maximisers, and a whole bunch of other things that I couldn't quite make sense of. Let's be honest, I was twenty, and I'd recently been heartbroken by a paleo-eating cross-fitter who wore Vibrams when we went out instead of shoes . . . so this all seemed highly aspirational. Australians don't tend to have a culture of talking about relationships requiring active, intentional love and care. I was riveted by it.

I wasn't one to die wondering, so I bought a copy of *The Five Love Languages* at the airport and started reading it on the plane. I was already piecing together a whole new world of uncommunicated emotion when, halfway through, the Fijian flight attendant stopped me as he came down the aisle and said, 'That book saved my marriage.' We spent the next half-hour talking about it.

The idea that there are five distinct 'love languages' is surprisingly familiar to many people. That's pretty spectacular for a concept introduced in a book in 1992 written by a Southern Baptist pastor that was aimed mostly at married Christian couples. Chapman asserted that everyone has a primary love language or two, meaning a category of behaviours that they most immediately associate with affection. The five love languages are:

- quality time
- physical touch
- acts of service
- giving and receiving gifts
- words of affirmation.

Let's be clear: this is not about you, but about how you reinforce your care, respect and commitment for the people in your life. Be it partners in life or partners in business, to thrive in a long-term relationship we have to be able to discern and adapt to the love language of the person we're engaging with. Do you show your team you appreciate them in the way *they* respond to being appreciated?

Doing a quick audit of the people closest to me, I could see this showing up. I tended to have stronger relationships with those who by default had the same love languages as me (words and touch). They delivered for me, and I delivered for them, almost unconsciously. I could also see those relationships where I was missing the mark. The friends I'd forgotten to buy a birthday present for, thinking it was enough to call, write a card and shout them a meal, because I was inclined to regift my presents but keep a card for the next ten years. My flight attendant friend was the same: his wife's language was gifts, and his was acts of service. He was unstacking dishwashers and mowing lawns, thinking she would interpret that as him caring for her, but she just wanted him to bring her home a bunch of flowers every once in a while, or take her out for dinner. Meanwhile, she was leaving little gifts in his luggage when he'd go away on long-haul shifts, and he would have just loved it if every now and again she dropped him at the airport.

The way that we unconsciously miss each other has fascinated me ever since. I see leaders thank their team by asking the EA to organise everyone a gift voucher, when what they'd really love is public recognition in front of their colleagues. I come across bosses mistakenly thinking the quantity of time spent walking the floor is delivering on the quality time in development and mentoring their direct reports so desperately want and need. Nowadays, the mobile phones, smartwatches and technology are a huge killer of the quality time love language. Have you been in a meeting where someone is passionately pitching their idea or giving the overview of their area of responsibility and instead of being present people are checking emails and scrolling LinkedIn pings? I call this the best of un-intentions. Relationships die from multiple tiny paper cuts more often than from a major tearing apart.

Chapman's original message and intent was a consistent urging towards learning *other* people's love languages and modifying one's own behaviour. Here are three simple ideas for doing this.

Tune into another's love language

This is a great conversation upfront, but if you're a born-and-bred Aussie like me, it can feel a bit challenging. The best way to guess people's love languages is to look at what they like to give out. Which clients make a point of sending Christmas cards? Which colleague stays behind to help you work on a presentation when they don't have to? Which of your team members always makes a point of buying you a coffee when they fetch theirs? I have LL'ed all my colleagues, fellow board directors and clients too, and I try to always be attentive to saying thanks and expressing admiration, affirmation and grati- tude in the language they like to receive it. It takes the same amount of effort on my part but has a fundamentally different result.

Put the love language of the people you interact with the most next to their names in your phone

This way, every time they pop into your consciousness you can be thinking about who you are engaging with and how you need to adapt for them. This isn't to be reductionist or to suggest that people can't or don't appreciate gestures in all shapes and forms, but there is something powerful to be said for speaking to someone in their own language. Try it.

Find a way of opening up about yours

People aren't mind-readers and subtlety is sometimes too subtle. Plus, when other people know your love language, they can see you giving praise, appreciation and love through your defaults as all the more meaningful. For example, one of my business partners is an enormous words of affirmation person, so I always try to make a point of writing thank-you emails (and handwritten cards) when they help me or giving them a shout-out publicly where possible.

Of all the practices that I have put into place that have profoundly transformed my life, this one takes the cake. I urge you to see past the 'love language' label and ask yourself, if leadership were a language of love, how might this affect what people are willing to do for and with you? Look at the people around you who love what they do. Chances are, they also love who they're doing it with.

EQ is the new IQ. It's the smarts we need to thrive as twenty-first-century leaders attempting to mobilise people to solve complex problems. Understanding people's emotions and knowing how to purposefully and effectively influence them is a core leadership capability. It's also one that's within the grasp of each and every one of us. By observing more, tuning into people's indicated preferences and choosing to adapt the way we deliver information and offer gratitude accordingly we can profoundly improve our relationships, team dynamics and collective success.

A question from the leading edge:

How does (insert person's name) like to be treated?

18

Diversify your dice

'Diversity may be the hardest thing for a society to live with, and perhaps the most dangerous thing for a society to be without.'

William Sloane Coffin Jr

I was nineteen when I was challenged into starting my first business by a mentor. They were observing some of the strategy and leadership development work I'd been doing for a few years in the community sector and pushed me on its potential for application to the commercial world. Emboldened, but knowing nothing about business, I reached two logical conclusions: I should buy a copy of *The Personal MBA* by Josh Kaufman and chew through the recommended 100-book reading list; and I should join a business forum to interact with and learn from people who were already in this business caper. I think my naive strategy was that, by osmosis, I would absorb the skills required to be able to successfully do my own thing.

I'll never forget the first business forum event I went to. It was at a yacht club on the waterfront in my hometown, and there were about 200 people there. I know I must have stuck out like a sore thumb (the next youngest person would have been at least double my age and my attempt to suit-up was a dead newbie giveaway) but boy did they make me feel it. Only two people spoke to me throughout the whole function, and I am neither a shrinking violet nor short on conversation. John and Peter crossed the floor at different times during the lunch, and deliberately sought me out. They became my first business mentors, though this description dramatically under-states the impact they've had on my life. They are two of the most caring, principled wise owls you'll meet and both brought completely different perspectives to my thinking.

One day, early in our mentoring relationship, John turned up to coffee and placed a dice in the middle of the table. Both John and Peter had unconventional ways of teaching so this wasn't completely out of place.

I was intrigued.

'What do you see?' John asked.

I couldn't work out what his angle was, so I gave the direct response: 'A dice.'

'Be more specific,' he pushed me.

'I can see a three,' I said.

John replied, 'Well, I can see a four. Which of us is right?'

Of course, we both were. This was exactly the prompt John was looking for to lead into one of the many teachable moments that would transpire over coffee that morning.

'Bingo,' he said. 'One of the most important lessons for you to learn early in your career and cultivate into a habit is being inten-tional about the diversity of perspectives in helping to inform your view of the whole.' He also told me that as a young woman I would be in many rooms where my perspective would be different from the status quo.

John challenged me that morning to focus on making two things a part of how I live and lead:

• When faced with a decision, ask yourself: how many sides of the dice have I got in view here? If I only see one or two, what can I do to bring more perspectives to the table?

- When you see a situation differently from those around you, particularly when there's a singularly entrenched view, don't shirk from what you see. Understand that, even if it doesn't change the ultimate decision, your alternative view enriches the process, so find a way to help people come around to your side of the dice for a moment.

And then John ordered a cappuccino.

I've reflected on that conversation many times since. In Australia, you are 40 per cent more likely to be a captain of industry if your name (ironically) is Peter or John than if you're a woman. According to Black Enterprise, 37 per cent of the S&P 500 companies did not have a single black board member in 2019, and only five of the Fortune 500 are led by a black CEO. S&P 500 currently has twenty-nine female CEOs, while the Fortune 500 last year hit an 'all-time high' of thirty-seven women leaders. Only five world leaders have been openly LGBTQIA+, and only 1.9 per cent of the world's 45,000 parliamentarians are under thirty. For all the conversation about diversity over the past few years, the dial has barely moved on seeing the idea in action in institutions and decision-making forums around the world.

No tokens allowed

A few years ago, Arwa Mahdawi came up with Rent-A-Minority, a way to initiate the difficult, icky, un-PC diversity conversations that are so necessary to move the dial. To quote from Arwa's homepage:

> 'Rent-A-Minority' is a revolutionary new service designed for those oh-shit moments where you've realised your award show, corporate brochure, conference panel is entirely composed of white men. For, like, the fifth year in a row. Suddenly you're being called out on Twitter, and you need to look not-racist and not-misogynist fast. Actually, doing something meaningful to disrupt institutional inequality would be way too much work; so why not just Rent-A-Minority instead?

If you haven't worked it out already, the site is a parody. It was never intended that people actually 'book' a minority to get better optics in the photos for the company newsletter or things like that. It was intended to make a provocative statement about the meaninglessness of a lot of well-meaning statements on diversity, and to use humour to assist in starting some all-too-uncomfortable conversations about that reality and how it could be done better. It's also a passion project for Mahdawi, who works for an advertising firm in New York. She is young, dynamic and half-Palestinian, half-English. She created the site because she was tired of seeing companies making superficial efforts to promote diversity, the kinds of tokenistic actions that are more about optics than true change. The straw that broke the camel's back was when a colleague lamented jealously to Arwa that 'being a female and brown must be such an advantage in advertising'.

Arwa tells me, 'He seemed to think that with all the talk around diversity these days, you [people like me] have it *easier* than a straight white guy like him. And I was particularly frustrated because he wasn't a moron, this was a well-meaning, smart guy. I think that in all of the talking about diversity we've actually made it harder.'

Arwa believes that all the talk without action has propagated a myth that every promotion is due to affirmative action. The unspoken implication is 'you didn't earn it, you only got it because the company has to seem politically correct and promote "people like you".' This is despite all the evidence to the counter regarding the lack of movement on structural inequality. For example, according to the World Economic Forum's Global Gender Gap Report in 2019, it'll take 99.5 years to achieve gender equality at the current rate of progress. In other words, the drawbridge might have opened slightly but it hasn't been lowered, and meanwhile it feels there are a few extra guards roaming the perimeter ready to snipe at those whose who try to enter.

Arwa saw Rent-A-Minority as the most effective way that she could help deal with a sober topic plaguing just about every industry. Using humour can break down barriers, while being real about the superficiality of box-ticking diversity initiatives enables allies to speak up in a way that feels less confrontational. Arwa comments, 'I think one of the issues with diversity is people get really depressed talking about it, or they get stressed – so I find humour is a good way to make a point to people whose ears might otherwise be closed.' While some (not-to-be-named) large companies have inquired sincerely about her service and missed the point entirely, many people have told her that the site was a powerful icebreaker for bringing the topic up with bosses and colleagues because, really, 'Thinking that diversity is an add-on you can silo is just ridiculous.'

Arwa challenges all of us to take responsibility for the matter – to call out and redress tokenistic efforts. She compares diversity to digital: inevitable.

> If you look at demographics, you know people are becoming more mixed race and the idea of gender is way less binary than it's ever been thanks to Gen Z. This is the new normal. If you don't keep up you will go extinct. This is your customer base. This is who you have to cater to by reflecting them in your leadership.

Being able to curate, empower and mobilise diverse teams is going to be an increasingly essential leadership skill.

When rolling the diversity dice, too many people play as though nothing's really riding on it. Bringing diverse minds to the decision-making table and empowering them once there is a crucial lever to mitigate unconscious bias, groupthink and overconfident voices. For example, in a 2006 study of mock juries in the US, when black people were added to the jury, white jurors processed the case facts more carefully and deliberated more effectively. And this is not to mention the benefits diversity offers in creating the friction and energy necessary to iterate better outcomes, foresee unexplored opportunities and join the dots on new solutions. In a 2009 analysis of 506 companies, it was found that firms with more racial or gender diversity had more sales revenue, more customers and greater profits. In 2017, a Boston Consulting Group study of 1700 companies across eight countries found that companies with more diverse management teams have 19 per cent higher revenues due to innovation.

Most importantly, be bold enough to call out tokenism – because not only does it not further diversity, it actively hinders the progress. Send a link to rentaminority.com as a not-so-subtle opener to a critical conversation.

The diversity tax

Vivienne Ming is a commanding presenter, repeatedly enrapturing audiences around the world on the topics of AI, bias and inclusion. She's also a serial entrepreneur, theoretical neuroscientist and big data specialist. Her brain astounds me.

Vivienne is passionate about diversity and inclusion, but she is conscious of trying not to preach to the choir. In order to find a way to reach the 'unconverted', Vivienne challenged herself to think about how to explain her research on discrimination, bias and inclusion in a way that a conservative would understand. 'I'm here for the third of you that think this is all bullshit,' she says when addressing her audiences. 'And I'm here to explain why you will not hit your hiring number if you don't understand how much talent you're currently missing.' Knowing the motivations of the nay-sayers, she has landed on what she describes as a vastly better metaphor than the glass ceiling: the diversity tax.

There are additional hurdles for minorities that can be easily translated into monetary hurdles: when people don't fit the 'norm', their difference amounts to a financial disability. When we frame it that way, we can have a fairly honest discussion about the tangible cost of a lack of diversity. And through this dispassionate lens, it's clear that this economic disparity hurts the economy. 'It has nothing to do with your explicit beliefs about fairness; this is loss in the economy. It's a tax that doesn't pay for roads. It doesn't build bridges. It's just a loss. And like any tax, it comes with compounding interest. This is the money that could have been growing in our economy over time.'

What does Vivienne calculate as the 'tax on being different'? To arrive at a dollar figure, Vivienne built models that measured how good people were at the jobs they were never given the chance to do. This provided her with the 'cost' (or tax) of the lifetime opportunity cost of lost work. This included things the bill for extra degrees, or the extra experience needed to have the same opportunities as men from the dominant demographic group. These are the results from a few of her calculations: GBP 38,000 (USD 54,000) for being a gay man in England; between USD 100,000 and USD 300,000 for women in the US tech industry; USD 800,000 to USD 1.5 million for women in Hong Kong or Singapore in the tech industry. It's staggering. As Vivienne concludes from her findings: 'We are bad at valuing other people, and we are worse the more different they are to us.'

This work for Vivienne is deeply personal. Because before Vivienne was who she is now – a tall blonde who commands a stage with her witty repartee as she discusses the use of deep neural networks to overcome corporate diversity issues – she was Evan Smith, a Californian maths whizz and star kicker for the high school football team, who was secretly uncomfortable in his own skin. Vivienne grew up the privileged son of a middle-class doctor and his wife, with plenty of bourgeoise entitlement and the expectation of winning a Nobel Prize. Vivienne didn't transition until her thirties, and her journey wasn't without its challenges. In our interview, Vivienne tells me: 'You know, in nineteen versions of my life out of twenty, there's a night in 1995 where I pull the trigger, and that's the end. But in this one version of reality I didn't. I came up with a completely arbitrary reason to be alive, which was living a life that makes other people's lives better.'

To that end, Vivienne then calculated the *benefit* of difference – the flipside of her earlier calculation of the 'tax on diversity'. In this particular study, by compiling a database of entrepreneurs, tracing where they were based, how much money they raised and how many jobs they created, Vivienne deduced that over a decade, LGBTQIA+ entrepreneurs created 3 million jobs after they moved from less inclusive places – think Hialeah, Florida – to more inclusive places, like New York. Vivienne points out that conservative politicians 'love to extol the virtues of less regulation and lower taxes, yet these entrepreneurs chose to move to more heavily taxed places with stricter regulations but better attitudes towards diversity and inclusion'. And those places enjoyed the economic benefits.

Vivienne adds from her own research the importance of representation. When she was first doing work on AI in education, she came across a paper that was seeking to understand why high-performing students from under-represented backgrounds have either not applied for elite universities or have turned them down. She says it's a classic example of making assumptions about a problem: on this question, the 'armchair philosopher interpretation' would be assuming the students need to stay home and support their family. Instead, the study Vivienne encountered debunked that idea by showing that the number one predictor, by far and away, was whether someone from their neighbourhood had gone to an elite university before them.

They just needed a role model, a proof point that someone like them can do it. Interestingly, celebrity role models had little power. Knowing Oprah or Obama had done it does not change the perception of what someone from a particular community can accomplish. The role model needed to be someone just like them.

Vivienne's story is an inspiring one. It also offers us some strategies for taking up Arwa's challenge of applying non-tokenistic approaches to diversity and inclusion. Using data to quantify the value of difference will be key for leaders seeking to make a difference. Can you develop your own diversity dataset?

Deliberately roll with difference

Choose people who see another side of the dice and insist they have a seat at the table of your team. Think about how you will qualify the value of diverse perspectives to side-step tokenism.

Interrogate data-based assumptions

Don't be what Vivienne calls a 'diversity lemming', assuming that the new diversity 'fad' will be effective. Test and measure new initiatives to ensure they're moving the dial.

Dial up the data

When your team tries a new approach to a challenge, find a way to evaluate the success or failure of doing things differently.

Listen in to the silence

Try to measure what is 'not there' as well as what is more readily visible; it's much easier to note who speaks, who's present, whose picture is in the report. Pay attention to absence too.

Combine data with storytelling

Numbers alone won't move the needle, so you need to connect the information to a story that enlivens human emotion. Why should people care? Is there a metaphor or concept, like the diversity tax, that can carry your message?

Data + heart, particularly when combined to illuminate a new insight or offer a fresh take, can be a powerful cocktail when it comes to pushing for progress on diversity. Think about how you shake (or stir) the two up.

'Just don't tell me it's as simple as measurement and money'

Cath Tanna is the CEO of EnergyAustralia, an electricity generation, electricity and gas retailing private company in Australia, owned by Hong Kong–listed CLP Group. They have a portfolio of thermal coal, natural gas, hydro-electric, solar energy and wind generation sites, and employ about 2500 people. There are few business leaders, globally, whom I respect more than the ferociously smart and deeply principled Cath. Embodying the power of an introverted leader, when Cath chooses to speak, people listen.

Cath joined EA in 2014. Before her arrival, the company became embroiled in a sexual harassment case. Cath got to work fixing the aspects of EnergyAustralia's culture that required the most immediate attention.

Then something else appeared on her radar.

In our interview, Cath explains to me, 'Every year in Australia, companies of a certain size have to report their gender pay gap to the Workplace Gender Equality Agency.' While this is a good thing (as the old adage goes 'what you measure matters'), Cath says the math is very rudimentary – far too simple to be meaningful. You simply add up the total payroll and divide it according to gender and report the gap. Getting to the root of a problem as persistent as pay equity, let alone solving it, was going to require better data and systems than what they had at their fingertips at the time.

The first thing Cath did was create a better measurement system. EA needed to define each job within the company, have the description independently evaluated in a transparent way, benchmark the remuneration to market, decide the ideal place to sit in the range and then review whether the person was being paid fairly and equitably.

It took about eighteen months to implement and by the time it was in place, Cath thinks she'd probably already signed a couple of gender pay reports.

But when the report arrived on her desk in 2017, something prompted her to pause before automatically signing it and ask for the first time, 'Why do we have a gap?'

To this day, Cath says one of the big unanswered questions she has of herself is why it took her until probably the third time she signed a gender equity report to ask that question. Her question was quickly followed by 'and what would it take to close it?' The reaction from her own people was that it would be hard, but Cath pushed them to come back to her with what 'hard' actually meant. When they resurfaced, everyone was pretty surprised that closing the gap would actually be achievable. 'It cost money, sure – there's no dodging it costs money. But the total investment at the time was $1.2 million. And even the people I asked the question of thought it was going to come out as a much bigger number.' About 350 women got a substantial pay increase, as did eighty men. To Cath, this is an important part of the story: this was about pay equity for both sexes.

The company went public with the story on International Women's Day and Cath was taken aback by how much interest there was. But that was because the media were interested in a different spin on the equity story. 'Unsurprisingly, the journalists wanted me to tell the story they had in their mind about how tough it had been to pull it off. *This must have been a battle! There must have been blood spilt on the boardroom floor. You must have had to sacrifice so much. What did you have to give up to get this over the line?*' Cath wonders whether that means sometimes, as leaders, we don't pursue some of these changes and reforms because we have a preconceived idea that it's going to be a battle we don't want to face. But Cath told the journalists what actually happened from her side of the dice: 'When we put the results of our analysis in a paper for the EnergyAustralia

Board, and I called the chairman to discuss it, he simply said, "Great. We should have done this ages ago."'

Reflecting on her leadership of EnergyAustralia, Cath acknowledges that the awareness that this was going to be her last executive role allowed her to unlock herself from self-imposed constraints and the sense that she had to conform to what was expected. She quotes a presentation she heard from a fellow Australian ASX20 CEO, Alison Watkins, who cited that thirty CEO jobs become available in any given year in Australia. Of these, 60 per cent go to internal candidates, which leaves twelve for external hires; of those, only two go to women. As Cath remarks, anyone who can do that maths can see the pressure to 'conform' is obvious, given your sex, in and of itself, makes you an 'unconventional' choice. When push comes to shove, most people end up defaulting to what they know and what they can defend to their shareholders. And yet Cath is a great example of the value that can be unlocked for staff, shareholders and community alike when there's a preparedness to give a leadership opportunity to someone who's different from the norm.

Cath encourages people to imagine themselves going into their last job as a CEO as if it were a football game, and to think about how they plan to be in the final quarter of that match.

> Wouldn't it be great if you could project yourself into that future where you get to do the last job? Where you get to be so true to yourself; exactly how you think it should be done in terms of doing the right thing? Totally unconstrained. If you could somehow bring that to your earlier career that would be amazing. That's what we need from and for the next generation of leaders.

An hour after our interview, a message from Cath popped into my inbox. She's forwarding me an email from the day earlier, 13 August, which marked Black Women's Equal Pay Day: black women have to work an extra 225 days to earn what white men did the year before and what white women earned four months earlier. Her message: we have so much more to do – so let's stop talking and get to work.

A question from the leading edge:

How many sides of the dice have you got in view with regards to the decision that's top of mind for you right now?

19

Look risk in the eye

'There is a tremendous bias against taking risks. Everyone is trying to optimize their ass-covering.'

Elon Musk

Hunches. Warnings. Reading between the lines. Some of us maintain a mindset of seeking out or at least heeding these harbingers of decision-making. Others prefer the bliss of ignorance and hope for the best when it comes to seeing around corners.

In reality, the future is simply a set of possibilities. Leaders, by definition, are the ones to go first into the future, to guide others along uncertain paths – and therefore they need to be looking ahead more than anyone. They can't just follow whoever is in front of them; they must summon the courage to confront whatever crosses the collective path. As such, good leaders must make a practice of seeking out and then sizing up both challenges and new opportunities for a moment, so that we are not relying on short-sighted assumptions. If strategy is the plan of action we follow into the future, we must fearlessly look risk in the eye, knowing 'being aware of its presence will provide us better coordinates to map out our strategy'.

Our ability as leaders to deal with risk could do with some general improvement. In 2016, it was estimated that 67 per cent of well-formulated strategies failed due to poor execution. According to a ten-year study of executive leadership conducted by the firm led by transformational change expert Ron Carucci, '61 per cent of executives told us they were not prepared for the strategic challenges they faced upon being appointed to senior leadership roles. It's not surprising, then, that 50–60 per cent of executives fail within the first eighteen months of being promoted or hired.'

How can we improve our own ability to deal with risk?

While not many of us can relate to being in the room with the chance to buy Google for the bargain price of $750,000 when hard-backed encyclopaedias still had relevance or to pick up Netflix for a song when the latest movie was encased in a DVD, most of us can probably relate to kicking ourselves for not grabbing an opportunity when it was right there in front of us. Oh well, we say, let bygones be bygones. But what if there was a way to turn the crystal-clear mirror of hindsight into – not a crystal ball – but a spyglass for the future? How can we make our decision-making more transparent to increase the chances of our ventures working out well?

Seeing around corners

A crucial moment occurs when we establish the collective approach at the start of a strategic endeavour. From this beginning point, we set expectations about our openness to different opinions in the way we invite perspectives into the problem-solving process. Any newly curated teams will be highly attuned to how we encourage the identification of blind spots and curve balls. Why not influence mishaps and mistakes at the time when we have the most significant degree of agency over them: before they arise?

We can start by where we focus our energy and analysis. Debate the assumptions that sit behind a decision or prediction. Do you agree with them or not? Should we have a high degree of confidence or a more moderate level? What needs to hold true for these predictions to come to life? And can any intervention at this point change our confidence score? What data has led to the conclusion reached? Is there countervailing evidence? Does the proposed approach remain the soundest way of concluding what tomorrow might look like? Looking risk in the eye requires interrogation: of the information at hand, of our own decision-making and of the possibilities that may arise. Crossing our fingers and hoping for a sunny day is not going to replace a wet-weather plan.

Intentional interrogation of assumptions

A great example of how to debate assumptions comes from the Israeli military in the form of a concept known as the 'The Tenth Man'. It was born out of the 1973 Yom Kippur War (known in the Arab world as the Ramadan War), waged by a coalition of Arab states led by Egypt and Syria against Israel – a coalition that Israel had underestimated as a threat to national security, to its detriment. The synchronised attack took the Israeli Defense Forces by surprise, in part because it began on one of the holiest days in the Jewish calendar (when many soldiers were away from their post in religious observance) and also because the Israeli military establishment was captivated and captured by what it called 'the concept of Arab intentions'. This preset worldview dictated that an all-out assault by the Arabs would not happen without the precursor of Arab unity. In other words, the military establishment was held captive by its own group-think and ultimately lost the war to its own assumptions.

In the postwar aftermath, hurting badly, the Israeli military was determined never be caught off guard in this way again. They initiated a concept called the 'Tenth Man' – an official devil's advocate role designed to ensure robust, healthy dissent was baked into the decision-making process. The basic premise is that if there are ten people in a room and nine agree, the role of the tenth is to disagree and point out flaws in whatever decision the group has reached.

What's interesting to me about the Israeli approach of the Tenth Man (or Woman!) is that they were attuned to the fact that specific responsibility and authority needed to be given to the dissenter. It wasn't enough, as you often see in corporate, societal or even classroom cultures, to just have a motherhood statement about welcoming all opinions and perspectives. Most of us have been in that room where someone's offered up an opinion the boss or client doesn't want to hear, and instead of taking it on board to reshape a strategy, it gets shut down. This potential nugget of dissonant gold, more often than not, becomes a CLM (career-limiting move) for the person who voiced it.

The Israeli military gave the Tenth Man both a brief to challenge conventional and received wisdom, and the authority to search for arguments, facts and information to substantiate the counter argument. They also lowered the bar. Importantly, only one anomaly is sufficient to at least warrant a re-examination of the proposed course of action. We can often get stuck in a decision-making equivalent of 'innocent until proven guilty', being, 'we're right until we have overwhelming evidence to the contrary' . . . But let's be honest: by that point (like the Israelis in the Yom Kippur War) we're already resigned to the history of decisions not taken. The Tenth Man is also responsible for looking to subjects and data sources that may not have received sufficient attention up the pointier end of the chain of command. For example, they are nominated to be a sounding board for lower-level analysts who might wish to raise a view but don't feel sufficiently empowered. Their reports are tabled at the very top of the military decision-making tree and must be responded to. Even if these assertions are to be rebuffed, they cannot be ignored. As the saying goes in the military, to be forewarned is to be forearmed.

The Tenth Man idea is interesting because it offers a practical structure for bringing rigorous debate to life, even in a context far from a military operation. Countless organisations I know believe in the merit of good debate but don't actually implement it around their decision-making tables. And structure matters, because a whole range of psychological, situation and cultural forces make it difficult to encourage diversity: it's easier when people agree; we have dead-lines to meet; and, the longer we've worked on a problem, the harder it becomes to see it from a different perspective. Making it some-one's 'job', even if it's as unofficial as nominating a 'project dissenter' or 'meeting counterpart' to generate some dissenting thoughts or evidence can be a game changer. You can see concepts of this at work in organisations deploying 'red teaming': this is when a team, internally or externally, uses an adversarial approach to rigorously challenge the organisation's plans, policies, systems and assumptions.

The interrogation of assumptions need not be adversarial; instead, we can think of it as saving a space for difference. We are defending the time and bandwidth to seek out counter arguments, as opposed to attacking those already on the table. When mandatory, opening up decision-making can be an objective process rather than a defen-sive discussion. This notion also breaks down hierarchical leadership in a healthy way. Who wants to build castles in the sand if they will be destroyed by the waves of reality?

The power of premortems

When it comes to trying to forecast risk, one of the most effective exercises I've come across is a premortem. This process is designed to look ahead at the challenges that could cause everything to fail, and create a plan to navigate around them.

We've likely watched enough *CSI* and *Law & Order* to know what a post-mortem is and, in essence, a premortem is its opposite. As Gary Klein, a psychologist who specialises in studying decision-making, explains:

> A premortem . . . comes at the beginning of a project rather than the end, so that the project can be improved rather than autopsied. Unlike a typical critiquing session, in which project team members are asked what *might* go wrong, the premortem operates on the assumption that the 'patient' [the idea, the project, the business]

has died, and so asks what *did* go wrong. The team members' task is to generate plausible reasons for the project's failure.

Effectively, this is like playing a business version of the board game Cluedo. We nominate which aspects of the project (marketing, sales, competitive threats) are our equivalents of Colonel Mustard, Mrs Plum and Mr Green. Then we identify what the specific murder weapon might be. For example, we may nominate that a seed investment in a particularly disruptive technology could enhance the viability of a competitor's business model, and be the most likely cause of death for our own venture.

To avoid group-think, it's worth starting this process at an individual level by inviting everyone in the room to independently and anonymously write down every reason they can think of for the failure – especially reasons that they wouldn't usually mention. Then these can be shared and combined.

Once the team is clear on the premortem list, it's time to work out what on the list deserves attention. A simple filter I use is a two-by-two grid with likelihood and impact on the two axes. We're looking for those items from the list that belong in that top right corner – high impact and a high likelihood of eventuating. These are the ones we need to devote our time and effort to brainstorming solutions for.

I've not worked for or with an organisation that didn't engage in some form of pre-launch risk analysis and post-launch evaluation. But, I believe risk practices in most businesses are quite perilous for two reasons: the identified risks are confined to a tome-sized risk report compiled by a Chief Risk Officer and never owned or understood by the broader leadership team; and post-mortems are too subjective and get overridden by ego, protectionism and finger-pointing, making future finetuning almost impossible.

More helpfully than typical analyses, a premortem primes a team's mindset; it 'sensitises the team to pick up early signs of trouble once the project gets underway'. By flagging potential risks, the team's consciousness remains alert to their appearance. We get a sense of what the lead indicators of trouble are, allowing us to calibrate faster once we've pressed 'go'. Continual iterations and course corrections use these red flags as reference points. As Gary says, 'In the end, a premortem may be the best way to circumvent any need for a painful postmortem.' Start by adding one more agenda item to your meeting before you initiate your next project and invite everyone to do a little hypothetical sleuthing.

Creating a culture of feedback

A large part of bringing greater transparency to decision-making comes from adopting a feedback mindset. The Tenth Man is about ensuring we receive divergent feedback that challenges accepted wisdom. The premortem is about getting feedback at a more helpful stage in the process. It's also worth pausing to take stock of the environment we're inviting feedback into.

I was given a fish tank for my eighteenth birthday that came with a quite spectacular-looking Chinese fighter fish. The quite spectacular fighter fish stayed alive in its new home for all of two days. Embarrassed by my inability to care for my recently received gift, I purchased another fish . . . this one didn't make it to thirty-six hours. Turns out my little brother had – incorrectly – read that fighting fish loved saltwater, so he'd kindly poured a good amount of table salt into the tank. It wouldn't have mattered what I'd introduced to that tank: nothing was going to thrive until I had identified the issue and ensured the right conditions for flourishing.

In the fishbowl that is our professional lives, we will thrive in a healthy culture of feedback. We spoke in Part One of the personal feedback relationships we need for ourselves to thrive as leaders. Now we contemplate setting up feedback forums so our business ideas can thrive. The dynamism of the world we're working in means we must be a willing subject to responses, criticism and suggestions along development processes. As entrepreneur and Stanford professor Steve Blank says, 'No business plan survives first contact with the customer.' I love that quote. No matter how brilliantly we've concocted an idea in the cocoon of our head or on the pristine office whiteboard, it will be completely flipped on its head the moment we put it into play with real people.

We need to know: what do good feedback conditions look like?

Personally, I think nobody offers us more of a breadcrumb trail to follow when it comes to feedback done well than Pixar, the American animated film studio now owned by Disney. From *A Bug's Life* to *Toy Story* to *Finding Nemo, Monsters, Inc.* and *The Incredibles*, its films have been a success at the box office and at awards nights. It may not be just luck: corporate trainer and behavioural scientist Joe Hirsch has found that 'behind the box office magic sits an active feedback system that's built on candour, communication, and a surprising openness to other people's ideas'.

Edwin Catmull, one of Pixar's founders, came out with a book called *Creativity, Inc.* (co-written with Amy Wallace). He devotes a section of the book to feedback and makes four major points:

Every idea starts as an ugly baby

This is the phrase Ed uses to describe Pixar's early ideas. He says they're 'awkward and unformed, vulnerable and incompetent'. Ed challenges the notion that great works are born out of sublime inspiration, in fact arguing that this misconception is wholly unhelpful to the creative process and organisational culture.

Feedback requires candour, trust and empathy

While judging an idea too quickly can abruptly halt the creative process, being too positive about an idea can also have negative effects. The only way an ugly baby idea can dial up its appeal is through honest feedback. If we think about ideas as an extension of the creators, I think we'd engage in feedback differently. In Pixar's case, they've found it helps to have a common language or approach with which people are encouraged to give feedback known as 'plussing'. Plussing means you may only criticise an idea if you can also make a constructive suggestion. No snipers allowed!

Keep the cooks out of the kitchen

As touched on in Chapter 18, we know that one of the most important catalysts of creativity is being able to source ideas from diverse perspectives. Synthesising concepts from disparate domains and joining dots in a novel manner requires a healthy disregard for proven recipes. At Pixar, there is a nominated 'Brains Trust' composed of a diverse cross-section of the company's top directors and producers. The trust is charged with giving feedback to films in development. Importantly, everyone on the Brains Trust is a filmmaker and is capable of putting themselves in a director's shoes. Equally critically, this group meet every morning to critique the previous day's work. This approach avoids emotional attachment and the sunk-cost bias down the line. By making small, regular cuts and changes, Pixar enables a rapid design cycle that dunks ideas as quickly as they're dreamt up, meaning there's less investment put into them before evaluation is made.

The purpose is to move forward

One of the most surprising reflections Ed shares in his forensic dissection of the Pixar creative process is that not one of the creative geniuses he's worked with could articulate what it was that they were working towards when they started. He says a lot of people misappropriate what feedback is intended to do – we think it's about providing everyone with a retrospective opportunity to give input, but it's actually a form of momentum designed to move the process forward.

We therefore need to become barometers of the intention of feedback, at a collective and individual level. The moment ego and politics are allowed to hold sway over a feedback process is the moment we've lost the room. Part of what's critical in the Pixar story is the notion of the importance of discipline and intention when it comes to feedback: creating the space for it to flow regularly and ensuring everyone is mission-aligned and delivering feedback in support of the collective direction.

Recording lessons from failure

Now to the final stage in the process: feedback after the fact. Lessons not learnt are soon to be repeated. Whether we've manufactured or overestimated a risk, or have to adapt our approach to avoid or better mitigate against similar threats in the future, feedback cycles are critical to recalibration. We touched on the power of feedback to our individual growth and development in Part One, but now we're talking about feedback of leaders in context, as leaders of purpose, process and people.

That being said, there's some consistency in that, of all the feedback conversations we find ourselves in, the ones that come after a failure are typically the hardest. This is painful for a multitude of reasons. Firstly, we innately want to be able to blame someone or something. We're looking for a scapegoat or a fall guy. If we can just fire the person, change providers or target a readier customer, then *ta-da*: all will be well again.

If only it were that simple. Holding the mirror up and admitting our own culpability in missteps and misfires can feel like it threatens our survival on an atomic level.

In his book *Black Box Thinking*, journalist and former professional table tennis player Matthew Syed makes the case that all paths to success run through failure. Not only that, but we should also make an active point of learning from the mistakes of others because, as Matthew puts it, 'You can't live long enough to make them all yourself.' He encourages us to borrow from the aviation system of 'black box' reviews.

In the early 1900s, aviation was one of the riskiest forms of transportation: in 1912, more than half the US Army's pilots died in peacetime crashes. However, the industry has learned so much since then that in 2014, there was just one crash for every 8.3 million take-offs across the major airlines.

This success is partly because within the aviation world, the forensic examination of 'what went wrong' is done at arm's length. Only a handful of institutions in the world have the capability to read black box flight recorders, so there's no 'internal investigation' process that muddies the waters and allows politics to creep in. Furthermore, professionals have no reason not to cooperate, because any evidence they provide can't be used against them in court. This all means that any time a tragedy does occur, procedures are reformed to reduce the risk of them happening again. Near-misses also contribute to this process. There's also a collective industry approach to learning: once a report is published, there's an expectation of industry-wide compliance with the new protocols, processes and training methods within twelve months.

In contrast to this focus on process, Matthew points out that the healthcare sector has a different ethos whereby talent alone is considered the predictor for success. The focus on the individual rather than the institutional processes means that 'there is a tendency to become defensive, to try and cover up the mistake because you don't want to look untalented or to become self-justifying.'

Looking at the data, Matthew says the *Journal of Patient Safety* showed that in US hospitals 400,000 people are killed in 'preventable medical error' every year. A paper in the *British Medical Journal* in 2016 put the number around 250,000, putting it as the third leading cause of death in America. There are patterns, what accident investigators call 'signatures', to many of the deaths that occur in hospitals. Open reporting and honest evaluation can expose these patterns, meaning procedures can be improved to make sure the patterns no longer occur, but all too often, this doesn't happen. Doctors and hospitals, by contrast, rise and fall by their surgical success rates. Funding, tenure and promotion are often tacked to success. Such a culture not only leads to dysfunctional reviews of failure but perverse decision-making in the first instance.

Matthew argues that if US medical professionals had the same approach to learning from their mistakes as the aviation industry – if they saw them as opportunities for improvement and learning rather than something to be covered up – the numbers would likely be very different. But they don't. Independent investigation and safe space protection are equally vital in healthcare as in aviation. People must be assured that if defective processes lead to mistakes, they can speak up without fear of negative repercussions such as blame – only then can meaningful change occur.

Matthew summarises:

> This, then, is what we might call 'black box thinking.' For organisations beyond aviation, it is not about creating a literal black box; rather, it is about the willingness and tenacity to investigate the lessons that often exist when we fail, but which we rarely exploit. It is about creating systems and cultures that enable organisations to learn from errors, rather than being threatened by them.

Leaning into failure is a vulnerable process. It's not crowded at the leading edge because it's easier to switch off, tune out, make an excuse or pretend it didn't happen. But an easier life never made a better person, or a better world. If leading requires going first into the future, then forging the safest possible path requires wide open eyes and peripheral vision. When you're smart about how you look risk in the eye, more often than not it'll blink first.

A question from the leading edge:

What step have you built into your decision-making process to invite dissenting opinion and challenge assumptions?

Method

For decades we've brought method to the madness – now it's time to bring a little madness to the method

20

Design
for
inclusion

'Diversity is being invited to the party; inclusion is being asked to dance.'

Vernā Myers, VP of Inclusion, Netflix

We all know what it feels like to be excluded. These experiences affront our need for belonging, and are often so deeply traumatic that we carry the memory (and scars) long after the moment has passed. It could be that time when we were the last to be picked on the team or weren't picked at all; when we got rejected for the job we really wanted; or when we were laughed at for saying or wearing the wrong thing. It's amazing how vividly we can recall these experiences. My earliest memory of being excluded harks back to when I was ten and was kicked off my football team after four years because the decision was taken that girls weren't allowed to play any more. I can recall that moment and the tears I cried for hours on end as though it was yesterday.

Many organisations have now made progress on diversity within their workforces but, without the necessary inclusion to go with it, that diversity is robbed of the oxygen it needs to breathe. The act of inclusion enables diversity, not the other way around – which is why 'diversity' is in the Mindset section of this book and 'inclusion' belongs to Method.

Lessons from space

Pamela Melroy is a powerhouse. She served as pilot on space shuttle missions STS-92 and STS-112 and commanded mission STS-120 and has just been appointed by President Biden to serve as the Deputy Administrator of NASA. Interviewing her sent my brain into orbit – it's definitely not every day I get to talk to an astronaut about how to undertake a mission to repair the International Space Station. But, as fascinating as I found hearing about her experiences in space, the part of our conversation that captivated me most was learning about how teamwork happens 400 kilometres above Earth.

In Pam's view there are three key components to making a diverse team an inclusive, cohesive one: establishing a unifying mission; taking the time to develop a shared culture or team bond; and acknowledging and enabling the value of all the constituent parts.

Pam is quick to point out that, when you're working in a landscape as politically charged and big budget as international space missions, you don't always (read: pretty close to never) have a choice about the teams you lead. As Pam describes it, she was leading a 'mini-model United Nations' and 'dealing with a significant set of cultural variations'. Pam tells me, 'I flew with an Italian, a Japanese, a Russian. They all have very, very different approaches to problem-solving and also a layer of cultural behaviour that you have to learn to get comfortable with.'

Pam believes one of the most successful practices NASA instituted to help ensure these diverse stakeholders could work together, let alone operate in the high-pressure and high-risk environment that is space, was to send its crews off on a National Outdoor Leadership program. She tells me with a smile, 'I went sea kayaking with my [third] space crew for ten days and, with my second crew, we went hiking in the canyonlands of Utah. You have to bring everything with you. And if you don't have it, you have to learn to live without it.'

These outdoor adventures exposed the astronaut crews to pressure and strain in unknown environments where they had varying levels of competency and comfort. This context forced the groups to begin learning how to make decisions together, share the load, solve conflict, and accommodate one another's strengths and weaknesses. 'Astronauts all want the hardest job in the room. The key that I learnt from other tremendous leaders ahead of me is to actually value each person for the unique personal and professional attributes that they bring to the crew, and then make a point of highlighting them to everyone in the crew.' I love the specificity required in this practice.

While Pam understood the importance of the exercise before her mission to the International Space Station, the critical need to take the time to set and embed a group culture amongst her diverse team members was brought home when they had an emergency in space. A solar array – the solar panels used to generate electricity for the space station – tore. And 400 kilometres above the Earth's surface, Pam and her team had to work out how the hell to fix it, working closely with the NASA flight director and robotics team thousands of kilometres away to undertake a series of hair-raising operations to stitch up the solar array and repair it.

There are some hard and fast operational rules in space to keep astronauts safe, one of which is to stay within a thirty-minute space-walk of the airlock because that's as long as the secondary oxygen supply in your space suit will last. In this particular operation, the repair site was more than an hour away from the airlock, right at the tip of the robotic arm at the edges of the space station. Fixing the array was going to require ingenuity and improvisation.

Tasks were quickly identified and allocated, and before long astronauts were checking the electrical insulation tape supplies, the robotics team was running practice drills and others were poring over diagrams to work out the best way to approach the problem.

Pam recalls floating up to the ceiling of the airlock for a minute, as the rest of the crew busily got to work, so she could get as close to a bird's-eye view of the situation as one can get.

I just watched my crew for a while, and I listened to them . . . They were all saying, 'We've got to do this.' And, 'We've got to do that.' And, 'We're going to do this.' It was an absolutely peak moment in my life as a leader because this gamble that I had taken on the ground – that setting up the culture right would mean, whether I was in the room or not, everyone was going to work together successfully – paid off. They were going to be focused. They were going to be experts in what they needed to be and think of everything that they possibly could to create a solution . . . And they didn't need me to tell them what to do to make that happen.

It turns out that building inclusion into your team is the first step for rocket science as much as anything else.

Psychological safety

Back here on Earth, in a two-year study code-named Project Aristotle (a tribute to the quote credited to Aristotle, 'the whole is greater than the sum of its parts'), Google aimed to answer the question: 'What makes a team effective at Google?' The study identified five core features of the company's most effective teams but went as far as to say that the first factor was so critical that its absence would make high performance unattainable. That first factor was 'psychological safety', which Google defined as when 'team members feel safe to take risks and be vulnerable in front of one another'. In other words, team performance critically relies on people feeling confident that no-one on the team will embarrass or punish anyone else for admitting a mistake, asking a question, challenging the norms or offering a new idea.

Google's findings are consistent with the work of Amy Edmondson, whom many attribute with coining the term 'psychological safety'. Amy defines the concept as a 'shared belief held by members of a team that the team is safe for interpersonal risk-taking'. In the mid-1990s, Amy conducted research to discover whether high-performing medical teams made more or fewer mistakes than low-performing teams. First she determined whether teams were considered high- or low-performing from survey data, and then compared that with the number of mistakes made. However, the comparison was surprising: the highest-performing teams were actually making more mistakes than the lower-performing teams. That didn't seem to make sense – what was going on?

We've all felt vulnerable when we suggest a new idea at work, and we know it's even riskier to challenge someone else's ideas or decisions, particularly if that someone is your boss, or just someone in a more senior role or with more experience. We don't want to look dumb; we don't want to be laughed at; we actually just want to fit in. As diversity and inclusion consultant Felicity Menzies puts it:

> [We] engage in impression management techniques . . . [and] avoid situations that could potentially bruise our ego or result in social exclusion or loss of status, or that may attract substantial penalties such as a financial punishment or reduced opportunities for career progression. When we perceive these risks to be high, we seek to avoid being perceived as ignorant, incompetent or deviant and therefore refrain from offering novel ideas or from admitting mistakes.

In short, the further up the tree we go, the less inclined we are to put ourselves out on a limb.

In her book *The Fearless Organisation*, Amy Edmondson describes a eureka moment she had when reflecting on her counter-intuitive findings. 'What if the better teams had a climate of openness,' she writes, 'that made it easier to report and discuss error? The good teams, I suddenly thought, don't *make* more mistakes; they *report* more.'

In other words, if you want to cultivate great teams, you need to encourage – and expect – new ideas. Create a space where it is normalised to ask employees for their feedback, and be genuinely receptive to it. And importantly, support those employees to speak up if they've made a mistake by helping them understand that mistakes are what improve processes.

Here are some yes/no questions to test what psychological safety 'looks' like, from the Westrum model of measuring organisational culture:

1. In my team, new information is actively sought.
2. In my team, failures are learning opportunities, and messengers of them are not punished.
3. In my team, responsibilities are shared.
4. In my team, cross-functional collaboration is encouraged and rewarded.
5. In my team, failure causes enquiry.
6. In my team, we welcome calculated risk-taking.
7. In my team, new ideas are welcomed.

If you answered yes to most, you've probably got a fairly inclusive culture – at least, inclusive of *your* point of view. The next question to ask is whether others who maybe don't look, think or have a title/position like you would be likely to feel the same. To have true inclusion, *everyone* must feel that security.

One of the key revelations of Amy's work is the role of psychological safety in the context of diversity. Her research shows that in the absence of psychological safety, homogenous teams outperformed diverse ones. But with the presence of psychological safety, a diverse team will outperform a homogenous team. In particular, while a homogenous team may be well suited to delivering standardised, routine tasks, diverse teams were far more likely to produce 'breakthrough' (aka high) performance.

One of the critical nuggets in Amy's work is this: whether we're talking about bringing diverse cultures, genders or different personality types together, it's not enough to get them sitting around a table. If it's not psychologically safe for diverse views and opinions to be expressed, then we're not getting the benefit and bottom-line business value out of diversity.

This broadens our focus: we now need to think about the safety of the culture we've created as leaders. Google, for example, now measures psychological safety throughout its organisation and offers training and development to managers whose scores don't hit the Google benchmark. We also need to teach leaders how to encourage people to move from automatic social behaviours that stifle innovative collaboration towards joint problem-solving. Here are three methods to help achieve this goal.

Open up to level up

Too often, people will look for the barrier to blame rather than the opportunity to jump higher. When different perspectives become resources not obstacles, behaviours such as listening, engaging, making offers and posing questions emerge to move us beyond what we already know.

Fail forward

There are three main types of failure: preventable (we know how to do something right but got it wrong); complex (accident caused by several variables coming together in an unfamiliar way or context) and intelligent (failures linked with research, innovation and discovery). Communicating clearly that intelligence failures are a natural, integral part of innovation allows our people to understand that top performers are not those who never fail but those who learn and share their lessons of failure widely.

Compound learning

Failure only holds value if we take learning from it. The US Army uses four simple 'action review questions':
- What did we intend to do?
- What actually happened?

- What is the difference, and why?
- What will we do the same, and what will we do differently next time?

If we want creativity, high performance and smart risk-taking, it is critical we make the cultures we're building and the teams we're leading psychologically safe.

Empowering the inclusion of difference: thinking hats

One of the ways to start making it psychologically safe to voice different perspectives is to require our teams to practise it methodically. While Chapter 18 ('Diversify your dice') allowed us to see how to bring diverse mindsets to the table, the 'Six Thinking Hats' method enables the whole team to partake in different perspectives. The game originated from the creative thinking expert Edward de Bono and facilitates parallel thinking: simultaneous thinking along separate, specific tracks. This enables teams to actively participate in thinking processes in a detailed and cohesive way and move from group-think to thinking like a group.

The premise is that the human brain deliberates in several distinct ways which can be purposefully called upon. Edward identifies six trains of thought and suggests we put on each 'hat' for a limited period to view the problem or opportunity from that angle. The six types of thinking are ranked in order of complexity: knowledge, comprehension, application, analysis, synthesis and evaluation. Or in more everyday parlance:

- The big picture (blue)
- Facts and information (white)
- Feelings and emotions (red)
- Critical judgement (black)
- Positive (yellow)
- New ideas (green)

The idea is you sequence the order in which you 'wear these hats' to support the goal you're trying to achieve. All processes start and end with the blue hat to anchor the process in the bigger picture. There are particular sequences of hats which encompass and structure the thinking towards a particular goal. For example, blue, white, black, green, blue is the hat order for 'identifying solutions'. It works best if the team members agree together on the order in which they will put on their thinking caps and why.

The process can start as simply as identifying your goal and deciding which hat (after blue) would be the most useful to try on. Typically we try hats on for a short period of time (just two to five minutes can be useful). It's helpful to agree the time boundaries before we start. Once we've tried a hat on for size, pause and evaluate the outcomes of the thinking done up to that point: are they helping to achieve the goal? What hat is needed next? When it feels as though we're done, put the blue hat on and see if the team has a clearer vision for how to proceed with the challenge ahead. It can also be worth discussing which hat felt the most comfortable to wear, so the team builds a recognition of its own different thinking styles.

Inclusive culture design

The very essence of inclusion means that it can't be the icing on the cake; it has to be baked into the foundations. If we want to see inclusion as a lived reality in our teams, companies, cultures and communities we need to build it into the very structure of the way they're formed and run, not just layer it on top and hope the inclusion icing will be sweet enough to trickle its way down through the status quo. There are few people better placed to guide us further through this topic than Steve Pemberton. Steve brings a perspective that is refreshing, both in its honesty and its optimism. He has risen up the ranks of corporate America to become one of the nation's most respected voices on diversity and inclusion.

Steve is the Chief Human Resources Officer at Workhuman, where he works with HR leaders and senior management executives worldwide to help build workplaces where every employee feels recognised, respected and appreciated for who they are and what they do. Previously, Steve was vice president of diversity and inclusion at Walgreens. Under his leadership, Walgreens reached record levels of performance on nearly every measure of diversity and inclusion from representation to supplier diversity spend. In 2015, he was appointed by United States Secretary of Labor Thomas Perez to serve on the Advisory Committee for the Competitive Integrated Employment of People with Disabilities. In the same year, he was awarded the prestigious Horizon Award by the United States Congress. But his passion for inclusion goes far beyond his professional role scope; for Steve, it's deeply personal.

If you google Steve you'll see that his triumphant life journey was made into a film titled *A Chance in the World*: a babysitter had made the comment about Steve when he was only eighteen months old that those were his odds of being successful or even happy in his life. By the time he was three, Steve had landed in an abusive foster home. His parents, both drug addicts (his father was African American and his mother Irish American), had split up long before then. As journalist Barbara Palmer notes, from his early childhood, Steve was contending 'with painful questions about his identity and where he fit in'.

Steve insists in our interview he's no different from anyone else in that a lot of our views about diversity, equality and inclusion are reflections of the messaging we received from our family, community and broader society in our formative years.

> The issue of race really was at the centre of my life journey, in many ways before it even began. When I was taken from my mother, the system was really struggling to know what to do with me and that was because they were trying to figure out *what* I was rather than *who* I was . . . Is he white? Is he black? Is he something in between?

For Steve, this instilled what he describes as one of the first lessons of inclusion: if your first orientation towards inclusion or equity is someone's race or other demographic attribute, you are likely propagating the damage that labels do to people's lives. Steve reflects, 'Rather than being focused on who I was, they were focused on what I was, which was a child born to a mother battling alcoholism and almost certainly some mental health issues, and a father who was not present. As a result I remain keenly aware of the damage that labels do.'

We have to catch ourselves when labels rear their reductive heads. Be curious as to what reaching for a label might reveal about your own insecurities or fears. Consider where those labels come from: where were you taught them? Did we absorb them unconsciously from societal norms and cues? Whose agenda are we rolling out?

If we object to a behaviour, rather than plastering a label on it, why not combine curiosity with clarity? When I hear someone jumping to a conclusion, such as 'he's too entitled to understand' or 'she's such a corporate climber', I find it helpful to dismantle the label with a question and clearly articulate the behaviour. For example, if we're frustrated by a junior employee's approach, as opposed to just saying 'they're just *so* young' to express our frustration, we can inquire why they did a task in a certain way. Maybe they saw the opportunity to improve a process? Or thought they could put a fresh spin on it? They also could have been cutting corners. Regardless, nothing is served by us using an aspect of their identity to label their behaviour. We have to delve deeper and be more nuanced.

When it comes to inclusion, a huge and often underappreciated role, according to Steve, comes in the form of allies. Minorities, in any context, are historically clear on where they stand when it comes to matters of their own rights. They have marched, they have protested and they have voted. The ambiguity that gives hate oxygen comes from 'allies who won't stand with us or who won't say to their friends, that's wrong'. Steve says, 'Ally-ship means taking a strong stance when it does not involve you. In the numbers game of social progress that is what's required for those who traffic in hate to realise they're outnumbered.' We inspire 'ally-ship' by becoming an ally ourselves. Whom (or what cause) are you allying with? That can mean taking on a role of consciously supporting, sponsoring or advocating for a particular cause. It can also mean lending your time to a mission. Ally-ship is the actionable component of having a deeper sense of purpose as a leader. It has to be authentic and mean- ingful. Part of rallying our supporters is first allying them.

Steve's framing of the notion of inclusion is powerful: it's diver- sity in action. He challenges organisations to move beyond paying lip-service to inclusion and making it a strategic goal. Steve believes diversity is most powerful when it exists in verb form: 'diversify'. As he points out, diversification is the bedrock of the two core pillars of US society: democracy (checks and balances as diversified gover- nance) and finance (diversified investment portfolios). Why is it so much of a stretch for us to see diversified, inclusive teams as a pillar of business?

I ask Steve to define the hallmarks of leaders who are successful in establishing inclusive cultures. He offers me two characteristics.

1 They don't declare victory
The ecosystem of diversity and inclusion is dynamic. It cannot be a case of 'we have arrived, we're all set'. We never stop trying to be a better writer, better student, better husband, wife, father. Those who treat inclusion as a journey of discovery and empowerment, rather than a destination, understand the importance of maintain- ing a healthy ecosystem.

2 They don't confuse activity with accomplishment
There is a lot of activity in the inclusion and diversity space. But that's not the same as holding yourself accountable. Steve says the single consistent approach is to focus on strengths first. For example, when he arrived at Walgreens they were already donating millions of dollars to pharmacy schools and had been instrumental

in creating a pipeline of African American pharmacists. Steve identified this strength and amplified it, which allowed him to identify underlying hotspots and concerns and solve them.

Managing the tension between embracing the journey and satisfying the needs of stakeholders to be able to see and measure progress requires some disciplined methodology. When it comes to recruiting for diversity, the job advertisement, language, package, interview process and selection criteria all need to be geared to attract and measure the diversity of candidates. Once we have representation, we need to be able to measure mobility within the organisation and watch whether or not these demographic groups are ascending within the company. Critically, Steve says recognition should be the foundation of diversity and inclusion efforts. In his work, he's discovered a direct correlation between recognition (specifically the amount of recognition a person receives and the value of that recognition) and career success. Recognition affects perceived value, which is correlated with promotions and increased opportunities. Steve argues we need to do a better job of measuring recognition in order to ensure it is fairly distributed according to contribution.

Representation in and of itself is not sufficient; recognition allows for the measurement of culture and progress. Recognition takes the values off the wall and writes them into the culture in a way that you can measure.

As leaders we're orchestrating a dynamic, ever-evolving dance with diverse ideas, diverse challenges and diverse people. We'd be crazy to leave future-stars on the sidelines waiting to be asked to shine.

A question from the leading edge:

Who should you ask to the dance?

21

Build the case for change

'There is nothing more difficult to take in hand, more perilous to conduct or more uncertain in its success, than to take the lead in the introduction of a new order of things.'

Niccolò Machiavelli

Change might be inevitable but growth is intentional. We don't get improvement and success by chance; we get it by consciously choosing to change – in ways that push our limits and pursue new opportunities. We get it by constantly seeking and leading from the edge. A perspective attributed to Darwin reads, 'It's not the strongest of the species that survives, nor the most intelligent, it's the one most adaptable for change.' The ability to initiate and navigate change is one of the most critical capabilities demanded of twenty-first-century leaders.

People don't resist change; they resist being changed

For something that is such a ubiquitous part of life (seasons, hairstyles, software upgrades: we're constantly engaging with change), change cops a lot of flack in an organisational setting. Change resistance, change fatigue and flat-out change-induced mutinies are not uncommon topics.

A few years ago, I walked in to facilitate a strategy day and was met with an extremely quiet, cold room full of crossed arms. This wasn't a strategic session prompted by universal consensus that the business needed to transform . . . far from it. This was a day organised by a CEO who'd been brought in by the board to shake up the place and who was struggling six months in to get any kind of resonance with his message. While the results were declining year on year, they weren't terrible. Some people thought it was the market's fault; some people thought it was just a blip caused by their competitor's brilliant marketing campaign. But the board, watching sliding revenue and an increasing exodus of young talent thought otherwise and moved swiftly, hiring a new CEO with a brief to 'transform'. Only, or so I was told heading into the day, everyone else seemed quite happy to just keep kicking along with the status quo. Perhaps that was why my reception was so stony.

I decided I'd better grab a second coffee and take a somewhat high-risk approach: I called out the frostiness straightaway. Then, instead of starting by talking about purpose and aspirational goals and targets, I asked everyone to write down all the reasons why the new CEO's proposed change was not going to work and stick them on the wall. Boy did that get the chatter and the activity levels flowing! To say that twenty minutes later we had one hell of a sticker-filled wall would be an understatement. There was no shortage of criticism, including lot of: 'We've tried that before, and it didn't work', 'It's too radical', 'There's too much red tape', and 'We can't be sure it'll work'. Plus 'They won't fund it', 'We don't have the authority' and 'I'm not sure our shareholders/stakeholders/customers will go for it' – the list went on. There was one that just read, 'It's stupid.' Enough said, apparently.

The goal of this exercise was to allow the space for concerns, opposition and challenge to surface. When I'm guiding leaders through change processes, I believe one of the most critical components is to make sure we create this space. Once we've sorted the wheat from the chaff with regards to identifying resistance that has merit, I encourage leaders to deliberately extract a response to the question, 'If I was to turn your "No" into a "Yes" what would I have to do?'

I find this method useful on two fronts. First, we're surfacing the unspoken assumptions that are powerfully shaping the behavioural undercurrents. Second, we are keeping a conversation moving, when blocking will be the enemy. It's similar to the method we touched on in Chapter 9 about doing the work to have an opinion: we're collectively taking our opinions out and giving them a good whack with our metaphorical cricket bat to see if they hold up to scrutiny in the light of day.

When these assumptions are identified, we as leaders need to have the grace to see them not as a source of frustration but as a gift. 'I've just had the two or three "reasons we can't" enumerated to me, and they're all tackleable!' We can put the concerns raised on the top of our to-do list and make it our mission to alleviate them. In every context I've worked in, people who feel heard can begin to see a path ahead.

Why, what and how

The final part of the exercise that day was to use the opposite wall and more sticky notes to elucidate the 'reasons we have to change'. What's critical here is not getting lost in a numbers game (more often than not the reasons opposing will outnumber the reasons for; it's part of how we're wired). Far more valuable is finding what I call the 'Super Objective', a term borrowed from the seminal work of the actor, director, writer and teacher Konstantin Stanislavski. He shifted the world of drama away from results-oriented acting ('I want to look sad') to motive-oriented acting ('I want what the character wants, and if I feel that fully, it will show through'). The Super Objective, or 'spine of a character', represents the inner battle that creates the emotional tension between the character and the narrative. In a corporate context it equates to the purpose that lights the motivational fire in the team's belly: the reason they'll put in extra effort, try again after a setback or pursue goals that are many years in the making. It is the riveting stuff, and change will not happen in our organisations without it.

If we can articulate that we're fighting for something that matters, we can spark the fire of change in even the staunchest opposition. On this particular day, scribbled in green marker on a yellow sticky note was, 'Because we won't exist in five years if we don't.' I picked this one off the board first and asked people to give their reactions to what it would mean if this statement was true. People talked about having been at the company for five, eight and eighteen years. They spoke of how the team felt like a second family, how they had families to look after and mortgages to pay, how they couldn't afford for this not to work. With the conversation that opened up, we didn't need another one of the notes on the board because we'd tapped into the fundamental human emotion of the room. People simultaneously understood the reason the change had to happen as well as the genuine reservations and concerns.

The key thing about a Super Objective is it is always based in a fundamental human need. Things like 'keeping our customers happy' and 'achieving record sales' are objectives, but they're not Super Objectives. Not unless you make it real by bringing in a real-life customer who has a powerful story that can help people frame the impact of what 'keeping our customers happy' means. Building the case for change starts with leveraging some of the ideas we touched on in Chapter 16. How do you tap into the drivers of your people, to a fundamental human truth? How do you take the change initiative from professional to personal?

Back in our facilitation session, we moved from the why into discussing the what and the how. But the energy in the room had

already shifted. People now seemed far more accepting of the idea
that change needed to happen and were leaning into it.

In this way, we began to work through some general principles
for improving the ability to implement successful change that can
be captured under three broad, cascading categories.

- Why: there is a compelling case for getting something done.
- What: when the outcomes of successful change are clear and
  compelling.
- How: the processes for implementing the change are transparent around the support that will be available for these key
  areas: systems – HR and management systems (e.g., budgeting,
  technology, and talent); socially – by engaging all; leadership –
  leaders invest both their time and passion in the change; and
  analytics – the progress of the change is tracked, so there is both
  accountability and learning.

Build a roadmap

Once we've got buy-in for the why of our change, we need to convert
intention to a high-level action plan. One of the most valuable reference points I've found is the idea that you need to build a rough
map for the road trip. Just as you wouldn't depart on a road trip
without checking you've got a tank full of petrol and snacks for
the journey, you'll also need to think about the resources needed,
the scope or objective, and costs involved in the plan.

Roadmaps are *not* your detailed implementation plans. These
have a critical role in the implementation and will need to be
developed in the next phase by people who are closer to each
particular facet of the change. Right now, we're focused on the
macro: key steps and milestones, critical actions and a general
sense of the pace. I find it helpful to think about and provide
high-level guidance around these five points from the Prosci ECM
Roadmap:

- Current state – how things are done today

- Future state – how things are done once this initiative is fully implemented
- Transition state – how we move from the current state to the future state
- Technical side – the systems and mechanisms required to reach the future state
- People side – building the support and buy-in that is needed to reach the future state

You'll often see leaders use frameworks like thirty-, sixty- and ninety-day plans to break down a change initiative into chunks that focus employees and stakeholders on the immediate task at hand. A plan using frameworks such as these maintains one eye on the horizon. Ideally, you want to find a way of presenting this not just in words but as an image of the end-to-end overview of the direction, deliverables and deadlines.

Empowering change champions

Organisational transformation requires empowerment and participation at all levels. One of the most common questions I'm asked after keynote presentations is what the difference is between a champion of change and a change agent? They may sound like they are responsible for the same tasks, and they do overlap, but technically they are quite distinct. Using Don Harrison's four organisational roles – champions, agents, sponsors and targets, aka CAST – is an approach I find useful for thinking about how we break down a change initiative. Keep in mind, we all have the potential to move between categories during the scope of the initiative. Most importantly, avoid an 'us and them' mentality.

Champions

Champions of change believe in the change and attempt to obtain commitment and resources for it but may not have the line authority or the direct accountability required to make it happen. You might pick these people for reasons of visibility, to tap into their energy or because they have a particular passion for the initiative or change at hand.

Agents

Agents of change are assigned responsibility to implement change and are evaluated on their ability to get the project implemented. They are primarily responsible for the tactical change project implementation activity, including strategy, design, deployment, and evaluation of the change.

Sponsors

There are two types of sponsors. They either authorise, legitimise and demonstrate ownership for the change (authorising sponsors) or they reinforce their personal commitment through their own visible, active behaviour (reinforcing sponsors). Sponsors often serve as powerful signals that something is to be taken seriously.

Targets

Targets are the people who may change their behaviour, emotions, knowledge and perceptions as a result of the initiative. By this, we mean identifying who we want to target for change. Generally, targets of change will fall into two categories: people who might be directly experiencing the problem or are at risk, and people who contribute to the problem through their actions or lack of actions.

There are two big mistakes commonly made in selecting these roles: choosing based on titles or technical ability. Who we actually want to empower are people who have trust and influence as our champions and agents. Use the CAST filter as a way of helping you get the right fit for each of the key roles in your change team.

Critical culture

Louis Gerstner Jr, former chief executive of IBM, led one of the most successful business transformations in history. When he took over as CEO in 1993, a year the company posted an $8 billion loss, and IBM shares that had sold for $43 in 1987 could be had for $12. Larry Ellison, of rival Oracle, was quoted as saying that his company no longer thought about IBM because 'they're not dead but they're irrelevant'. By 2001 IBM had posted an $8 billion profit. One important lesson Lou learnt from the experience was that when it comes to change, 'culture is everything'. Business people today understand this. In a study by PWC's Katzenbach Center, 84 per cent said that the organisation's culture was critical to the success of change management, and 64 per cent saw it as more essential than strategy or operating model. Yet change leaders often fail to overcome cultural resistance and make the most of cultural support. Among respondents whose companies were unable to sustain change over time, a startling 76 per cent reported that executives failed to take account of the existing culture when designing the transformation effort. Leaders must examine which elements of the culture are already aligned with the change and emphasise these, ideally bringing them to the attention to the people who will be most affected by the change. Equally important is the need to call out and stamp out elements of culture and behaviour that are misaligned. This includes, at the extreme, those who will not be able to make the journey.

Fostering a culture entails 'getting the right people on the bus' – as coined so eloquently by Jim Collins. This means hiring employees who buy into the progressive components of the culture and make it a part of how they work every day. It also means getting the wrong people off the bus, and that's often the hardest part. One of the harsh realities of change initiatives is that some people will find themselves without a seat. Sometimes the new world order will require different skills, though increasingly it never ceases to amaze me how capable people are of pivoting if the culture of the organisation is one that facilitates and permits learning. More often than not, the final decision comes down to cultural fit or lack thereof – which if we're not careful becomes a cover for becoming less diverse. It's important to acknowledge the cultural spectrum here and to give people time and grace to adapt to new circumstances and initiatives, but we also cannot allow cultural contagion. No one person is bigger than the team.

For example, Sir Richard Branson has told me how he won't hire anyone, irrespective of how impressive they might have been in the interview, if they weren't kind to the receptionist on their way in. I turned down a board position once because the chair, whom I was meeting for the first time at a corporate function, mistook me as one of the function staff and condescendingly unleashed his anger on me at being seated at table 23. It didn't matter how much he changed his tune once I was sitting next to him behind my designated name card; I'd seen how he'd treated me when he thought I was the waiter.

The hardest and yet the most important people to move off the bus are those whom I term the 'toxic high-performers': they get results, but they erode culture in the process. Think a sales executive who wins big contracts but bullies their younger team members, or the IT executive who white-ants the rest of the management team, diminishing confidence in the organisation's strategic direction. Despite their job skills, they're usually not worth the price of keeping them around because they pose a direct threat to the company's culture.

Getting rid of these employees is 100 per cent the right thing to do, but how we do it matters just as much. Some kind of awkward 'this just isn't working' doesn't suffice, and it confuses people. By the objective measures in their scorecard, more often than not, these people are figuratively killing it. This is the problem when culture is amorphous. Few companies successfully understand and shape their culture. Fewer still can articulate how it supports their mission statement, let alone truly incorporate it into everything they do. Does your company put its culture at the core of everything, from performance criteria to performance management to documentation? The most effective companies do this, using their culture to bring out the best in their employees and mitigate the risk of those 'toxic high-performers'. How? By making it a key part of all aspects of the employee life cycle, with documentation to show how it is done. This is arguably one of the most important things a leader can implement early in the change process: define or reset your cultural expectations, and make culture a quantifiable part of the performance evaluations for all employees.

In 2019, Atlassian announced that it was no longer going to tolerate 'brilliant jerks' who deliver results for the company but make life hell for their co-workers. The company shifted to a performance review model whereby two-thirds of every review now has nothing to do with job skills. Instead, equal weighting is given to how each of its 3000 employees affects others on their team, and to how they live the company values. Atlassian says the change aims to 'more fairly measure people on how they bring their whole self to work'. The goal was to make sure the company was rewarding the right behaviours.

Atlassian was clear that the reason for resetting the performance targets was less about shuffling people out and more about de-biasing the performance system. The global head of talent, Bek Chee, says, 'We recognise things are not the way they used to be, yet companies haven't evolved [from] thirty years ago when they were primarily made up often of white men. Tech standards have evolved; we have new ways of working, new demographics and generational change.'

Atlassian employees can receive one of three grading levels on each element, based on 'growth mindset language' – rather than a score, they either get an exceptional year, a great year or an off year. 'We crowdsourced from within the organisation, that was one of the suggestions that came from our employees,' Bek says. 'The reason that language is really important is it does not mean you are a certain type of person or a certain type of performer; it means you had a great year or an exceptional year.'

Imposed values are rarely 'valued' as much as crowdsourced values. The sense of self-directed ownership over culture also allows people to feel more ownership over the change initiative. IBM recognised this need when they rolled out a new initiative on culture in 2003. A clear set of definitions and cultural traits had been developed by the leadership team. However, they then flipped the ownership in a 'values jam' that was hosted online and open to anyone in the company to post their ideas for a 72-hour period. The feedback was incorporated and the interactive value set given over to the people of the company as co-creators.

In Atlassian's case, Bek says appealing to the Millennial and Gen Y and Z crowd was a huge part of it. The company have a young workforce profile but are also cognisant of the broader intergenerational shift within the workforce. 'We know the next generation is very socially conscious; they have a different set of expectations. They're kind of no-bullshit. They don't want to hear a company say, "You can bring your whole self to work, we're diverse, we're socially conscious" and not have that backed up.'

Some leaders resist this advice. They would argue (and I've heard them argue!) that this sort of move is molly-coddling Millennials. Some treat their company culture like it's intangible and can't be pinned down. Others will argue that employees can be fired for any reason, at any time. That may be so, but it's much more manageable from a legal standpoint if you can point to your established, documented reasoning for why a particular employee doesn't fit with the culture. Beyond the legal reasoning, research increasingly shows that culture can improve operational and even financial results, so tracking it should be a key part of every company's HR processes. As companies like Atlassian explain, this isn't about appeasing Millennials with a participation trophy mentality.

'Our top performers we know nail it in terms of living values and being part of the team and delivering in their role,' says Bek.

> I don't think this is a peanut butter approach [a business term that refers to anything, such as time, money or energy, that has been spread too far to be useful] by any means. I definitely think some people could look at a system that has values and team and culture tied into it and get concerned, but we know from our own experience and research that these behaviours encourage collaboration and lead to high performance. It's not just, 'Oh they're friendly, and they smile.'

When you change course, you open up the opportunity to redefine behaviour and reset expectations. Culture, in return, supports the case for change and provides the core strength to sustain people through times of change. And there's a more fundamental reason to place culture at the centre: it's simply a better way to treat people.

A question from the leading edge:

Is your why for change more compelling than your 'why not'?

22

Yes, and

'Life is improvisation.'

Tina Fey

During my year of fear, I took myself along to an improvisation class. It terrified me – which is somewhat odd because I absolutely love being on stage and, to be honest, the bigger the audience, the better. But there is something I found deeply unnerving about improv. I thought at first perhaps it was the lack of control but that didn't make sense. In my speaking work I revel in letting the audience take control of discussion and feel energised by the unpredictability of where a room might want to take things on any given day. There was just something about the high degree of living right on the edge that comes with improv: failure or embarrassment seems only ever a moment away.

In the class, one of the first exercises we did was to line up across the room, and the instructors started telling a story. We were urged to step forward at any time from the line (there's no going in order in improv!) and pick up the conversation using the phrase 'yes, and' in order to take things in whatever direction we liked.

As I later found out, 'yes, and' is a central pillar of improvisation. It's also known as the acceptance principle. Basically, when someone in a scene states something, you accept it as truth: 'yes'. After this endorsement is the reciprocal build: 'and'. When we entered into the exercise that day, it was never to undermine or disagree; it was to accept and then build.

One of the things that quickly becomes apparent in improv is the level of trust required from the group. When we step forward, we're trusting ourselves and backing our ability to float a new idea into the conversation. We're also trusting that someone else will step in, speak up and not leave us hanging.

'Nerves', my improv instructor said, 'are selfish.' That phrase took some stomaching; I mean, it's only human to get nervous, right? But what he meant was if we're nervous, we're focused inward. And from a place of self-focus, we won't be able to suspend our ego, concerns and fears in a way that will allow us to fully submit to the creative process and be available to our peers. We'll also violate the principle of 'yes, and' because coming from a place focused on self-protection or self-preservation doesn't give other perform-ers in the scene anything to build on. The scene will crumble, and those involved will likely feel a little bruised from the experience. Improv works on the principle of making your partner look good and trusting that they'll do the same for you. Similarly, leaders can no longer afford to be internally focused in the brave new world of collective uncertainty.

Why does improv matter for leaders?

We are all effectively improvising every day in our working and personal lives, responding to each scenario that greets us. For collab-oration to function optimally, we need everyone participating in the same agenda: to work together at peak intelligence as a team and create a process or product that delights the audience. We are simultaneously a leader and a follower. We must learn the art of building a great ensemble and the craft of adapting and being agile. Critically, to achieve this, our focus has to shift from being about ourselves to whoever we are 'for'.

Three MIT Sloane professors, Edivandro Carlos Conforto, Eric Rebentisch and Daniel Amaral, conducted extensive research into the principles of agility and adaptability in project teams. In many ways being 'adaptive' and 'agile' are just fancy corporate (Silicon Valley) speak for improvisation. They conducted studies across seventeen different industries and seventy-six different countries. As the research team characterised it, innovation projects (which are inherently challenging due to their uncertainty and rapidly evolving nature) require improvisation skills. To be successful, the project team must be able to respond quickly to changes, including recognising opportunities to improve the product and deliver results under time and cost pressures. They found that projects with extreme changes in requirements (90 per cent or more) employed 41 per cent more improvisation practices than projects that had relatively stable requirements (10 per cent or fewer changes). This suggests that higher levels of improvisation, deliberate or not, are more likely to happen in projects that have fluid and unstable specifications. In other words, as the world of work becomes increasingly volatile, the more critical it becomes to feel comfortable improvising.

'Yes, and' is perhaps as much a philosophy as it is an improvisation method. It encourages the pursuit of a common goal while maintaining an individual intellectual perspective. In my experience 'yes, and' actually allows people to flourish. As business improv expert Bob Kulhan puts it in his book *Getting to 'Yes And'*, 'Unconditional acceptance is not the same as unequivocal agreement.' There is still room left for healthy, respectful contention. People also often mistake improvisation for being entirely unstructured but there are parameters and rules that create the right conditions for improvisational brainstorming to thrive. The origins stem from David Alger at the Pan Theater in San Francisco, and at their core are the specific rules of improv. Here are the first eight and some ways to bring them into your leadership approach.

Establish the location

Good improv needs to be grounded. We're standing on an empty stage or in an empty office meeting room: we need to breathe life into it. By imbuing it with characteristics that add colour and dimension, we build a dynamic between ourselves and others on stage. An equivalent in the business context might be localising your conversation in the historical company roots or the heartbeat of the community you live in and serve. Giving people 'place' provides crucial context for the way a 'yes, and' narrative evolves.

Insert 'yes, and . . .'

In meetings and team scenarios, we naturally care about being right. By replacing the more common 'yes, but' with the more open 'yes, and', we hear other perspectives with openness and insert a bit of distance between brain and ego. We can get out of our own way and encourage others to be more receptive to what we have to say. Try using it in your next few meetings and observe the conversational shifts.

Add new information

Improvisation, like collaboration, only moves forward if we add new information. Saying 'yes, and' doesn't mean there won't be any conflict, but this type of open, positive approach to disagreement acts as a catalyst for progression. Adding new information means piggy-backing on the idea you've heard: 'yes, and perhaps we could develop a freemium version of the product for non-profits' or 'yes, and if we collaborated with a marketing firm we could make it happen twice as fast'. It's incredible how people respond when you acknowledge their opinions then voice your own afterwards. It's a softening mechanism, with significant and unintended returns.

Unblock

The opposite of 'yes, and' is blocking or denial. This stops or destroys the addition of new information; worse, it white-ants what has already been established. Sometimes blocking comes from a distorted assumption that saying 'no' elevates our own opinions and contribution. Pay attention to moments when you are using blocking language and try switching to 'yes, and' instead.

Avoid asking questions

In the world of improv, asking questions is akin to blocking. It means you're not committing to making a choice. 'Why?' and 'How?' imply the need for justification or edification. Here we're going for gut instincts, momentum and the exploration that spontaneous response allows us. Reflexive questions like "Why should I?" or "What for?" don't support your partner or move the conversation along; instead, think about how you could turn your question into a suggestion: 'yes, and we could try to find another pathway over here?'

Play in the present and use the moment

You've got to be hyper-present for improv to work. What is the body language of your partner revealing? Are they moving away or towards? Are they smiling or looking nervous? What do they need from you? These questions can be good prompts in a business setting too, to help you tune into the receptivity of the client or stakeholder. While there are varying opinions on the exact breakdown between verbal and non-verbal communication, there's universal agreement that body language matters even more than verbal, with around a sixty/forty split. Even in a virtual meeting, body language plays a big part.

Be specific and provide colourful details

Details are the lifeblood of momentum. Each detail provides a clue as to what is essential. Without detail, we remain suspended in sweeping generalisations and abstracts. Detail adds more dimensions and therefore, better opportunity for springboarding. There's a big difference between saying, 'You're the best doctor there is, that's why they chose you' to saying, 'Angela, you're the best trauma surgeon in Sydney. That's why the governor has decided to route all the emergency response to the tornado through our hospital.'

Change, change, change

At its core, improv is about change. To hold our 'audience', there needs to be some kind of change. There needs to be a journey, a twist, a revelation, a challenge. We want to see people experience the ramifications of their choices. We want to see them give themselves over to the moment and to their instinctive response to the 'yes, and' offered by their partners. Here, the audience is your team; your people want to be emotionally invested. We want to feel like we're taking risks and moving forward. We want to see potential realised in front of our eyes, and the only way to do that is to change continually.

Exercises to bring improv to life

There is all manner of improv exercises that you can tap into to help bring some collaborative energy to your workplace. Try bringing one of these to life at the start of your next brainstorming session or when you're looking to shift the energy of your people.

To break the ice: word-at-a-time story

Everyone sits in a circle (or zoom grid if needs be!). Source a focus or title for the story you're about to co-create from the group, e.g. 'The Best Product Ever Released'. The story is told rapidly, one word at a time around the circle, and the end of a sentence is indicated by a player saying 'stop'. It doesn't have to make sense, but people do have to try to build sentences, not just throw in meaningless words to get a quick laugh. The goal is to see how long you can keep going before the story descends into chaos. Try two or three times, picking a different theme each time to help the group build the muscle. This is a powerful exercise to build listening skills and collectively develop a narrative. It's much harder than it sounds.

For collaboration: problem and solution

This exercise (used by the team at CSZ Berlin) is a conversation between two people that always follows the same structure, but where the participants have to fill in the gaps:

A: I have a problem [describe problem].

B: Here, I have a [completely random object].

A: Great! Now I can [comes up with a solution]. Thank you!

A and B high-five and then two more people have a go.

This is a great one for catalysing creativity. You're not sure what problem you'll be thrown but you have to offer an instant response and collectively you have to 'solve' a problem. Kickstart your next brainstorming session.

For ideation: 'yes, and'

Break people into pairs and invite the first person to suggest an activity (for example, 'Let's go on a holiday'), and the second person responds and says 'yes, and . . .' before adding something to the idea. It can help to begin with something unrelated to work to kick creativity into gear before bringing the focus to things that might have more real or relevant ramifications, such as ideating on new services, cross-selling to existing clients or how to handle tricky customers.

Lessons from Lonely Planet

Gus Balbontin is an investor, adviser and adventurer. He has so much energy he could move a mountain. The Argentinian is also the former executive director and CTO of Lonely Planet, where he led one of the world's most loved brands through significant disruption. Gus argues it was his solid background in hitchhiking that both landed him with a foot in the door at Lonely Planet and enabled him to find the road for these paperback traveller's bibles to survive a digital transformation.

The revolution was upon Lonely Planet and Gus considers himself lucky to have been in the trenches. He tells me:

It was amazing, all of the media, newspapers, magazines, TV, books, music, all of that sector that communicated in some way with humans in various methods . . . The entire thing was flipped on its head by the first wave of digitisation.

As Gus points out, there was no blueprint, and the business was 'scrambling' to respond. Gus credits Lonely Planet's ability to pivot to the 'wonderful group of humans' he was working alongside. He is convinced when disruption is reverberating through the very core of your business model, you can't slate innovation as the responsibility of one particular group or department; it has to be everyone's responsibility. The culture of the group is critical.

'Innovation,' says Gus, 'starts with each of us.' Here Gus calls up the significance of his time adventuring in his youth, heading out with little more than a backpack and a smile. The true essence of 'yes, and' – having to source a roof over his head, get a lift to the next town, pull together an entire cross-country adventure once it was already underway. He's since become a student of improv and has brought the technique into several companies and start-ups he works with. He says hitchhiking and improv have built within him not just a capacity to think on his feet but a joy in doing so.

Critical to Lonely Planet's cultural response was stripping out the structure that didn't serve innovation. Gus has strong opinions on KPIs. He thinks people would follow them off a cliff. In his mind, KPIs require us to 'pay the tax of reviewing them every single day'. He warns, 'Be careful how many you have because it's a fair tax to pay. Pick one or two indicators that will give you a real sense of progress. But make sure they don't kill common sense.'

Gus says we need to find a way to resist the human tendency to make things 'complex, bigger and to always delay it till later'. One of his favourite exercises to run with teams is to engage in improvisational brainstorming using those three factors as prompts: how do we make it 'simpler/smaller/easier'?

> Innovation is [composed] of three characteristics: curiosity, courage and resilience. Don't be owned by your work systems. Everything you do in business can feel like concrete; if it isn't adaptable, then it's rigid and unadaptable. If you can't follow the customer, their needs and wants, you will become the concrete.

In an increasingly dynamic world, developing a disposition for adaptation translates to a competitive advantage.

At the core of improv, three questions help us build an adaptive disposition and are worth asking of ourselves and of our teams:

- What can I notice here? (Spoken and unspoken)
- What can I accept here? (Especially if and when it differs from my pre-existing perspective)
- How can I build on these ideas or perspectives? (Create and collaborate versus apply judgement and debate)

Improvisation in a crisis

COVID-19 was an incredible example of organisations, communities and governments improvising in response to a challenging set of circumstances. Globally, as we entered into unprecedented economic shutdown, social distancing and mobility restrictions, we were challenged to improvise and innovate as we attempted to minimise the lives lost to the coronavirus pandemic. So many aspects of our 'normal' were yanked away. Businesses were shut, physical human contact was halted and borders were closed. We had to develop novel, value-adding responses to new circumstances quickly. Gin companies pivoted into the production of hand sanitiser. Clothing manufacturers repurposed their supplies and workforce to produce face masks. Cafes and restaurants closed premises and launched delivery-only options with everything from vacuum-packed cocktails to produce boxes complete with YouTube videos from chefs on how to put the meals together. Italian engineers at start-up Issinova built a prototype at pace to reverse engineer 3D printing of respirator venturi valves.

A once-in-a-century pandemic forced us to make it up as we went. Was it survival of the fittest? Or survival of the fastest when it came to trying something new? The beautiful thing that improvisation brings to leadership is the will of the collective to survive, the intricate reliance we have on each other comes to the fore. If improvisation can get us through a global pandemic, maybe 'business as usual' needs a little more 'business as unusual'.

A question from the leading edge:

When did you last truly feel the thrill of improvising with your team?

23

Navigate from polarisation to participation

'No-one is exempt from the call to find common ground.'

Barack Obama

Between polar opposites, by nature, lies common ground. When we think of the Earth's poles, they are both covered in ice (and hopefully will remain so), just at opposite ends of the same globe. When we think of the far left and far right of politics, they are equally didactic and rigid to other ideas: for example, some extreme environmental progressives in Australia also espouse anti-vaccination beliefs, denying science in much the same way as extreme environmental conservatives.

When a photographic image is polarised, we see the same shapes, in a different light. When we think about polarisation as two disconnected views, we miss the energy and tension held in their opposites and the dynamic debate that can be unlocked as result. And when we ignore, chastise or belittle people with extreme opinions, they rarely 'see the light'; rather, they solidify their perspective and retreat to their own corner of the bigger picture. Progressing outcomes for companies, communities and countries will routinely involve leaders engaging with a spectrum of opinions. In the quest for more common ground, we've got to learn the method of constructive depolarisation.

Reem the Reformer

I first met Reem Abu Hassan on a bus in Melbourne. Reem was in town for the International Women's Forum and after a night's festivities we were all jostling for seats on the bus. I sat next to Reem. What strikes you first about Reem is her warmth; she's one of those people who just seems to build instant rapport. We were chatting furiously about the conference, and the state of the world and her family for about twenty minutes before a mentor of mine, Lisa, turned around from the row of seats in front and said, 'Holly, has Reem told you about how she set up Jordan's first-ever shelter for domestic violence and how she crusaded to vanquish "honour crimes" from Jordanian society?' Suffice to say, I needed the bus to travel the length of Australia that night to accommodate the questions that unlocked!

The fact someone had to tell me Reem's accomplishments gives you a sense of her humility but the more I've come to understand the process of how Reem works, the more I realise it's part of the superpower she's honed over decades of working in and on policy reform: Reem listens first. She wants to understand what makes you tick. Because in what makes you tick, as she says, 'lies the common ground and the lever for change'. Reem tells me, 'If you don't know history, you'll struggle to play any role in the future of anything.'

Before I get into sharing what Reem has achieved, and how she's achieved it, it's critical to understand the tension between the religious and traditional tribal culture and the desire among Jordanians to be a modern part of the international community.

Reem says she was fortunate to grow up in a family with enlightened grandfathers on both sides, as well as an enlightened grandmother, who was one of the first teachers in Jordan. Reem had a father who encouraged his wife to work and his daughter to study law. Reem undertook her original degree in Jordan, where to study law meant to study religious principles and cultural traditions, as much as more formal legal precedent and acts of parliament. At university, Reem was exposed to the writing of Moroccan psychologist Fatima Mernissi, whose book *Beyond the Veil* argued that it was the male interpretation of the Quran, as opposed to the principles of Islam itself, that posed an issue for women.

Mernissi's text proved pivotal in shaping Reem's method of depolarisation: she believed that Islam *could* be a way to promote women's empowerment, they just needed to find the right interpretation. Reem says, 'I would look always to bring the conversation back to foundational principles. Instead of fighting against text and culture, I chose to fight *with* them.'

Reem's reforms have focused primarily on women's rights in Jordan, specifically with regard to domestic violence and honour crimes. Honour crimes refer to the murder of a family member due to a perpetrator's belief that the victim has brought dishonour to their family. In the late 1980s and early 1990s Jordan became known internationally for its honour crimes. At the same time Jordan was preparing to participate in the Fourth World Women's Conference in 1995; there was pressure to review the Jordanian criminal law and Reem was given the brief.

Reem breaks her method down into three parts.

Get everyone working from the same facts

Reem began her deep dive by spending three days poring over the court transcripts and decisions in every honour killing case. When Reem looked at the perpetrators they were often black sheep of the family and almost all of them would get a sentence of six months to three years: that's it. Reem dug deeper. What was the source of this lenient punishment for murder? Surprisingly, not the Quran, but colonialism. It was a legacy from Syrian criminal law which was adopted from the French. This didn't excuse the fact that France had long ago moved on and Jordan hadn't, but for Reem this new light was a breakthrough.

Reem's campaign commenced: this is not part of Islam.

Her ability to make the new appear old – changing the way these killers were treated in line with Islam – disarmed her opponents. She had found the thread she needed to pull to enable a dynamic debate.

Get to the root of the actual problem

Reem wanted to understand why honour killings were getting such lenient sentences. She met with the head of the courts and respectfully asked to understand the process and their thinking when sentencing people convicted of honour crimes. It boiled down to a lenient sentence being given if a person commits the crime in a fit of fury. Reem believes there is strength in finding the weakest link in polarised debate. She discovered the very first investigation by a public prosecutor failed to require the evidentiary burden for a more severe sentence in court. From there on, precedent was set and followed. In shining a light on the original leniency, she was able to challenge the precedent and set in motion a different outcome.

Deal with things in a way that doesn't trigger sensitivity

Reem asked the Minister of Justice for permission to conduct a review of investigations, and proposed that three dedicated homicide public prosecutors be appointed to deal with homicides. Reem says it was important the prosecutors were given a broader brief than just 'honour killings', because the term is highly emotive and inflames part of the political spectrum. She used the broader prosecutor remit as the indirect strategy to lift investigation standards and demand more evidence. Equally, there was a push to make one of the prosecutors female, but Reem was of the belief that the initial wave of precedent needed to be established by male prosecutors.

The plan was put in motion and it began to work. The prosecutors started to escalate stronger cases that would correlate to harsher sentences, including in some instances capital punishment. In this way, Reem says, they changed the messaging on the issue: 'The message to families was, are you going to let your son sacrifice his future? He may face potential capital punishment or sixteen years' hard labour? Is it worth it?'

Further, Reem says what was really important was that the ideation process, as well as the solution, were Jordanian.

> Especially when you're talking about culture, family or society, you have to show that you're not just importing opinions from the West. International standards are within our culture, but we need to find them . . . to find that principle in the international treaty that resonates with Islamic principle, or a cultural tradition that I have.

Depolarisation – and calling Bullshift

The term 'depolarisation' comes from biology. Depolarisation represents a sudden change in a cell due to a shift in electric charge distribution, resulting in less negative charge within the cell. The scientific focus on discharging the negative is useful; after all, detaching people from their polarised positions can help to relieve tension and negativity. How can we depolarise the issues dividing the people we lead?

Andrew Horabin is a professional speaker, facilitator, author, comedian and award-winning singer and songwriter. He runs a company called Bullshift, which is all about helping shift the 'bull' out of workplaces. The process starts by noticing the 'bulls' – the unconscious reactions that can charge without our awareness – and then making the 'shifts' to a more conscious response. Everyone from the Australian Army's elite special forces to championship-winning sporting teams have called on Andrew and his team to assist them with changing their workplace communication. More often than not, he meets organisations at a point where division and competition are the dominant features of the culture; his goal is to help bring a higher consciousness to the way people communicate.

In Andrew's experience, one of the big reasons we're wedded to our view of the world is because once we form a belief, we invest in it. We filter data (consciously or unconsciously) to look for evidence that reinforces the beliefs we already have. Layer on the idea that it might be a belief we've taught our kids or built a marriage on or made a career out of, and you can start to see Andrew's point that the more invested you are, the more that is at stake when you contemplate letting go of your bullshit.

To get people to detach from the security of their invested opinions, Andrew says we have to get them to look at the unconscious beliefs those opinions are attached to. 'We have to help people to distinguish between themselves, and whatever the thing is. The project, the tasks, the relationship, the role, the title, whatever it is. Would this still be a good idea if you hadn't thought of it? Or if you hadn't already spent three months on it?' When people can't distinguish where the object of conflict stops and they start, they'll look at everything through the filter of 'me' and with a shallow consciousness and no willingness to question or change.

One of the methods Andrew uses to separate a person from their tightly held belief is to break them free from the binary of 'either/or'. When it comes to constructive depolarisation, moving people from a place of two opposing possibilities onto a spectrum of possibilities immediately brings fluidity to their thinking. 'Instead of either/or what does "both, and" look like? As in, what if you're both right *and* there's also some other thing we haven't thought of yet? And then it's about how we get everybody collectively to go looking for that third position.'

Andrew classifies relationships into four levels on a spectrum: adversarial, competitive, cooperative and collaborative. The methods of communicating are entirely different at each level; in summary:

- Adversarial: a need to win and to see someone else lose. Even a willingness for both to lose, as long as the other party loses.

- Competitive (the norm): siloed leaders identify with their 'team' and not the collective. Conversation takes on the form of debate.
- Cooperative: people trying to get on and not get in each other's way. Conversation is couched in language that softens opinions, and people are careful in the way that they offer their perspective.
- Collaborative: a willingness to have openness and honesty, and strive to challenge and question assumptions, to rigorously investigate the data, rather than just go with a preordained position.

According to Andrew, 'Anyone on the scale from competitive to cooperative will form a view before they arrive at the meeting.' Whereas at the collaborative level, we come into the room open to having a perspective changed. As leaders, our responsibility to find common ground is not easy. We must confront not only our deepest held beliefs and those of the people around us. As we strive for diversity in the workplace, we must see it as a positive that common ground is not necessarily common, but common good relies upon finding it.

Constructing a dialogue

Differing opinions and healthy debate are necessary for a group to keep evolving. But what happens when real and raw conflict is unearthed in the process?

Conflicts need to be handled quickly, professionally, fairly and with a workable agreement in mind or else the organisation suffers and the argument can turn the place into a feudal battleground. Conflicting goals turn into personal vendettas, and nothing meaningful can or will be accomplished until the situation is de-escalated, and the affected relationships are reset. People's talents will go unused, and the organisation's services, products and customers will suffer the consequences.

One of the things I'm forever grateful for is that my Year 10 Society and Environment teacher enrolled me in a conflict resolution and mediation competition called SCRAM (school conflict resolution and mediation). For the best part of a year, we were continually presented with conflict scenarios and rotated through playing the warring parties or the mediator seeking to find a resolution. It etched into my muscle memory the framework for how you go about de-escalating a situation and looking to find a path forward. It imbued in me such a love of the process that I have pursued studying the art and craft of mediation ever since.

Depolarisation is at its most constructive when human emotion is expressed constructively in order to allow our humanity back in. We can also be mindful of taking steps to build trust, encourage productive conflict and prevent or deal with the unhelpful friction. Surveying people can be a good way of surfacing observations on team culture. Further, you can implement these strategies.

Welcome dissent that's focused on tasks, strategies and mission

Sometimes bringing in an external provocateur to tease out issues and get beyond surface conversations can be useful. You can also think about how to use anonymous suggestions or comment submissions or calls for questions if you're worried that people may not speak freely otherwise.

Find ways of building your team's appetite for healthy debate and disagreement

We've explored this before – in chapters 18 and 19 – but think about how you consciously build diversity into teams. Consider appointing a rotating devil's advocate – the Israeli 'Tenth Man' tactic – as a good way to stir up productive conflict.

Create accountability

Many disagreements arise because it's not clear who has the final authority to make a decision, so make sure roles are clearly established and communicated.

Empower people to be their own solution

You can't take the perks of working in an empowered organisation if you're not prepared to take on the responsibility. If employees want to be given autonomy to manage their own work, they also need to manage their own conflict.

Provide training

Most of us hate conflict; to be honest, we should probably be a little worried about people who love it. We prefer to be amicable, liked and positive, so conflict often goes unresolved for so long that it becomes a much bigger problem than it needs to be. Given we're better at not doing conflict than doing it, it's unlikely when we periodically find ourselves jumping in that we'll 'nail it'; it'd be like not running for a year and then deciding to put our shoes on and run 5 kilometres (uphill!). We can help people learn the conflict-resolution skills they need by suggesting books, podcasts or even courses. Or merely giving them simple guidance, like preparing in advance the three most important things they want to say about the conflict.

Crucial conversations

Mediation might be too structured an approach for the conflict resolution you find yourself in, and it's hard to be objective about managing a process when you're a party to the subject matter under discussion. In this instance, it can be helpful to have a framework for how to navigate high-stakes conversations. The book I have leant on more times than I can count is *Crucial Conversations* by Kerry Patterson, Joseph Grenny, Ron McMillan and Al Swizler. I first came across the book when I was working in the mining industry, and I had to interact routinely with a manager who did not like me one iota and went out of their way to make my life difficult. I've found that the more times I undertake the process laid out in the book, the more it becomes second nature.

The premise for *Crucial Conversations* intrigued me. The authors had gone on a research expedition seeking to identify the distinguishing features that made high-performing companies stand out. But instead of finding a common management strategy, they discovered that 'the edge' came down to an ability to navigate crucial conversations, be they high stakes or high emotions.

Crucial conversations exist all around us: from performance appraisals to conversations about bullying or harassment. Within our personal lives, too, crucial conversations range from income and lifestyle to conversations about sexual intimacy. Clifford Notarius and Howard Markham, two marriage scholars, examined couples during heated arguments and discovered that people tended to fall into one of three behavioural groups: those who get emotionally drawn in and resort to threats or name-calling; those who silently fume; and those who speak openly, honestly and effectively. Upon analysis, of course, they found those in the third camp were more likely to stay together.

When we look at communities instead of couples, findings have shown that how a community deals with problems is more important than the number of problems they have. If issues are embraced and discussed openly and honestly, communities were 'healthier' than those who tried to ignore them.

As *Crucial Conversations* points out, it is human nature to avoid pain and discomfort. Leading in the working environment is no different. We are often masters at avoiding these conversations, or when we do find ourselves in them, they can bring out the worst in us. We are wired this way genetically through centuries of fighting for survival ahead of intelligent persuasiveness. But research has shown that healthy relationships, careers, organisations and communities all draw from the same source of power: the ability to talk openly about high-stakes, emotional, controversial topics.

Crucial Conversations provides a simple model based on seven steps, four of which I'll focus on here.

Start with the heart (empathy and positive intent)

How we discuss something often matters more than what we discuss. It is easier to change yourself than it is to change another person. To change yourself doesn't mean to diminish your feelings, but it does mean choosing to approach the situation by being 'open' to holding multiple truths simultaneously.

Both verbal and non-verbal communication play a major role. The other person can often sense if you are not being authentic and speaking from a place of respect. But how do we feel respect for a person we don't respect? We need to find and focus on common ground. We can start with our weakness, because we all have weaknesses, and acknowledge that we're all equal in this regard.

Make it safe

This is a powerful idea and tool for me. I'd never consciously thought about the 'safety' of a conversation before. Now I view every important exchange through that lens. *Crucial Conversations* suggests an 'unsafe' conversation causes us to 'close down' and this manifests in three forms: masking (where we pretend to agree or be listening); avoiding (distraction techniques); and withdrawing. We need to be on the lookout for signs that the other person does not feel 'safe' – perhaps a tightening of eyes or a change in energy, language or tone.

People will only be as open as it feels safe for them to do so. And openness is critical to the flow of information: it is the enabler of dialogue.

The biggest takeaway for conducting crucial conversations is the idea of triple processing: content, context and self.

When we sense a situation is becoming unsafe (for example, if someone has created a negative meaning from what's been said), we need to move from the content to the context by staying focused on the desired outcome. A good way to do this is to restate positive intent. For example, 'Can we just switch gear for a minute? My goal here is not to make you feel guilty. My intent is purely to help us both find a way through this together.' The third layer involves a high level of self-awareness as well as self-observation: watching ourselves as if we were watching another person.

Listening, *really* listening, is the key to establishing safety. *Crucial Conversations* offers suggestions like asking, 'I'd really like to get your opinion on . . .' to get the ball rolling or paraphrasing (by saying something like, 'Let me see if I've got this right . . .') as a way of acknowledging their story and getting out of the emotion and into the language.

Don't get hooked by emotion (or hook them)

It is critical not to let our emotions take over. A great way to keep them in check is to acknowledge them. Are we angry? Hurt? Demoralised? When emotions (and words that wound) start flying around, then it's easy to get 'hooked'. To keep from getting hooked there are three things we can do: stay focused on the end goal; refuse to play the game; and avoid the sucker's choice – we can often find ourselves in a situation where we think there are only two solutions: to shut up and let it go; or to express 'brutal' honesty.

To find the middle ground, try the STATE tools:

- Share the facts: 'We can agree that . . .'
- Tell your story: 'The story I'm telling myself about that is . . .'
- Ask for the other person's story: 'I'd appreciate hearing your side . . .'
- Talk tentatively: 'Shall we . . .' or 'Perhaps the most sensible thing to do is . . .'
- Encourage testing: 'So if we both agree that . . .' or 'A logical action may be to . . .'

Separate facts from the story

What is fact and what is opinion? It's worth noting that scores of stories can be created from the same set of facts. The key is avoiding getting stuck in the three unhelpful storyline patterns: victim stories (it's not my fault); villain stories (it's my fault); and helpless stories (there's nothing I can do). The goal is to create a bigger, shared story. Again, *Crucial Conversations* has an easy-to-recall ABC acronym for us:

- Agree: find the areas that you do agree on (people can sometimes obsess on just 5 to 10 per cent points of difference, ignoring the 95 per cent of aligned perspective).
- Build: our education system and culture raise us to be critical, so we are better at tearing things down than building up. The principle of 'yes, and . . .' that we touched on in the last chapter can be incredibly useful here.
- Compare: we should not set up the other person's point of view to be wrong, but just different. Often an opening statement like 'I think I see things differently . . .' helps.

Not only did these steps help me resolve the conflict I was in with my manager at the time, but they provide a framework that I've used in a multitude of contexts in my professional and personal life since.

To borrow Martin Luther King Jr's words: 'Power without love is reckless and abusive, and love without power is sentimental and anaemic. Power at its best is love implementing the demands of justice, and justice at its best is power correcting everything that stands against love.'

A question from the leading edge:

How safe do you make it to invite dialogue about the things that are uncomfortable?

24

Apply critical curiosity

'It's not the answer that enlightens but the question.'

Eugène Ionesco

Have you ever had that moment of meeting someone who is just so kick-ass impressive that you think, 'Jeez, I want to be them when I grow up!' It's got nothing to do with age; I just hope that one day I professionally 'grow up' to the level of capability and contribution of Genevieve Bell. Genevieve is a Doc Marten–wearing, occasional f-bomb-dropping anthropologist best known for her work at the intersection of cultural practice and technological development.

Genevieve is the daughter of renowned Australian anthropologist Diane Bell, and though she was born in Sydney she was raised in a number of Australian communities, including Melbourne, Canberra and in several Indigenous communities in the Northern Territory. She followed her mum's footsteps into anthropology, collecting her master's degree and PhD from Stanford, also teaching Anthropology and Native American Studies at the university while she completed the latter.

At Intel, Genevieve developed User Experience as a practical way of designing for the customer, and a recognised competency in data science. She became a Vice President in 2014 and Senior

Fellow in 2016 and has been inducted into the Women in Technology International Hall of Fame and named one of the 100 Most Creative People in Business by Fast Company. Nowadays, Genevieve is back in Australia disrupting academia by building a whole new branch of engineering at the Australian National University.

Look to history not for answers but better questions

Genevieve fuses a combination of anthropological training and deep understanding of human history and culture with her experience as a pioneering architect of our technological present and future. Who better to quiz on how to ask better questions?

In our interview, Genevieve begins by explaining we have to understand the inherent limitations of most of the questions we're currently asking. First, one of the problems with many questions is they presuppose the shape of the answers: 'Effectively, in the framing of your questions, you're setting the world up for a multiple-choice answer and never an open-ended one.' Often, the way we frame the question also frames the way someone can answer it, because we've dictated the terms and the conceptual model.

When it comes to good questions in the research field, there is some low-hanging fruit in terms of areas for improvement (in increasing degree of difficulty):

- Ask yourself: why am I asking this question? Why now?
- Are you asking your question in a sufficiently open-ended way so you're not predetermining the answer?
- Are you asking questions to open up space or to delay (or delegate) having to take action?

Sitting at a slightly higher order is Genevieve's challenge that we move from 'problem-solving to question-framing'. I like to think of this in talent terms as hiring problem finders, not just problem solvers. This involves suspending our often tightly held opinion that we know the right problem to tackle. Instead what is required is to work out where the right moment for intervention is. 'We have to stop the autopilot of taking the task at hand as the only way the thing can or ought to be done. We have to take a step backwards and sometimes sideways and find a different way to look at the space.' This means undoing habits. As we discussed in Chapter 11, this gets harder to practise the more established you become in your field. 'An important habit of leaders, but a really hard habit to maintain, is to maintain your ability to be surprised and your ability not to know,' Genevieve explains, acknowledging it comes more naturally to her from her background in anthropology. The foundation of ethnographic interviews (the fancy anthropological term for the part of the research where participants are observed in their real-life environment) is:

> being able to allow the person to whom you're talking to be the expert. This means distancing yourself as the questioner, because often asking questions is a power thing. You have the power to ask the question. So how do you frame a question that lets someone else be an expert? Can your line of questioning empower someone else be more relevant or more important than you?

Genevieve credits her mum with instilling this practice in her by encouraging 'critical curiosity'. At the end of every day, instead of asking Genevieve and her sibling what they had learnt that day, she asked, 'What surprised you?' I recommend this becoming a question you ask friends, clients, co-workers and kids – it leads down all sorts of interesting paths. Genevieve explains, 'Because when you're surprised what you're effectively doing is encountering a moment in which the world doesn't work the way you thought it did. Or where your vision of how things should unfold or your knowledge base got challenged, right?'

Despite having critical curiosity hardwired into her as a kid, Genevieve's professional circles have at times worked just as hard to beat the habit out of her. People have told her repeatedly that such vulnerable questions make her look weak. But Genevieve believes few things are more critical for modern leaders than the ability to integrate question-asking into our leadership practices. Once again, when exploring a different angle of leadership on the edge, we come back to the foundation point that it is imperative that people are not afraid to tell us things we don't know – and, conversely, that we're not afraid to ask questions we don't know the answers to.

For Genevieve, as with Reem in Chapter 23, that learning journey starts with understanding history. It is, for example, a misconception that artificial intelligence (AI) is a recent technology. The term was coined in 1956 and people have been theorising about it, research-ing it and developing it ever since. Genevieve reminds us AI was not invented in the last ten minutes by some supernerd in Silicon Valley. But she says we can start to interrogate the history and the clues inextricably linked to who funded it, who built it, where they came from and what problems they were trying to solve. When you under-stand that IBM, Bell Telephone and Rand were at the forefront of the first AI conference, which desperately wanted to create a machine that could make sense of what was then the feared superpower of the communist USSR (both to gain intelligence and launch missiles before they did), you begin to understand that, more than sixty years on, we're still building a thing that was imagined at the height of the Cold War for a very particular purpose. These worl-dviews from the 1950s are built into the technology we are now talking about. It's only through interrogating history that we see the challenges in a system that aren't always visible.

Being able to go backwards in history doesn't necessarily tell you what the answer is, because the world now is completely different to 1956, but it does help generate the questions we should be asking now. For example, who else should be in the room for this conver-sation? Because we know women and ethnic minorities weren't, in 1956. Or how would we think about putting cultural data and ecological data into this conversation? Or are there other people we should be talking to? I've always thought that what history does is let you ask a better set of questions.

Somewhat nervously, I ask Genevieve whether there's such a thing as too big a question. There's a tension in me about how we seek to tackle enormous questions, such as how to combat climate change or end poverty, while simultaneously enabling people not to feel overwhelmed by the scale. Big questions can see people rule themselves out of being able to engage in the conversation, let alone being part of the solution. She quotes from Martin Luther King Jr's 'Letter from Birmingham Jail', one of few examples of the written word that makes the hair on the back of my neck stand up:

> *For years now I have heard the word 'Wait!' It rings in the ear of every Negro with piercing familiarity. This 'Wait' has almost always meant 'Never.' We must come to see, with one of our distinguished jurists, that 'justice too long delayed is justice denied.'*

When people say the question is too big, Genevieve tells me, she hears 'The Letter from Birmingham Jail' ringing in her head and she thinks, *Ask it again.* At a minimum, she believes 'every damn day' we need to be asking ourselves, 'What's the world that we imagined we're building? And who's doing the imagining? And whose interests are being served in that? And the second question that flows from that is: who is that system silent to or unable to see?'

Genevieve finishes our conversation recounting the most alarming bit of data that came across her desk during the COVID pandemic. It was a study about pulse meters (also known as oximeters – they're a little device you put on your finger that reads blood oxygenation). These devices became of critical importance in 2020 because one of the characteristics of COVID is that your oxygen levels drop really low without the accompanying signs and signals;

often, by the time people were arriving at ICUs, they had a much diminished lung capacity without showing the usual symptoms. Pulse meters became one of the go-to tools to assess whether or not COVID patients' lungs were functioning. The technology is simple and has been around in various forms since the 1970s. It basically sends a light pulse through your skin to be able to count the blood flow. Which works like a charm ... if your skin is white. Light goes through black skin, for example, completely differently, meaning the technology that played a critical part in the medical response to the pandemic was systematically not recognising the illness in one of the most vulnerable populations.

Genevieve riles against the chain of unasked questions that brought us to this point.

> In 1950 maybe you didn't know but in 2020 you have no damn excuse. There are no excuses left. There are no uses in 2020 for building technology that doesn't see through black skin or doesn't recognise black faces or systematically disenfranchises Aboriginal people or reproduces inequities against women or poisons the environment or can't hear women's voices or doesn't recognise that people live in wheelchairs or isn't good with forms of cognitive disenfranchisement and disempowerment or doesn't recognise domestic violence or whatever. There are no excuses left. In 2020 there are no reasons you can't know those things.

We all need to learn our history, do our homework and make better questioning part of our leadership practice.

Trust the question and listen beyond the answer

Few people have prompted me to think more deeply about the quality of the questions we ask and their relationship to the answers we give than Malcolm Gladwell. The multi-time *New York Times*–bestselling author of books like *The Tipping Point* and *Outliers* has made a career of reminding us how wrong we can be about what we take for granted as truth. He's challenged an entire generation of leaders to think differently about the world, question our assumptions and take unusual angles on popular subjects that we *think* we know.

I interviewed Malcolm on stage in 2019 at the Energy Disruptors Forum I co-founded in Calgary. We spoke about how to get conversational cut-through in a noisy world, whether distrust is the epidemic it's reported to be and what lessons leaders and innovators are yet to excavate from history.

Against the backdrop of a social media minute (41.6 million messages will be sent over Facebook Messenger and WhatsApp, 347,222 people are scrolling Instagram, 87,500 people posting to Twitter and 4.5 million videos on YouTube are being watched), it's easy to see why people worry that truth is dead and facts are no longer able to be trusted. But Malcolm starts our conversation by rejecting my assertion that it's hard to ask our questions and find real answers amid the noise. He argues that there's never been a better time to seek out and to tell compelling stories about our existence. Paradoxically, though, he argues that the trick to doing so lies not in speaking but in listening.

As Malcolm unpacks his reply, the 'mind of Gladwell' meanders between trust, inequality, social context and cultural subtext. When I inquire whether he believes we have a trust crisis, he emphatically replies 'no'. He points out that fifteen years ago, the concept of hitting a button on a cellular device, waiting for a random car to show up, hopping into said random car, to be driven by a stranger, while relying on a phone to map the correct route and then hopping out with no exchange of money or credit card swiping was simply incomprehensible. It seems trust is crowd-sourced these days; it's not lost, but it has morphed.

Malcolm argues that on a macro level, we are insanely more trusting than we ever have been. We simply don't have the time to walk around wondering if we should trust the bank, if we should trust the childcare helper looking after the kids, if we should trust the cafe owner making our food, or even the Uber driver in charge of our safety. 'Evolution selected us to trust people implicitly unless we are given overwhelming evidence to the contrary,' says Malcolm.

If trust enables us to form groups, communicate and collaborate more effectively, does trust also facilitate us excluding or dismissing alternative people and viewpoints? In the age of the 24-hour news cycle, short-termism and fake news, can we trust what is presented to us by known (aka 'trusted') entities? The modus operandi of echo chamber leaders is not just to close off external voices but also to openly discredit and distrust them. Why? Because trust is oxygen for belief formation; without it, there can be no life. In his latest book, *Talking to Strangers*, Malcolm terms this phenomenon 'default to truth'.

This shortcut route to belief formation means that, often without the time, resources or motivation to make anything other than an assumption, we consume narratives without a lens of critical thinking. How does this affect collaboration with diverse minds? Growth into new markets? Innovative products to new customers? Malcolm suggests that we 'read people from across cultures, the same way we read simplistic TV'. Unless we have some imperative to know what another person thinks, we only ask questions relevant to our answers and we only hear pertinent answers to our questions. In terms of today's need for critical curiosity or disrupt by design, 'like-mindedness' is of course, catastrophic.

As an example, Malcolm discusses tech innovation and the incredibly slow adoption of key inventions such as the telephone. The telephone took a generation to catch on because its inventors did not comprehend the social context of the innovation; they saw it as a business-to-business tool, and modelled it on the telegraph, actively discouraging women from using it and not seeing the value in bringing it to rural areas. It took twenty years from when the technical capability emerged for the phone to find its social footing. Malcolm says, 'Social context wins over technically useful innovation, every time.'

If trust is built on our limited reference points (biologically embedded by clan-living over a few hundred thousand years), the real question for leaders, thinkers, collaborators and decision-makers is, can we trust ourselves?

When we ask a question, we naturally assess the validity of the source: have they done their research, which side of politics do they sit on, what's their real agenda? In this way, questions are the keys to understanding what's not said. But our answers are just as biased and much more commonly trusted as a source of truth. When I ask how we get outside the box to debunk traditional thinking or ask better questions, Malcolm replies, 'if you are willing to do your homework, you will automatically be in a position to tell a story that the rest of the media is not telling.'

I'd suggest that by listening beyond our own need to be heard, we begin to hear and ask better questions. By collaborating beyond the answer we want to hear, we will shift the zeitgeist of what's permissible. We live in the world our questions create. Question wisely.

Methods for better questioning

Whether you've admired the 'a-ha' moment when Denny Crane masterfully corners someone in cross-examination on *Boston Legal* or appreciated how Oprah was able to unlock such extraordinary vulnerability from a guest on her couch, you know not all questions are created equal. But every one of us is capable of powerfully transforming the interactions we're in by asking different questions.

Here are a few useful prompts to think through your intention and pre-prepare questions you might like to ask.

Conversation destinations

I often think about conversation 'destinations' as places I'm eager to visit with a person. These may be based on a personal insight or research, or these may open up while we're in the conversation. Depending on the 'why' of the conversation we're having, I might choose to prioritise one or the other. I will also be factoring in the comfort level I'm sensing. Conversations are an exercise in building trust, so the more I actively listen and the safer I make the other person feel, the more likely they are to open up.

Not landing an outcome

Not every interaction will land you the outcome you want, so it's also important you are able to be present in the journey and find meaning and significance in it. People know when you're half-listening or when you're trying to strong arm a conversation in a pre-determined direction. Here, you're only doing yourself a disservice. Conversations are a dance; you've got to allow your partner to lead and to surprise you.

Open to anything

Being open for me first and foremost means being a blank canvas for the answers the person will offer you. I never order my questions, I trust in the magic of the conversation to organically unfold. Otherwise, I disconnect my listening ability and play a game of conversational ping-pong. To this end, we need to bring questions that keep the ball in play, inviting so much more than a 'yes' or a 'no' (unless we're trying to corner a politician into actually giving their position on a particular subject).

Throughout both seasons of my *Coffee Pods* podcast I always asked my guests the one thing they'd like to encourage listeners to go and do tomorrow. In more than eighty podcasts, I never got close to receiving the same response. When we create the space and offer an open-ended prompt, we're often surprised by what people chose to fill it with.

Share of ourselves first

When it comes to taking a conversation from closed to open, it helps if we lead by example. We can't expect people to share of themselves if we don't initiate by demonstrating some vulnerability too. This tells our counterpart they're not alone. For example, if we're asking someone for honest feedback on how we could improve the culture of the workplace, we might start by sharing a self-reflection on how we could adapt our leadership style to make a contribution.

Finish on a question

One of my favourite things I like to invite audiences and teams to mull over at the end of the conversation or session we've conducted is, 'What's the question I/we didn't ask?' This is a tricky one to throw at people on the spot, but it's a great one to leave as food for thought and to allow people the time and space to circle back with their opinions. Another one I'll often end on after a meeting or strategic planning session is, 'What's the question you're left thinking about?' I find this can be both a useful check and a good way of surfacing questions that didn't arise in the moment.

As leaders deal with more complex, dynamic and unpredictable challenges, we see that having all the answers is now less important than asking the right questions. Where we once thought of questions as purely subjective, and answers as more concretely objective, it's time for a paradigm shift. Questions are rooted in our core and in our collective cause. The change we are leading defines the questions that we ask – ask them deeply. Answers on the other hand, should be flexible, able to change with new information and take in new perspectives. Trust the question. Listen beyond the answer.

A question from the leading edge:

Can you pause, after your brain generates an initial question, and ask yourself, 'What's the better question?'

Mastery

Only once we acknowledge ourselves as part of the system will we become capable of changing it

25

Inspire and empower followership

'One measure of a leader is the calibre of the people who choose to follow them.'

Anon.

Something has always deeply resonated with me about the ability of humankind to move mountains when we come together and inspire and empower others to follow. To me, this is true leadership mastery.

[Sound of a record scratching] . . . Let's be clear, we're not talking in this chapter about mastering Instagram and Twitter followership. Nor are we talking about slacktivism (the lazy follower-building practices supporting a political or social cause by online petitions). We are also not talking about politics: political campaigning is an artform of a different kind (or a gross waste of money, depending on your worldview).

We are talking about the mastery of inspiring others to take action, become part of a movement and lend their own influence. If we can do this, our ideas and organisations can achieve a multiplier effect with a reach beyond those who are already on board.

Inspiring and empowering followership is critical because change is a numbers game – a compounding numbers game. We therefore need to rally a critical mass of people who are committed to making something happen. Change also takes time, so we must build sufficient energy into the system to see an idea through to fruition (we'll touch on this further in the next chapter). We have to find a way not only of inspiring hearts and minds to amplify our voices and strengthen our push for change to carry more weight, but also of sharing the load of the movement to make the momentum sustainable.

The power of the first follower

Before we talk about first follower, we should probably step back for a moment: what even is a 'follower'? A follower is someone who gives full support and loyalty to another. They move or travel behind someone or something and in doing so they give essential momentum and support. In his legendary three-minute TED talk, Derek Sivers, founder of CD Baby, the largest seller of independent music on the web, breaks down the sequence of events that lead to starting a successful movement. His specific focus is on the power of what he terms the 'first follower'. Recruiting this person is so important, Derek suggests, that it'll make or break a movement. Referencing a viral video of a large group of college kids hanging out on the grass at a music festival, Shivers illustrates how a 'shirtless guy' gets a dance movement started, flailing his arms around and looking a bit ridiculous as he dances by himself. But then another guy joins him in the same wild dance, after which a few others get involved and before long, crowds of people are running to be part of the fun. If you haven't seen it, *you* should get involved!

It's this first follower who transforms 'shirtless guy' into a leader, thanks to four factors:

The confident leader

The shirtless guy moves confidently, unafraid to stand out from the crowd or face ridicule. As a leader, you must do the same – when you go, go confidently.

The first follower

Derek explains that the first person to follow a leader is actually displaying an underrated form of leadership: 'Leadership is over-glorified. It's really the first follower who transformed the lone nut into a leader.'

Treat followers as equals

The lone dancer hugged his new friend before starting to dance with him, and that gesture was significant. If you treat the first few followers, often known as early adopters or influencers, as equals, you'll earn their trust and continued loyalty. This in turn leads to others noticing and feeling more comfortable joining in too.

Bring followers into the fold

Once enough people have joined in, the few who haven't usually start to feel uneasy or out of place. When ideas or products reach a tipping point, all of a sudden it's the non-adopters who stand out as though they're the ones on their own.

As Derek observes, first followership is a form of leadership all on its own. When it comes to inspiring followership, we have to hold true to our purpose and remove all the barriers that might exist for people wanting to get on board.

Make following frictionless

Vicki Saunders is an award-winning mentor and leading advocate for entrepreneurship as a way of creating positive transformation in the world. More specifically, Vicki is founder of SheEO, which she describes as a global community of radically generous women supporting women-led ventures working on the World's To Do List. The Canadian powerhouse is one of the World Economic Forum's Global Leaders for Tomorrow. She has the poise and grace of a ballet dancer and the relentless tenacity of a dog with a bone. It's a potent combination.

Vicki was compelled to set up SheEO after observing the treatment of a young female mentee interacting with advisers and funders as she sought to grow her business. People were telling this promising young entrepreneur that she wouldn't be CEO for long, that investors would want to bring in a male CEO. Having taken her own company public, Vicki was all too familiar with the fact that only 2.7 per cent of venture capital goes to women. From 2010 to 2019, the amount of money raised by all-female teams grew to about $6 billion USD from $1 billion, while all-male teams saw funding soar to $195 billion USD from $31 billion. A minuscule 0.2% goes to women of colour. She was determined to ensure the reality for this emerging generation was different to that of her own.

The SheEO model brings together 500 women (called Activators) in each year's cohort, who contribute $1100 as an 'act of radical generosity'. The money is pooled and lent out at 0 per cent interest to five women-led ventures selected by the activators. All ventures generate revenue, have export potential and are creating a better world through their business model or their product and service. The loans are paid back over five years and then lent out again, creating a perpetual fund which, in our interview, Vicki says, 'We will pass on to our daughters, nieces and granddaughters.' The 500 women Activators in each cohort become the de-facto 'team' for the five selected ventures, bringing their buying power as early customers, their expertise and advice and their vast networks to help grow the businesses.

Vicki set an audacious goal when she launched SheEO: she wanted to empower 1 million Activators to back 10,000 female-led ventures and create a $1 billion perpetual fund to support women for generations to come. At its pre-COVID growth rate, the organisation is on track to do that by 2026.

But as Vicki touched on when I spoke with her, the quantum and the momentum that the community have now built belies how difficult the start was.

'The biggest surprise was how hard it was to get the first 500 . . . to build our first community of Activators,' says Vicki.

When we were going to market, we partnered with a bank in Canada and the woman there was a total maverick. She and I spent hours talking about what we were going to do with our waiting list, '*Oh my god, what are we going to do with all the women that are on the waiting list? Because we're only going to do 1000 women.*' Well, that just did not happen. It was super, super tough. I had to do seventy-five events in living rooms and corporate offices to get 500 women to sign up.

In part, Vicki says it was down to the fact that there were so many new components to the model. Not only were women statistically less exposed to investing but, even for those who were familiar with the concept, this was also a very different model. Vicki initially tried explaining everything in one go but she observed that if people found even one thing they didn't like, they'd opt out. This was one of Vicki's most important lessons: do not explain every element, in one go, up-front. Why? First, it was a total information overload; second, all these concerns would and could be dealt with through a culture of continual improvement, so in time would be irrelevant.

The next step for Vicki in empowering a followership was making it as simple as possible to join. All it takes to be an Activator in Canada, the USA, the UK, Australia and New Zealand is $1100. All it takes to apply to be a potential SheEO venture is to be running a female-led business with revenue greater than $50,000 in the currency of whichever country you're in. Just one criterion for each, rather than multiple conditions to meet. When it comes to being an investor, Vicki keeps it simple too: 'Two questions, why you and why now? That's it.'

The more obstacles you can remove from inspiring followership, the less friction there is, the better. Keep it simple and you'll start to scale.

Scale your purpose

As it stands in the world right now, there are an estimated 79.5 million displaced people, half of whom are under the age of eighteen. Wars and climate change are already forcing millions of people to leave their homes every day. By 2050, the World Bank estimates that 143 million people will be displaced by climate change alone.

Not prepared to sit idly and watch, Mark Butcher, then editor-at-large of *TechCrunch* in Europe, posted a call-out on Facebook in response to a 2015 picture showing the lifeless body of a refugee named Aylan on a Turkish beach in 2015 that had gone viral. By Butcher's calculation about 87 per cent of displaced people were living in an area with access to at least 2G or 3G technology, which meant technology had even greater proximity than aid and humanitarian organisations. Butcher decided to call that latent capacity into action. In his post, Butcher urged the tech community to respond to the refugee crisis, proposing an initial action that would begin simply with concerned individuals and organisations sharing information about projects, products, hackathons, events and so on relevant to the topic. A few days later, 300 people were brought together in London for a first conference, followed by a hackathon. Many cities and countries across the world (Oslo, Sydney, Paris, Turin) did the same over the following weeks. Emboldened by the goal of creating technology that empowers displaced people around the world, and guided by the overarching principles of starting with the displaced people (human-centred design), the groups aimed to make their targeted users not only beneficiaries of the technology, but empower them to build it as co-creators.

From those enthusiastic beginnings, Techfugees has grown into a community of more than 18,000 hackers, technologists, humanitarians, academics, entrepreneurs and curious minds running programs and events in twenty-five countries. One in four participants in those networking and creation spaces had a refugee background. Since 2019, Techfugees has also created an accelerated program that would permit refugees to scale up their tech projects through the Global Challenges Competition. Having met some of the incredible people involved in the global movement, let me tell you: they are passion personified. They believe so much in what Techfugees does and they cannot wait to tell you all about it.

There are three main reasons Techfugees has been able to be so successful at scaling its purpose-based followership across many countries.

Guiding principles, local autonomy

Organisational structure protocol is kept at a minimum, with the team instead focused on ensuring all chapters around the world operate according to eight guiding principles, while sensitising and creating the local conditions that can enable their ethical and long-term impact.

It is so refreshing to see the 'club' model leap forward a millennium to a structure without the protocol, hierarchy and procedure of old. This operating model is built on trust and the positive social peer pressure of being part of a visible, impact-oriented global movement. The movement's eight guiding principles are:

- Human-centred design: start with displaced people
- Empowerment: from refugees to Techfugees
- Data governance and transparency: don't collect data for data's sake!
- Open source: sharing is caring
- Inclusive tech: because we are all in this together
- Sustainability: good intentions are great to start with but sustainability is the key to real impact
- Human rights–based approach: integration isn't just about challenges of refugees, it is a (very) political battle too
- No solutionism: remember – tech is just a tool

The Techfugees team believes that if volunteers are living these principles, no further guidelines are required. For anyone wanting to scale and empower followership, it's worth establishing your guiding principles early on. What I like about Techfugees is they provide guardrails to make sure the movement has consistency across the world but they allow a level of autonomy that is empowering to those involved.

Inspire first, then empower

The movement has spawned some incredible success stories. As of early 2020, Techfugees had ideated and accelerated 185 projects since 2015. For example, Refugee Talent, an Australian hackathon winner, is an online platform matching refugees with employers while Bureaucrazy, a German victor, is an official processes translator that helps 'decode' all the various government process and assistance steps refugees have to navigate.

Interestingly, Techfugees found that 33 per cent of projects with support were up and running within a year, versus only 16 per cent of those without support. As Techfugees has grown, the organisation has intentionally built a model that seeks to both involve as many people in hackathons as possible and to wrap support around teams that want to pursue their idea in full. Winners get incubation, funding, mentorship, access to premises, technology perks, visibility and volunteer assistance.

Offer optionality

Through building a network of global partners (from Google Copenhagen to Cisco France) and developing a model where all participating teams pitch to a room full of local stakeholders, Techfugees have seen a lot more ideas gather interest, backing and support than just those anointed the 'winners'. In 2018 they launched a 'workathon' where companies were able as part of their corporate social responsibility to work with the winners of the previous year's Global Challenges competition. Being able to diversify the form of Techfugees has enabled a range of diverse stakeholders to help and contribute in different ways. It's helping tap the organisation into resources and achieve a scale and sophistication of outcomes that would have been much harder to arrive at otherwise.

The takeaway: mastering a followership stems from being purpose-driven, but also allowing that drive to make inroads in different directions. Deliberately create multiple pathways for the destination called impact.

Lessons from the ultimate organiser

Whether we are organising a social movement or rallying support for a new initiative at work, building and mobilising our base is a non-negotiable skillset for leaders hoping to influence. Meet Jane McAlevey, an organiser like no other. Jane is unbelievably good at rallying, empowering and preaching to the 'non-converted'. Organising is the true process by which people come to change their opinions or their views – in other words, it's the work of 'base expansion'. If you've read about Stacey Abrams and her impact on voter participation in the 2020 US election, you've read about organising. Before you can begin to mobilise your already-converted, you need to build a base of support. This is Jane's superpower, though she readily acknowledges in our interview that it's a challenge: 'It puts you in direct contact every day with people who have no shared political values whatsoever and you're often tasked with engaging them at a time of intense politicisation or polarisation.'

Jane has worked across the US and advised around the world, from Fridays for Future to union movements across multiple continents. I first came across her work in a sensational podcast with Vox's Ezra Klein, where Jane gives a masterclass in political organising. I had never heard a leader speak about change the way she does and was struck by how practical and people-first her approach was, and the clarity of her theory of change. She stressed the importance of disciplined process and structure. Most of us, she argues, are capable of building to 90 per cent unity across very diverse people without too much trouble but we don't know the process of how to actually do it.

Fascinated, I reached out and Jane was kind enough to give me a seventy-minute deep-dive into organising, from which I took three big learnings in particular:

Lesson 1: Nothing matters more than trust

When Jane was a young organiser she made the decision to live and work in every part of the US: 'Every single corner, and in the middle and everything in between.' She knew she wanted to be a national organiser and influence national policy, so she strategically and consciously moved to different parts of the country to understand the very different cultures that exist: you can't organise if you don't understand where people come from.

It was at a chance visit to the civil rights archives at the Highlander Centre, a social justice training school in Tennessee, where Jane heard the story of the civil rights movement told a different way for the first time. She learnt of all of the incredible black women who were trusted leaders in their churches, informally because they didn't and couldn't have the title of minister, but who were actually doing the work of getting people out to march in the streets, rallying the masses for boycotts. It was then that a seed was planted in Jane's mind: followership is a relationship that starts and ends with trust.

Ever since, in every situation Jane has found herself in, her formula for organising successfully has been to focus on finding the people who elicit trust, and figure out what else needs to be done to help them go from leading some to leading many.

Lesson 2: Raise an organic leader's expectations and form a collective identity

Most of the time, an organic leader isn't interested in being a part of collective action. They're talented and more often than not their employer already knows it. If they're reluctant to the idea of collective action or taking a stand, you can bet your bottom dollar they're going to resist being in any sort of official leadership role. Your conversation with them has to do two things:

- Start with their own self-interest and help them to go beyond: What do they want to change? While not everyone has an opinion on what they'd change about, say, the entire nation's insurance policy, everyone has things they'd change about their workplace. Or street. Or community. Building a bridge from individual to collective identity starts with truly understanding what matters to them. That forms your foundation.

- Connecting participation to an outcome: This involves painting a really clear picture for people of how it's only with their participation that we stand a chance of solving the problem. Jane says this goes hand-in-hand with helping organic leaders understand who they are and the role that they play – maybe they don't understand the influence they already have or, because they haven't 'chosen' leadership, they don't want to be put into a position where they have to play a different part. 'It's about showing them the results of their work, whereby they actually start to comprehend that they're playing a much bigger role than they realised.'

Lesson 3: Use structure to build durable power

Jane describes this as the first test of informal leadership. Can a person 'bring out' (whether in signatures or presence at a protest) a majority of their colleagues/network/community and lead them to action? After all, having 25,000 people turn out for a climate rally is great but if you can't follow up with them, you've got very little return for effort. Durable power requires building a community whom you can rally, re-energise and redirect to future activities and campaigns. Protests, she says, are 'feel-good politics': they're great but they're not going to change the power structure. You've got to get more concrete.

For example, when advising Greta Thunberg's 'Fridays for the Future' group, who famously stage school walk-outs on Fridays, Jane counselled Greta not to change the group but intentionally structure the way she was organising. Starting to build a network based on a school-by-school infrastructure would add up to a neighbourhood-by-neighbourhood infrastructure and, in the case of students, allow Greta to organise parents as well. 'You need to build durable, long-lasting power that is sustainable and repeatable. And power like that needs structure.'

Jane is frequently asked about the viability of this advice for environments that don't naturally lend themselves to structure. She advises: 'You must look at everything as a way to build structure. Unless and until you create a human structure against which you can measure, you don't know what you're doing, or what it's adding up to. You have to start to think about human social relationships, which is what organisers do, and how to chart and systematise them.'

Lesson 4: Build a coalition of the trusted

Key to all of the above is identifying the natural, organic leaders. And as I've learnt, in corporate contexts as much as in civil society, they're often not the people with the fancy titles. We're talking about the people that are most trusted. The people who are turned to when someone has a problem. The people other people ask the opinion of when a situation arises, because they're sort of the organisational barometer. It's got nothing to do with who makes a great speech or who's first to offer their opinion in a meeting.

We need to be careful not to view belief in a cause as an audition for being the ultimate first follower. Instead, we must bear in mind, that the ultimate first followers are people whom others trust. These community pillars are the ones who will inspire ever-greater followership.

'If young people can learn two things,' Jane tells me, 'it's how to understand who's an activist versus who's a high-capacity informal, trusted leader; and then how you can actually move that person. That's the art.' We can learn a lot about followership and how to cultivate our own high-capacity informal, trusted leadership in a way that would encourage others to follow, by tracing our own patterns of followership. I believe that just as good mentors are simultaneously mentees, good leaders are simultaneously good followers. When I think about the people I've followed, they are all people of the utmost integrity, who exude an infectious passion for their cause and for whom I'd walk to the ends of the earth if they needed me to.

Followership is always a two-way flow: I draw energy from the movement even as I give my all to sustain it. Rather than the spark and fuel of a combustion engine, sustainable followership is like clean energy storage, ready to supercharge your power supply when you need it. If you have these first followers around you, don't ever let them go. Treat them as the under-acknowledged leaders you know them to be.

A question from the leading edge:

How are you embracing and empowering your followers?

26
Sustain momentum

'It's not about speed; it's about momentum.'

Anon.

I went to circus school when I was a kid (yep, I was *that* cool!). I was staying with my uncle and cousin for a week and, probably at a loss of what to do with a pair of bored tweens, my uncle enrolled the two of us in circus school. It was awesome and, amazingly, there's a lot of it I still use now to provide analogies for the ways I think, or as part of my own practices. For example, I have found few more powerful mindfulness activities than juggling. I'm convinced you cannot be in your head and juggle four balls at the same time (though most of us feel like this perpetually at work!). If you check my suitcase, you find that to this day I always travel with juggling balls.

Circus school was also the first time I'd tried slacklining, whereby you rig up a 'line' close to the ground between two trees and then attempt to walk across it. You might have seen people doing it in the park and making it look easy, but I find it insanely hard because it is so dynamic. There will be a momentary glimmer of balance – a microsecond of stability – and then in the next instant you're totally off-kilter again. (I faceplanted into the grass several times.) Lifting and tentatively placing your feet, one in front of the other, humbles you because at no point is making it across a sure thing. And while confidence is critical, if you get cocky and lose focus you're done for. The more you can sensitise yourself to the minor tremors in the line and intuit how you need to respond to them (do I need to adjust? Can I just ride it out?), the more likely you are to stop minor tremors from becoming major shakes in the line that will cause you to topple.

This is the tightrope all leaders of change must walk. You're not just managing your own expectations, you're managing your people's, which means treading a fine line between being transparent about just how challenging you're finding the initiative, and giving people the hope and aspiration to sustain momentum. The best leaders I've met not only have the vision for the evolution that's needed, but also understand the dynamic slackline they are walking. They are able to keep iterating strategies to spur their teams on and maintain balance when those inevitable tremors threaten confidence and progress.

Make change real

While we have explored implementing change in Chapter 21, it is precisely during times of change that challenges of sustaining momentum are highlighted. Someone who has experienced this in one of Australia's largest organisations is David Thodey, one of the giants of Australian business. The former managing director of IBM, with a degree in social anthropology and computer programming, is one of the most respected chairmen in the nation. But David is probably best known for his turnaround leadership of Australian telco giant, Telstra. When David came to Telstra, their net promoter scores (the ones that ask whether you'd recommend the company to your family and friends) would have made most business executives cry. Public sentiment was so bad that Telstra employees would change out of their uniforms before they travelled home on public transport. David walked into an organisation that was beyond change fatigue, he tells me; they had severe 30/60/90-day plan burnout and 'time for transformation' trauma-induced exhaustion.

David recognised that cynicism about change arises when people are continually being pitched a message about organisational culture that's at complete odds with the everyday behaviour. For David, tackling the two big issues of customer malaise and internal cultural change aligned in what he called a 'customer connection' program. David knew he needed to align the change behind a single thought; when he stepped back, he realised Telstra was all about connecting people.

'We were suddenly able to have really honest discussions with each other about what our customers were saying and what the change in our culture needed to look like.' From this place of trust and honesty, David led the team to imagine what being 'customer connected' at every level of the business would look like. The focus on tangible changes brought the workforce together and created a new momentum. 'And that was very powerful, but it wasn't easy. It took probably two to three years to get through it. But that momentum grew and grew and grew.'

In parallel to the cultural change program, David and his executives pitched an audacious idea to the board: customer-centricity and customer advocacy should be the number one metric and target in the organisation, and everything should be redesigned accordingly. They knew that to drive fundamental change there needed to be an accountability system alongside the shifting values. David describes it as a huge, gutsy decision for the board. 'We made the decision to pay our employees more based on customer service than we did on financial results. And to do that, you have to really believe that satisfied customers buy more from you and stay with you for longer.'

Change extends far beyond digitisation and market volatility, as David points out. People and markets are always changing, and in whatever context we're leading, we will need to sustain this momentum of adaptation alongside our customer. 'The big question is, how do you create an organisation that doesn't lurch from a burning platform to a transformation into another transformation?

We need to create organisations that are sustainable, that are sort of self-regulating.' But the 'agile 'organisation of today is continually judging itself by the market, not by what we think of ourselves. David says that as a leader of change, 'You're about an orientation of never quite there, because you never arrive with customers, customers are that demanding.'

David's bold and long-term approach to revolutionising Telstra was successful: Telstra's value more than doubled from below $40 billion to above $80 billion while he was in charge. For him, the years-long process reinforced that mastering sustainable change requires three things.

Start with yourself first

If you don't start from an authentic and sustainable place, you'll never gain momentum let alone keep up the pace. Change is unsettling for everyone, at all levels of an organisation. When it's on the cards, everyone looks to the CEO and leadership team for support and guidance. If you as a leader can embrace change first, you can motivate others while also setting the tone and modelling the new behaviours and expectations.

Deal systematically with the 'human side'

The ten principles for change management by John Jones, DeAnne Aguirre and Matthew Calderstone state, 'New leaders will be asked to step up; jobs will be changed; new skills and capabilities must be developed; and employees will be uncertain and resistant. Dealing with these issues on a reactive, case-by-case basis puts speed, morale and results at risk.' A formal approach for supporting people through change – beginning with the leadership team and then engaging key stakeholders – should be developed early, and adapted in response to highly disciplined data collection and analysis, planning and implementation. As the change evolves, so do the 'human' impacts, whether they be upskilling, mental health or role transition. This process will need to be continually revisited so it adds (and doesn't detract) from momentum.

Be clear on the values and the vision

Being able to articulate why change is required and writing a formal vision statement can help you ensure everyone is on the same page. The three steps set out by Jones, Aguirre and Calderstone can help you do this:

- 'Confront reality and articulate a convincing need for change.
- Demonstrate faith that the company has a viable future and trust in the leadership to get us there.
- Provide a roadmap to guide behaviour and decision-making. Leaders must then customise this message for various internal audiences, describing the pending change, in terms that matter to the individuals.' Having a compelling destination and a clear roadmap (that you can track progress against) are key to maintaining momentum.

Transformation requires consistent energy and enthusiasm over a period of time, and you often need to remind everyone involved of the significant opportunities that lie ahead. But all too often, change efforts start with a big bang, and quickly lose their firepower when people declare victory too soon. When it comes to losing the momentum for change, there are few things that undermine our efforts so much as words that lack the backing of ongoing action. To sustain that forward impetus, we need to combine an audacious aspiration with tangible signs of hope and progress that demonstrate to our followers how far we've come.

Continual 'chunking'

A major threat to sustained momentum with change initiatives is lack of bandwidth. Everyone is so busy with their existing portfolio of work that change slips through the cracks. That's where chunking change down into manageable parts can help.

In conjunction with a number of companies who were looking to find a way of building momentum for 'new', I've developed a simple tool called 24/7/1. These organisations understand that innovation is essential to the ongoing viability of their business and important enough to take beyond mere lip service, but struggled to find a simple structure that didn't require massive distraction . . . or at least that didn't involve dreaded Gantt charts.

Instead, 24/7/1 builds momentum.

24: Day One, pick your target

It could be the rollout of the new company strategy, a company value you want to see embodied more or a new behaviour you want to drive. Within twenty-four hours, you have to take an initial step towards doing something about it. Whatever it is, it needs to be a step so small (i.e. utterly doable) that it's inexcusable for you not to get it done within twenty-four hours.

7: Week One, the bold next step

This time, you will want to take a more significant action step. You might meet one of the people you connected with for a conversation, or swap your usual role for a day for one that's customer-facing and can ground you in customer feedback. Whatever it is, it's slightly bigger than the twenty-four-hour action step but still eminently doable within a week.

1: Month One, pilot change

You need to take an even bigger action step this time. You might make a change to your operational plan based on the conversations you've had with the seasoned innovators. Perhaps you might pick a low-hanging-fruit example of one of the pieces of customer feedback and attempt to pilot a solution. Whatever you choose, it needs to be bigger than the twenty-four-hour and the seven-day action steps, but achievable within a month. And at the end of that month, you need to take all your insights, learnings, connections and experiences and roll that into the creation of a new 24/7/1.

Some organisations I know have chosen to make this method part of their operating rhythm and internal learning culture by creating start-of-month 24/7/1 meet-ups. By allowing people both to reflect on steps and progress made and to make a commitment to the month ahead, they find the exercise both engages positive social peer pressure and also allows the learnings to be collective. The tool can scale behaviour change in a positive and sustainable way.

Learn from Mother Nature

You might have heard terms like 'bio-empathy' and 'bio-mimicry' start to punctuate leadership conversations in environmentally conscious organisations. Bio-mimicry involves learning from strategies found in nature and mimicking them to solve human design challenges. After all, as Janine Benyus, a biologist and one of the leaders of the global bio-mimicry movement, points out, 'When we look at what is truly sustainable, the only real model that has worked over long periods of time is the natural world.' Bio-empathy is defined more broadly as seeing things from nature's point of view and understanding and learning from its patterns.

When we consider growth through a natural lens, we think fundamentally differently from when we view it through the traditional leadership (or capitalist) model of getting bigger, going faster, being busier. The prevailing corporate structure is one of competing and racing and consuming in silos where we don't connect our actions beyond our immediate productivity system. Nature, by contrast, grows in cycles. The seasons hold expansion, and decline. Waste and compost also become part of growth. Nature is competitive, fiercely so, but in a way that maintains the balance of the whole, and that doesn't allow the overall ecosystem to degrade. While humans maximise, nature optimises. Nature's natural restorative properties allow for rejuvenation and renewal: something we could learn from! There's a movement gaining traction that argues 'bio-leadership' is the right way forward – and perhaps the only one.

Examples abound everywhere of leaders who are already doing this. In Chapter 1 we discussed Simon Sinek's 'infinite game', where the concept of winning is not focused on competition but on the evolution of the game. For example, when one of the world's fastest trains (the Shinkansen Bullet, which moves at up to 320 kilometres per hour between Tokyo and Kyoto) faced a noise problem, the project's chief engineer, Eiji Nakatsu, sought to learn from nature. Every time the train emerged from a tunnel, the pressure change produced an almighty thunderclap that was causing residents 400 metres away to complain. Nakatsu, who (like my best friend) happens to be an avid ornithologist, wondered whether there was something in nature that travelled quickly and smoothly between mediums. The answer? The humble kingfisher. By modelling the front end of the train after the beak of the kingfisher (which dives into the water with a minimal splash to feast on fish), the train not only got quieter but also uses 15 per cent less electricity and runs 10 per cent faster.

Becoming a bio-empathic leader

In addition to learning from nature to shape our leadership, bio-empathy challenges us to take a more sustainable, holistic approach to the work that we do. Bio-leadership can be summed up with three core pillars:

- Change through ourselves: as agents of action
- Change through our communities: influencing action through our broader organisations, systems and planet
- Change through a new paradigm of leadership: readjusting the lens and narrative through which we define progress and success in the world

Companies looking to embrace bio-leadership are taking on these changes, from overhauling their supply chains to be more ethical and sustainable to entirely redefining their reason for existing around a much more conscious mission statement. Ben and Jerry's Ice-cream, for example, came out in support of the Paris Climate Accord in 2015, adopting a new climate goal across its entire value chain and aptly titling its campaign, 'If it's melted, it's ruined'. The company has installed a solar array at its Vermont factory that generates one-third of that plant's electricity plus a bio-digester in its Dutch factory that turns ice-cream waste from the manufacturing processes into clean energy that helps power the plant. The company is also helping pioneer technology for climate-friendly (i.e. Hydrochloro-fluorocarbon free) freezer cases as part of their aspiration to make the finest quality ice cream using business practices that promote and respect the earth and the environment.

On an individual level, there are probably few better examples of bio-leadership than Paul Polman. As Unilever's CEO, Paul has become a prominent voice on corporate social responsibility. When Paul took over Unilever, he stopped issuing quarterly guidance, signalling to Wall Street that he was not going to make decisions to improve the short-term stock price. He then began rolling out the Sustainable Living Plan, a long-term strategy to make Unilever a more environmentally and socially responsible business. The ten-year plan charted three main goals: improving the health and well-being of more than one billion people by 2020; reducing the company's environmental impact by half by 2020; and improving the economic livelihoods of millions of women and smallholder farmers in Unilever's supply chain by 2020. While the company didn't hit all of its targets, it did manage to reach 1.3 billion people through its health and hygiene programs, reduce consumer waste of its products by 32 per cent, and achieve zero waste to landfill across all factories. It also reduced greenhouse gas emissions from its own manufacturing by 65 per cent, and achieved 100 per cent renewable grid electricity across all sites.

Importantly, the Sustainable Living Plan was both purposeful and profitable, a trait of the balance inherent in bio-leadership. For example, Domestos is a toilet cleaner sold in thirty-five countries that aims to enhance health and wellbeing by improving sanitation. The Domestos business unit committed to help 25 million people around the world gain access to toilets by 2020 and it set up the multi-sectoral Toilet Board Coalition to pursue this. Amazingly, the coalition managed to exceed expectations and improve sanitation access for 28 million people. The key chemical compound has minimal environmental impact because of its rapid degradation, but even then, Unilever has announced a £1 billion effort to implement a cleaning range free of fossil fuels. Unilever are convinced that their purposeful, planet-friendly business is more profitable. After all, building more toilets potentially means more sales of toilet cleaner.

Given the rising importance of purpose across life and work for employees, bio-leadership is not just about tapping into purpose for progress; it's also about establishing new organisational eco-systems that allow for more adaptive, connected and regenerative ways of sustaining the momentum of change.

To build genuinely sustainable momentum, we need to create the space to properly explore what being 'sustainable' means when it comes to people, planet and profit in our respective contexts. Take a moment to conduct an audit of your current activities and their impacts across people, planet and profit: is there an area where you could set a goal to shake up the way that you do things for the better? What would a more sustainable way of doing things look like?

Cultivate an attitude that sustains you

Unhappy leaders do not create happy work environments. It's hard to achieve much of anything from a place of unhappiness.

The importance of happiness features prominently in the career reflections of Gail Kelly. When she was in her early twenties,

Gail Kelly was deeply unhappy, teaching Latin at a school in Johannesburg, South Africa. Recognising the need for a sustainable career, she left at the end of the term to begin work instead as a bank teller. On 1 February 2015, she retired as CEO of Westpac, Australia's second-largest bank and the twelfth largest bank in the world in terms of market capitalisation, with $651.4 billion in assets and 40,000 employees. During her career, she was named the eighth most powerful woman in the world by Forbes, collected several honorary doctorates and Best Financial Service Executive of the Year awards, and raised four children (including triplets!) with her husband, Allan. During her time as CEO she had to lead the business through numerous initiatives to remain relevant to the ever-changing needs of customers and their increasingly technology-fuelled lives. Gail's journey is remarkable, and her advice when we speak is invaluable, in terms of how to navigate the personal challenges of leading any substantial, long-term change initiative:

Always find a passion point (for you and your people)

Gail talks a lot about loving what you do and doing what you love. This doesn't mean that you love every moment of every day, but it does mean that a core pillar of what you do must energise you. That way, you are tapping into your fuel storage every day.

Early in her banking career, Gail was tasked with leading 'the new Peoples Bank'. Nelson Mandela was two years into his presidency, the system of apartheid in South Africa was falling and the workforce was becoming more diverse each day with a blend of Zulus, Indians, Xhosas and returning fighters from various areas. Gail sought to hire staff from different backgrounds to ensure employees matched local customers. 'They were all coming into the workforce. The key focus was aligning people with a common interest,' she explained to me. To do this, Gail looked at what Mandela was doing at the macro scale. Basic strategies like storytelling workshops allowed people to realise that they cared about the same core things, such as family and jobs. They could connect around these passion points as a common reason to turn up to work each day.

Choose to be positive

Gail's philosophy is, 'You must stand guard at the door of your own mind and choose to be positive.' She notes that people sometimes roll their eyes when they hear her say 'choose to be positive' as one of the single most important lessons of her career, but her career experience suggests all too few people make that choice. Gail has met people who are at the professional pinnacle of their field of endeavour but who are deeply unhappy. For all they might have gained in terms of rungs up the career ladder or increase in the size of their pay, many, she reflects, have lost so much, including friends, partners, health – the things that are so crucial to sustain us.

Gail shared with me a habit she built to ground herself every day before she crossed the threshold into her home. Gail would drive into the carport each evening and, whether she'd had a bad day or not, she would sit in her car for a moment and fold down the car mirror in front of her in the driver's seat. There, on a sticky note, she had written: 'I can choose the attitude that I bring home tonight.' And then she would say out loud to herself, 'I choose to be positive. I choose to be warm. I choose to be welcoming.' And then she'd walk inside to her family.

Pick the right people to share the trenches with

Early in her career; Gail recalls listening to Jack Welch (the infamous CEO of GE) speak of a generosity gene, a gene Welch believed either was in you or wasn't. Gail inherently believes leaders need to provide evidence of generosity of spirit. She says, 'I'm playing a leading, steering, guiding and cheerleading role in lots of ways.' But equally, having the right people in the right roles means changing up team members, rotating the advisers that are providing us with insights, and creating a natural wave of renewable energy around us.

The key is this: every organisation needs to support its employees in the process of making transitions or changes. Nobody gives up power willingly. Inevitably change will involve some trauma because power, prestige, control and influence will be affected to some degree. Understanding where change is taking people and being cognisant of the different ways we can steer it gives us a higher chance of sustaining momentum.

Ultimately, the message of momentum that we as leaders need to unite our people around is this:

> *Kua tawhiti kē to haerenga mai,*
> *kia kore e haere tonu.*
> *He nui rawa o mahi,*
> *kia kore e mahi tonu.*
> We have come too far to not go further
> We have done too much to not to do more.
> (*Ta Hemi Henare* – Sir James Henare)

A question from the leading edge:

Supposing change is a long road, what can you do to embed sustainability into your business model, your ideas, your leadership or your movement?

27
Think in systems

'One's got to change the system, or one changes nothing.'

George Orwell

I adore kids. In my work and in writing *The Leading Edge* I've spent a lot of time with the next generation. Researching new world leadership has made me think deeply about the world they're going to inherit. I find their refreshing, unfiltered perspectives enlighten and challenge me. I also put a lot of credence in the line, 'If you can't explain it to a six-year-old, you don't understand it yourself'. When it comes to comprehending our work as a small section of a much larger, complex system, there's nothing quite like a child to remind you to stay focused on the bigger picture.

One morning, as a guest educator for a day, I was helping make macaroni necklaces. I say 'helping' but I might have been inadvertently making things worse because our attempts to glue the parts of the necklace puzzle were failing miserably. It just kept falling apart! Suddenly, a flame-haired student by the name of Gabriella tapped me on the shoulder. 'Maybe we shouldn't always try and fix broken things. Maybe we should start over and create something better,' she suggested. Suddenly macaroni art took on a whole new level of meaning.

We often bemoan broken systems. We also often don't have the luxury of deciding to press 'reset' and start over. But Gabriella's comment struck me as a reflection of profound importance for the kind of work that aims to tackle complex, large-scale problems. Ask yourself: are you focusing your efforts and energy on the right thing? Are you aware of the bigger system you're playing in?

What is systems thinking?

As one of the modern fathers of systems thinking, Peter Senge, puts it: systems thinking is a discipline for seeing wholes. It is a framework for seeing interrelationships rather than things, for seeing 'patterns of change' rather than static 'snapshots'. Systems thinking is challenging. We're juggling lots of different parts that have an array of interdependencies, which is why people often shy away from systems change: it's often a lot easier to just zone in on a part than to contend with the sum of all of them. But if we're going to solve intractable problems, we've got to be able to understand and think in systems, otherwise we risk developing solutions that are ineffective, take more time or resources to implement, or even make problems worse. This is why systems change sits squarely in the 'Mastery' section of this book.

Systems can be natural or human-made (for example the solar system or the railway system that connects a city), but when we talk about 'systems change' in this context, we're talking about deliberate intervention to transform a system's fundamental behaviour so that a new pattern can emerge. As an article from the World Economic Forum explains, 'Transforming a complex system – such as the energy, health or food system – is a monumental task requiring coordinated action from people with very different viewpoints. Systems-change initiatives often engage hundreds of organisations – governments, companies, civil society organisations, worker associations, research institutions and others – combining their capacities to achieve a shared goal.'

In my experience, ineffective leaders try to directly initiate change whereas more successful system leaders focus on creating conditions that can produce or foster change. In this way, change can eventually be self-sustaining. Systems leaders catalyse and empower collective action in others, rather than controlling or directing the action themselves.

Changing the world one STREAT at a time

Bec Scott, the co-founder and CEO of STREAT, is a shining example of a systems-change thinker at work. She was frustrated by the state of youth unemployment and homelessness in Australia, neither of which are new issues, unfortunately, and incredulous at how many people are still attempting to solve complex, interdependent problems like these with fragmented or siloed solutions. In our interview, Bec tells me it isn't uncommon to meet a young person who has ten different caseworkers across ten different services, none of whom is talking to another or even aware that the others exist. 'The problem is not that these young people are missing and invisible to the system. They're in the system, and an enormous amount of money is being spent on them in that system, and yet they're *still* in crisis.'

To start fixing a system, you've got to understand the barriers to change and your distinct advantage. Bec was determined to take effective action and she could see that the two most significant obstacles were the legacy issues of how the system operates and the funding model that perpetuates 'the tail wagging the dog'. Some community housing organisations, for example, are funded for the number of kids they house that means, ultimately, they're incentivised to enable a high turnover of young people as opposed to working on finding a permanent pathway out of crisis accommodation.

So, in 2008, Bec and her partner Kate started STREAT, a social enterprise aimed at giving disadvantaged young people the life skills, training and work experience they need to achieve some of their personal goals. Bec intentionally chose the social enterprise structure so she would have the freedom to innovate in a way that organisations that depend on government funding can't, having been told early on that STREAT's non-traditional work was 'too innovative for the government's innovation funding . . . that about sums it up!' she says with a smile.

In 2010 they launched their first venture, a coffee and food cart in Melbourne's Federation Square. The business employed young people at risk, with profits reinvested back into creating more opportunities through the STREAT organisation. The pitch to customers was simple: you need to eat, so why not eat with STREAT and help support disadvantaged young people at the same time? Since then, Bec and the team have built a portfolio of twelve businesses, across which they've served over 3 million meals, and provided over 250,000 hours of training to more than 3000 young people. And while they've provided their youth with a lot of practical support, such as finding stable housing, vocational skills, improved mental health and wellbeing – they consistently hear that the most important thing they've provided is a sense of belonging.

Bec has been completely purpose-driven right from the start, and I love how she entered into her endeavour with her eyes open to the systemic nature of these social challenges and a determination to try a different approach. Here are some of the strategies she identifies behind STREAT's success.

Get the goalposts right

STREAT's first goal was a ten-year one: to change the equivalent of a life every mealtime. That means 1095 kids a year or nearly 11,000 in their first decade of operation, which seemed an enormous number at the time. 'Your goal has got to be near enough that you could imagine sticking at the problem for the foreseeable future,' she explains, 'but hard enough that you're going to lie awake at night and go, "*How the hell is this possible?!*"' That's the sign that you're being radical enough with your wholesale idea. Incremental change doesn't catalyse systems thinking. Systems problems are those that demand big doses of creativity.

Learn from people on the margins

Bec believes this is an extraordinary power that we're not currently leveraging to change systems. 'Something happens when you're a kid on the margins and you're not used to being a part of the system, or you haven't got privilege – there's this sense of liminality. You're used to your head always sitting in a different space. In my case, it was being the queer kid in the highly religious town.'

Bec thinks this is part of why we're starting to see such great innovation from the social enterprise sector where, in Australia at least, half are run by women and founders are more culturally and linguistically diverse than in the traditional business sector.

> Marginalisation brings with it some extraordinary superpowers: extra empathy and compassion being two. People who know what it's like to have to try to survive have got some extraordinary skills: street savviness, survivorship, an ability to adapt and innovate that's nothing short of extraordinary. They also know why the systems are broken, and not in an academic or a theoretical way . . . because it's them the system 'broke' on.

If you don't have people from the 'margins' involved in your work already, think about how you can engage them (perhaps in a research or facilitator capacity) to begin to tap into these learnings and skills.

Pick a goal that has as much relevance to the customer as the team

If you do, everyone will want to come on the journey with you. To Bec, this is key to giving your organisation a touch stone and provides you as its leader with a story to keep telling, internally and externally. This sense of purpose enables 'a culture of bravery and a preparedness to give things a crack'.

Core to STREAT's success has been allowing customers to take a micro-moment of bravery and then connecting their values and identity to a bigger community. Early in STREAT's evolution, it conducted research with a partner organisation to understand what made customers come into STREAT. The research discovered two things:

- People who just came in to buy a coffee each morning were overwhelmed when you talked to them about the size of the problem they were helping to tackle. They didn't feel like they were making a dent.
- When the impact for all the STREAT coffee cart sites across Melbourne was aggregated, seeing that bigger combined number flipped hopelessness to optimism. People felt part of a positive movement and saw their decision as having significance in a way they hadn't before.

As a result, STREAT built a 'counter' to make the impact tangible, a machine that allowed customers to see their impact as they made their purchase. Photos of the young people being affected by STREAT appeared, showing numbers of the lives helped, 'So you never ever forgot that these are real humans.' The numbers aggregated all the STREAT sites in real time, meaning the numbers would accumulate and spin super-fast. People could viscerally feel that all around the city there were people making this same generous decision on this morning. Bec says that, in the customer's eyes, she could see them register, 'I'm not alone. And collectively today, we've made the change.'

What I think Bec and the STREAT team's story illustrates so beautifully is how you need first to understand the existing system and its shortcomings, and then create a solution that's systems-based and connects the components you've identified. Systems change is an ongoing and delicate balance between trying to get an individual to take that first micro action, and then scaling it by triggering a web of impact. It requires leaders with big vision and even bigger curiosity, not just to ask questions and chase answers from a variety of vantage points but also to effectively deploy those different skills and capabilities. Systems change is powered by empowerment.

Design to disrupt

Cyrill Gutsch is an award-winning designer, brand builder and product developer. Cyrill's life and career direction changed dramatically in 2012, when 'the German-born New Yorker learnt about the threat that ocean plastic poses to sea life from environmentalist Paul Watson'. Paul had been arrested by the German government for confronting the Japanese whaling fleet, putting his life at risk, in order to protect whales.

For Cyrill, the meeting awakened a deep-seated passion for the environmental cause. Up to that point, he admits in our interview that he had been totally preoccupied with his own career, 'and making money and winning awards and just ego-shooting'. Paul painted a grim picture for him of the looming reality: according to two leading marine scientists, without an urgent change to the status quo all life in the ocean will effectively collapse by 2048. Cyrill felt prepared to take on the challenge; the need for systems change was crystal clear.

Not one to sit on his hands, Cyrill converted his agency from a design company to an environmental organisation pretty much overnight. 'My partners and I decided that we were going to stop what we do, and now fight for the sea.' They believed the power for change lay in the hands of the consumer and that creative industries could shape this consumer mindset. Parley for the Oceans was born, to encourage other creatives to repurpose ocean waste, and find alternatives to plastic.

When I met Cyrill, hosting the Virgin Disruptors in London in 2016, I was blown away by the passion and conviction with which he spoke. As audacious as his goal seemed, his tone suggested it was eminently doable.

The truth is, at this moment we are sitting on the edge, and we are about to fall into this big black hole. And it's a beautiful moment because there's a lot of tension and that's what we need.

Behind every environmental problem we are looking at right now that's threatening our seas is a faulty, old-school and exploitative business model. It is up to us to come up with a new design concept.

According to Cyrill, plastic in and of itself is a design failure. The Parley for the Oceans team concluded it needed 'to find ways to synchronise the economic system of humankind with the ecosystem of nature, and make environmental protection fiscally lucrative for pacesetting companies'. In the way of the circular economy, the team wanted to invent its way out of systems failure.

Parley for the Oceans' approach was to make the strategy as simple as possible. The result is affectionately known as AIR: avoid, intercept and redesign.

Part of Cyrill's systems-based approach was to find one player in each market segment, in each consumer category, who redefines the rules. They would partner with them to question the way things were currently being done and rethink them, then find a way to make it profitable so the impact could scale. Parley for the Oceans' founding partner was Adidas. Together, Parley and Adidas launched their partnership and commitment to their shared vision at the United Nations in 2015 by unveiling a concept shoe made from reclaimed marine plastic waste. 'The Ultra Boost prototype featured an upper made of yarns and filaments reclaimed and recycled from ocean waste and illegal deep-sea gillnets.' The partners immediately began investing in research to bring the concept shoe and upcycled plastic into Adidas's global supply chain at a level that would make a real impact.

The Adidas Group also worked to phase out plastic bags in all of its retail stores within a year and, together with its partner COTY, stopped using plastic microbeads in licensed body-care products and asked staff to stop using plastic bottles in all meetings at its headquarters.

Meanwhile, Parley continued with the development of the world's first supply chain for upcycled marine waste, creating Ocean Plastic, which was used to produce 1 million pairs of Adidas shoes in 2017. In 2020, 15 million pairs of shoes were produced with Parley Ocean Plastic, along with shirts, socks and other performance wear. By the end of 2020, the brand aimed to ensure that more than 50 per cent of polyester used in its products is sourced from recycling; by 2024, Adidas aims to exclude virgin polyester completely.

Cyrill's quest shows the power of bringing a different lens and skillset to a problem. Who would have thought Adidas would be a natural partner for an environmental movement?

Intervening in the system through leverage points

Donella (known as Dana) Meadows was a Pew Scholar in Conservation and Environment and a MacArthur Fellow. It would be fair to say that she was one of the most influential environmental thinkers of the twentieth century. After receiving a PhD in biophysics from Harvard, she joined a team at MIT applying what were the relatively new tools of system dynamics to global problems. She was the principal author of *Limits to Growth* (1972), which sold more than 9 million copies in twenty-six languages, authored or co-authored eight more books and was nominated for a Pulitzer Prize in 1991.

What I know her for best is her influential thinking about systems. In 1996, Dana founded the Sustainability Institute (now the Academy for Systems Change), which aims to foster transitions to sustainable systems at all levels of society, from local to global.

Dana was a big believer in 'leverage points', places within any kind of complex system (a corporation, an economy, a living body, a city, an ecosystem) where a small shift in one thing can produce big changes in everything. While Dana's work goes into great depth as to the manipulation of leverage points, here I've developed this series of questions to focus on a challenge we are trying to solve, and understanding the system that sits around it. As we walk through the leverage points, think about how each could be used to affect the operating of the whole.

- What is the structure of the system?
- What are the physical attributes of the system?
- How does the communication of data flow throughout the system?
- Where are the open feedback loops in the system, available for new data flow?
- Where are the closed feedback loops that may reinforce the system in an unchecked manner?
- Who does and does not have access to information?
- What are the rules of the system? What are its scope, boundaries, degrees of freedom, and power?
- Is there the ability to change, evolve or self-organise within the system structure?
- Can you define the clear goals of the system?
- What is the mindset, paradigm or worldview that the system is built upon?
- How might the system transcend the paradigm? How might it entirely flip the way we are seeing the challenge to begin with?

Staring down the barrel of systems change can be overwhelming: change of this nature is complex and long term. Few cookie-cutter solutions apply and there aren't many easy photo ops, or predictable numbers for the annual report. For the next generation of leaders, climate change, a global pandemic, rising inequality and racial injustice have laid bare the flaws of many of our systems. Being the change we want to see in the world will require strong, intrinsic motivation, the curiosity and humility to deeply understand a problem and the burning desire to solve an intractable challenge or leave a legacy of a better way. But it will also require a new approach, necessarily a systems change approach, in this interconnected world. We'll need to build coalitions with unlikely collaborators, come up with innovative and strategic ways of deploying capital and unlocking value chains, and mobilising people at a grassroots level to join in and play their part.

Be the change you want to see in the system by changing the system.

A question from the leading edge:

Can you explain the part you are playing in the system you hope to change?

28

Grow others to grow others

'The key to greatness is to look for people's potential and spend time developing it.'

Peter Drucker

The greatest legacy we lead doesn't boil down to the execution of our strategic plan or our flawless implementation of a cost-reduction initiative; it comes down to a single question: did we leave people better than where we met them? Did we nourish, support and encourage? Did we take the time to coach and give feedback? Were we humble enough to share opportunities? Did we plant seeds and then, like any good gardener, did we attentively nurture them so they blossomed to their full potential? When we do this our leadership extends not just beyond our organisation but beyond our own lifetime, as those we've affected take the ideas and opportunities we've offered and add their own inspiration to pioneer the next wave of progress. Our leadership is not about us.

Level 5 leadership

Jim Collins is one of the most influential thought leaders of the last twenty-five years when it comes to business and leadership. A prodigious contributor to thought leadership in business, Jim first coined the term 'Level 5 Leadership' in his bestseller *Good to Great* after years of researching high-performance leadership. Jim noticed all high-performing organisations were headed by a 'Level 5 Leader', someone with a powerful mixture of personal humility and indomitable will. Level 5 leaders are incredibly ambitious, but their ambition is first and foremost for the cause, for the organisation and its purpose, not themselves. Jim challenges people to ask themselves: what cause do you serve with Level 5 ambition? By that he means something bigger than you. Jim distinguishes between Level 4 leaders, who are good at getting people to follow them, and Level 5 leaders, who are good at getting people to follow a cause.

It's perhaps unsurprising, given that focus, that Jim Collins was asked to spend a year as the chair of the Study of Leadership at the prestigious West Point Military Academy in 2012–13 to teach leadership best and brightest military cadets. But Jim says he was the one who ended up getting schooled. He summarises his observations with a presentation on seven key questions he believes all young leaders need to ask themselves. I recommend googling it – the ideas sitting beneath it are timeless.

I want to open this final chapter with a focus on three of Jim's questions.

How will you succeed by helping others succeed?

According to Jim, we are succeeding at our very best only when we are helping others succeed. One of Jim's profound observations from West Point was that when we're facing severe challenges, feeling inadequate or experiencing fear, there's extraordinary power in taking that moment of need and turning to someone else to ask: 'Can I help you?' It ignites the important idea that you are never alone. Jim says, 'It is impossible, in my view, to have a great life unless it is a meaningful life – and I believe it is very difficult to have a meaningful life without meaningful work.' Meaning, Jim says, is at the centre of a triangle that has 'service', 'success' and 'growth' on the three points. The next time you're feeling overwhelmed or afraid, instead of going inwards, try turning outwards and find opportunities to help others.

How will you build your unit or team into a pocket of greatness?

As touched in Chapter 21, Jim was the originator of the phrase 'getting the right people on the bus'. And with this concept he encourages us to think about our own minibus, not our career. Good to great CEOs, he says, became CEO when they 'focused on their unit of responsibility and, at every stage of their career, whatever they were running . . . they built their unit into a little pocket of greatness.' This starts with being rigorous about our people decisions: caring about people, investing in building culture, taking the time to tell people they matter and that we appreciate them. Making our team the very best it can be will naturally pay dividends for our own trajectory as a leader.

How will you change the lives of others?

Whether it's a lot or just a few, how will some people's lives be better and different because we were here on this planet? We've got to find a way to make ourselves useful. Service, Jim says, 'is a life choice, not a sector choice'. In other words, we're called to serve, whether we decide to work in the non-profit sector, public sector or the private sector. Whose lives will our life choices serve to improve?

The benefit of the possible

To describe Mark Brand as a chef is to do him a disservice. He's an entrepreneur, an educator, a facilitator *and* one hell of a chef. So much so that he is the executive chef of Pope Francis's Laudato and a visiting professor of innovation at Stanford. He is one of the most passionate human beings you'll encounter, and he's a self-described 'change enthusiast'. He is also not someone who takes the easy approach.

In our interview, Mark tells me how he decided to set up shop in the second-oldest building in Vancouver. Seemingly undeterred by the fact the location had played host to five failed restaurant attempts immediately prior to his move-in, Mark's restaurant quickly grew to award-winning acclaim. And then six years in, a team of consultants arrived . . .

Mark recalls being asked to sit in a meeting about launching an informal currency. It was a gift card of sorts for the Downtown Eastside where money would be crowd-sourced from the community and the value translated into $20 or $50 gift cards to be distributed to homeless people in the area. Mark didn't play his part. He knew his community. He'd been running a business for the past six years in the Downtown Eastside, which at the time held the unenviable title of being the largest open-air drug market in North America. He saw what happened when companies came down with Starbucks gift cards at Christmas: people patted themselves on the back for 'doing good' but with no connection to their intended impact. Gift cards got traded for crack cocaine, meth, heroin or something else the homeless needed a lot more than a vanilla latte.

Mark still gets angry talking about it with me. 'No research,' he says. 'They had done two years of planning on false assumptions.' Mark was so enraged he decided to do their job for them. The next day he texted a designer friend, and within two weeks he had 2000 poker chips adorned with the iconic pigs from Mark's store, a feature retained from the 1957 fit-up. They sold the poker chips to customers for $2.25; customers were able to give these to someone in need, and anyone who came in with one could redeem it for a sandwich. On the very first day, they did 120 redemptions, which Mark is quick to reframe as '240 people involved in 120 conversations between someone who has and somebody who has not.' That was the point: Mark's impact was 'humans engaging with other humans to understand the struggle they're going through and try to figure out how to help'. They've now served 2.4 million meals and counting.

Mark then created a second challenge. How do we scale up to meet the need? Again, he wanted to develop his model to find a new way forward. He wanted to empower people who traditionally faced barriers to being employed: 'People who have come out of recidivism, people on the street and people facing a developmental delay or developmental disability, people who have other issues.' Mark and the team worked with a multitude of agencies. And then started to employ people facing such issues. Some people with a developmental disability have now been there longer than the managing director. Mark says, 'They're the best.'

> So these folks come into work in our business, and I start to notice something really quickly. I realise nobody's ever sick. Nobody ever calls in with issues. Nobody ever complains ... And then what I also started to see is that people who were working in my business traditionally were way more excited to come to work because they could see our purpose beyond the people we were serving. They could also see that we were serving people inside. So morale was at an all-time high. This was amazing. My turnover dropped through the floor; people who have disabilities, physical or mental, turnover at less than 30 per cent per annum. Mine less than seven.

Mark goes on to talk further about his approach:

> Hospitality is not known for high retention: typically 75 per cent or more annual turnover in North America. It costs me $2000 to train an employee. If I'm a business of fifty people and have to spend $2000 on 75 per cent of them, do the math. That's a renovation. That's a whole salary – a CEO salary! And we don't have to do that. So when people are like, Yeah, I really wanted to hire somebody who's struggling, but I know it's gonna be a pain in the ass ... They literally have it backwards. It's the opposite. Your business gets more

stable; people are happier; you don't have to worry about it. Now, is this in every case? No. There's the cases of people who freaked out, or there's problems, or we've had deaths, of course – we're dealing with the hardest margins. But for the most part, 99 per cent of the time, they were the best people who were in my employment.

Mark says it's simple. Development and empowerment are only possible if you believe in people and seek to understand them. Mark calls it being 'for' people, akin to being in someone's cheer squad. People grow to be bigger and better versions of themselves. But no growth or commitment will happen in an environment where we don't start by feeling cared for and cared about. Mark not only gave people opportunities but he built a culture of encouragement and care, reinforced by training and support. It's better than giving someone the benefit of the doubt; it's giving them the benefit of the possible.

Mark's final words in our lengthy conversation were these: 'Stop making stupid assumptions about people and then not testing them. If you want to believe the worst of people, you'll get it. Raise the bar and you'll raise reality.'

Empowering words.

Calibrating a purpose-led culture
KA MATE! KA MATE!

It's a freezing night at Eden Park, Auckland. Despite being crammed in with 50,000 raucous Kiwis, you could hear a pin drop as the Maori war cry known as the Haka rings out from the fifteen All Blacks in the centre of the field. I'm a lone yellow jersey Aussie in a sea of black and white . . . and I'm unlikely to be smiling at the end of the evening.

In Chapter 1, we looked at the incredible success the All Blacks have had as a team, and how understanding their personal why and their team why played a part in their world dominance.

Now, I want to look at a couple of other lessons we can take from that awesome team.

In the book *Legacy*, we get an intimate look inside the All Blacks' high-performance culture. Author James Kerr shares the principles the All Blacks use in order to sustain their world number one status. The through line of their leadership? Humility.

Within our organisations, our movements, and our communities, leading with humility means instilling an awareness of the broader timeline. We occupy a moment of possibility, a fleck in the trajectory of humanity; what we choose to do with that moment might affect generations.

Sacrifice – find something you would die for and give your life to it

As Kerr writes, sacrifice is vital for the All Blacks, and there is no paradox – play to win, don't play not to lose. Don't be a good All Black, live and breathe being an All Black to your core. All Blacks are raised in a culture that says, 'Champions do extra'. Bleed on the field and know that your teammates will do the same for you. Be the first to arrive at the gym, be the last to leave.

As leaders today, we can be fearful of being too overwhelmed or burnt out, of never seeing our loved ones, because we feel as though we are already bleeding our life force into our work. But this misses the first mantra: 'Ask why'. In order to grow others, we must all be on board with the mission. Bring your loved ones into that mission. Allow your kids to know your passion. Maybe one day it will be theirs. To find something we would die for and give our lives to is never going to be about transactional work, because that is not the playing field of the leading edge.

Leading is sacrifice. We go first into the future. We shoulder the responsibility. We do for others what was not done for us. When we lead a team who are crystal clear on what they are playing for, sacrifice becomes an act of giving, rather than something being taken away.

Write your legacy – this is your time

All Blacks players are actively encouraged to leave the legacy stronger than they found it. They dare to dream of the way their own personal legacy might shape the broader folklore surrounding the team. When a player makes the All Blacks, they're given a small black book. The first page shows a jersey from the 1905 Originals, the first touring team. On the next page is another jersey, that of the 1924 Invincibles, and thereafter, pages of other jerseys until the present day, and then the rest of the pages are blank, waiting to be filled. By the player.

This philosophy that our leadership will live on, in and for future generations is what drives every single great leader I have had the chance to meet. This is why so many great leaders have an absence of ego, are seemingly free from fear and happy to give of themselves. They have dared to dream, so that we can too.

Wherever *The Leading Edge* meets you, know that you have the right to dream big. You are the unique coming together of the experiences, beliefs, opportunities and challenges of people that have shaped your life. Right now, you are in the process of shaping many lives to come. Your growth is the growth of the ecosystem. Your spark of change will light others up and stoke the fire in the belly of all those who believe in a better world.

The leading edge is about knowing the power of your mindsets, your methods and your mastery, and combining them to become a more holistic and empowered version of yourself, in order to make meaningful change.

A question from the leading edge:

How are you helping others to grow?

Epilogue: Maintaining perspective

On day two of writing this book, in the midst of the COVID-19 pandemic, my grandma, Dorothy, had a nasty fall that fractured both her shoulders and her right knee. The phone lines were down in their small country town due to a storm, so my 91-year-old grandfather mustered a gargantuan effort to get himself and his walking frame to the car, drive to the neighbours' house in the thick of the storm and inch his way down a precarious set of steps to reach someone with a mobile phone who could call an ambulance. I have no idea how he managed to do it but, if the two of them have taught me anything, it's that nothing is more powerful than love.

When the dust settled and Grandma was ensconced in a hospital bed, I'd call and ask the nurse to prop the phone up to her ear so we could talk. I'm not sure whether it was just the latest musings of her seemingly endless fountain of eighty-nine years of wisdom, or because of all the extra time she had to mull over the state of the world while confined to a hospital bed ('I hate sitting still but I can't move anything!', she'd lament), but our conversations grew even more reflective and philosophical than usual. Grandma shared stories I'd never heard before about her dad driving them into town to witness people camping on the riverbanks in the dire economic aftermath of the World War II, which he did to imbue his children with a sense of gratitude and civic responsibility. She told me more about working as a nurse with her best friend Ruth during the polio pandemic. She also mused about the state of the world a lot, frequently bemoaning 'the half-brains that seem to be running the show nowadays'.

One day, I asked her if she was hopeful that it could all turn around, if she thought we could find a way forward and through. The line went quiet as she paused to think for a minute. 'Oh, yes, infinitely,' she replied with her trademark, matter-of-fact conviction that I've come to know and love so much over the years.

Her confidence made me smile. But given her mediocre assessment of the current state of the world, I couldn't help but inquire: 'Why?'

'Because if I've learnt anything in my life it's that people rise to meet the challenges before them. But they also rise to the estimations we have of them. What I hope your generation does better than mine is realise the importance of believing in the potential of everyone. *Really* believing. I think it's the greatest force for good there is, in a war between what is and what could be.'

I think my grandma, as always, just might be right.

Notes

1 Anchor to purpose

5   'If you don't know . . .' Yogi Berra with Dave Kaplan, *When You Come to a Fork in the Road, Take It!: Inspiration and wisdom from one of baseball's greatest heroes*, Hyperion, New York, 2002, p. 53.

9   'We're in an age . . .' Mark Lobosco, 'Four trends changing the way you attract and retain talent', *LinkedIn Talent Blog*, 22 January 2020: https://business.linkedin.com/talent-solutions/blog/trends-and-research/2020/global-talent-trends-2020.

10 'They are the most successful . . .' Sports Travel and Hospitality Group, 'Global Travel Services for Rugby World Champions': https://sportstravelhospitality.com/case-studies/world-beating-travel-partner/.

10 'Richie wanted to take stock . . .' James Kerr, *Legacy: What the All Blacks Can Teach Us About the Business of Life*. Little, Brown and Company, Great Britain, 2015.

13 'Vision without action . . .' *Oxford Essential Quotations* (4th edn), Susan Ratcliffe (ed.), Oxford University Press, 2016. Originally from Joel Arthur Baker, *The Power of Vision* (1991 video).

13 'Early in Benjamin's life . . .' Benjamin Franklin, *The Autobiography of Benjamin Franklin*, Duke Classics, 2020.

2 Frame your choices

17 'There is a choice . . .' John Wooden. and Steve Jamison, *Wooden on Leadership*, McGraw-Hill, New York, 2005.

18 'As Leslie Ye writes, 'Choice . . .' Leslie Ye, 'The Psychology of Choice: How to Make Decisions Easier', HubSpot, 14 August 2018: https://blog.hubspot.com/sales/the-psychology-of-choice.

19 'Comedian Aziz Ansari teamed up . . .' Aziz Ansari and Eric Klinenberg, *Modern Romance: An investigation*, Penguin, New York, 2015.

19 'You do have time . . .' Seth Godin, 'Urgency and accountability are two sides of the same coin', *Seth's Blog*, https://seths.blog/2013/05/urgency-and-accountability-are-two-sides-of-the-innovation-coin/.

22 'The key findings showed that only 28 per cent . . .' Stacy Smith and Crystal Allene Cook, *Gender Stereotypes: An analysis of popular films and TV*, Geena Davis Institute on Gender in Media, 2008, https://seejane.org/wp-content/uploads/GDIGM_Gender_Stereotypes.pdf.

23 'The institute has shone a light on ...' *The Geena Benchmark Report: 2007–2017*, Geena Davis Institute on Gender in Media, 2019: https://seejane.org/research-informs-empowers/the-geena-benchmark-report-2007-2017/.

3 Own your narrative

28 'There's a power ...' Michelle Obama, *Becoming: A Guided Journal for Discovering your Voice*, Penguin Random House, New York, 2019.

30 'And since it's our destiny ...' Jim Loehr, *The Power of Story: Rewrite your destiny in business and in life*, Free Press, New York, 2007.

31 'In his prolific work ...' Marshall Ganz, 'What Is Public Narrative'?, The Community Organizing Website, 2007: https://comm-org.wisc.edu/syllabi/ganz/WhatisPublicNarrative5.19.08.htm.

31 'If we haven't talked ...' Marshall Ganz, 'Leading Change: Leadership, organization, and social movements', in Nitin Nohria and Rakesh Khurana (eds), *Handbook of Leadership Theory and Practice: A Harvard Business School centennial colloqium*, Harvard Business Press, Boston, 2010.

32 'In the 2014 Harvard ...' Paul J. Zak, 'Why Your Brain Loves Good Storytelling', *Harvard Business Review* [online], 2014: https://hbr.org/2014/10/why-your-brain-loves-good-storytelling.

32 'Black, queer, disabled and brilliant ...' Catie Monteiro, '"Black, queer, disabled and brilliant": Activist hopes to make history in space', *NBC News*, 27 June 2018: https://www.nbcnews.com/feature/nbc-out/black-queer-disabled-brilliant-activist-hopes-make-history-space-n886586.

33 'It's not just an adventure ...' 'No Looking Back: Eddie Ndopu makes space for a historic 2018', *African Leadership Academy*, 2018: https://www.africanleadershipacademy.org/blog/eddie-ndopu-makes-space-historic-2018/.

34 'If you don't have yourself ...' Larry Moss, *The Intent to Live: Achieving your true potential as an actor*, Bantam, New York, 2005.

34 'Hagen says every actor should ask themselves nine questions ...' Uta Hagen and Haskel Frankel, *Respect for Acting*, Macmillan, New York, 1973.

35 'If you're brave enough ...' Ibid.

36 'Owning our story and loving ourselves ...' Brené Brown: https://brenebrown.com/about/#close-popup.

37 'At the time of white settlement ...' Rona Glynn-McDonald, 'First Nations Languages', Common Ground, 2021: commonground.org.au/learn/indigenous-languages-avoiding-a-silent-future.

4 Build your bounce

39 'The greatest glory in living ...' Oliver Goldsmith, 'The Citizen of the World: or, Letters from a Chinese Philosopher, Residing in London, to His Friends in the East by Lien Chi Altangi', Letter VII and Letter XXII, Printed for George and Alex. Ewing, Dublin, Ireland, 1762, ECCO TCP: Eighteenth Century Collections Online, Text: https://quod.lib.umich.edu/e/ecco/004776950.0001.001/1:24?rgn=div1;view=fulltext, p89.

40 'Research on the epidemiology of trauma ...' C. Benjet et al., 'The epidemiology of traumatic event exposure worldwide: results from the World Mental Health Survey Consortium', *Psychological Medicine*, vol. 46, no. 2, 2016, pp. 327–43.

40 'Richard G. Tedeschi wrote . . .' Richard G. Tedeschi and Lawrence G. Calhoun, 'Posttraumatic growth: conceptual foundations and empirical evidence', *Psychological Inquiry*, vol. 15, no. 1, 2004, pp. 1–18.

40 'In her TED talk . . .' Kelly McGonigal, 'How to make stress your friend', TED, June 2013.

40 'University of Wisconsin researchers tracked . . .' A. Keller et al., 'Does the perception that stress affects health matter? The association with health and mortality. *Health Psychology*, vol. 31, no. 5, 2012, pp. 667–84.

40 'A study from the University of Buffalo . . .' M.J. Poulin, et al.,. 'Giving to others and the association between stress and mortality', *American Journal of Public Health*, vol. 103, no. 9, 2013, pp. 1649–55.

41 'When you choose to connect . . .' McGonigal, 'How to make stress your friend'.

41 'British elite athlete Tom Don . . .' *Tim Don: The Man with the Halo*, On Productions, 2018: youtube.com/watch?v=UhjIchwAkAU.

45 'One of the most simple and helpful checklists . . .' Mike Kyrios, STREAM Framework, *Flinders University website*: https://www.flinders.edu.au/institute-mental-health-wellbeing/stream.

47 'Yet we know that while mental health support . . .' Chestnut Global Partners, '2016 Top Trends in EAP and Wellness Report: An analysis of what is occurring in the fields of employee assistance, organizational health and workplace productivity industries', 2016; Mental Health Australia and KPMG, *Investing to Save: The economic benefits for Australia of investment in mental health reform*, 2018.

47 'One of his many fascinating findings . . .' G. M. Buchanan and M. E. P. Seligman (eds), *Explanatory Style*, Lawrence Erlbaum Associates, New Jersey, 1995.

47 'He began training people to . . .' Maria Konnikova, 'How People Learn to Become Resilient', *The New Yorker*, 11 February 2016: https://www.newyorker.com/science/maria-konnikova/the-secret-formula-for-resilience.

49 'In her latest book, *The Upside of Stress* . . .' McGonigal, Kelly, *The Upside of Stress: Why stress is good for you, and how to get good at it*, Avery, New York, 2015.

5 Stay hungry for feedback

50 'Feedback is a free education . . .' Anne Marie Houghtailing, *How I Created the Dollar out of Thin Air*, Chula Vista, 2013, quoted in James Nottingham and Jill Nottingham, *Challenging Learning Through Feedback: How to Get the Type, Tone and Quality*, Corwin Press, 2017.

51 'Nearly all – 96 per cent – of employees . . .' 'The global state of employee engagement', *Officevibe*, n.d. https://officevibe.com/guides/state-employee-engagement.

51 'Companies like Deloitte and Accenture . . .' 'Deloitte joins Abode and Accenture in dumping the annual performance review', *Impraise*, n.d. https://www.impraise.com/blog/deloitte-joins-adobe-and-accenture-in-dumping-performance-reviews.

52 'Approximately 6 per cent of Fortune 500 . . .' Lillian Cunningham, 'In a big move, Accenture will get rid of annual performance reviews and rankings', *Washington Post*, 21 July 2015.

52 'Research looking at the way teens . . .' Benjamin Williams, 'Living life online: Adolescent mental health and social media', *Psychiatry Advisor*, 7 December 2020: psychiatryadvisor.com/home/topics/child-adolescent-psychiatry/living-life-online-adolescent-mental-health-and-social-media/.

52 'When esteemed video game designer . . .' Jane McGonigal, 'Gaming can make a better world', TED, February 2010.

53 'As Jane points out . . .' Jane McGonigal, 'Gaming can make a better world'.

54 'Video games are unpredictable . . .' Darran Jamieson, 'Making Difficult Fun: How to Challenge Your Players', Envatotuts+, 20 May 2016: https://gamedevelopment.tutsplus.com/tutorials/making-difficult-fun-how-to-challenge-your-players--cms-25873.

55 'According to Francesca Gino . . .' Francesca Gino, 'Research: We tend to drop people who give us critical feedback', *Harvard Business Review*, 16 September 2016.

55 'Receiving honest criticism . . .' Paul Green Jr, Francesca Gino and Bradley Staats, 'Shopping for Confirmation: How disconfirming feedback shapes social networks', *Harvard Business School Working Paper*, No. 18–028, 2017.

56 'One of the most helpful books . . .' Douglas Stone and Sheila Heen, *Thanks for the Feedback: The science and art of receiving feedback well (even when it is off base, unfair, poorly delivered, and, frankly, you're not in the mood)*, Portfolio Penguin, London, 2015.

60 'In his book *What Got You Here* . . .' Marshall Goldsmith, *What Got You Here Won't Get You There*, Hyperion, 2007.

61 'The research of neuroscientist . . .' Larry Moss, *The Intent to Live: Achieving Your True Potential as an Actor*, Bantam, 2005.

6 Be four again

65 'Above all, never stop questioning . . .' from statement to William Miller, as quoted in *LIFE* magazine (2 May 1955). https://www.asl-associates.com/einstein quotes.htm.

65 'The numbers back it up . . .' For those interested, the five toughest questions were deemed to be: Why is water wet? Where does the sky end? What are shadows made of? Why is the sky blue? And how do fish breathe underwater? 'Mums asked nearly 300 questions a day by kids', *Business Standard*, 29 March 2013: https://www.business-standard.com/article/pti-stories/mums-asked-nearly-300-questions-a-day-by-kids-113032900197_1.html; Warren Berger, *A More Beautiful Question: The power of inquiry to spark breakthrough*, Bloomsbury, 2014.

65 'Study after study shows we stop . . .' Warren Berger, 'What Kills Questioning?' [book trailer for *A More Beautiful Question* by Warren Berger], 7 November 2013.

66 'In the famed MIT Marshmallow Challenge . . .' Stanford d.school, 'Resources: Spaghetti marshmallow challenge', https://dschool.stanford.edu/resources/spaghetti-marshmallow-challenge.

66 'When comparing the performance . . .' Tom Wujec, 'Build a tower, build a team', TED, February 2010.

67 'We have "killed creativity" . . .' Sir Ken Robinson, 'Do schools kill creativity?', TED, February 2006.

67 'Companies like Disney . . .' Walt Disney, 'Walt's Quotes', *D23*: https://d23.com/section/walt-disney-archives/walts-quotes/.

69 'According to Ian Leslie . . .' Ian Leslie, *Curious: The desire to know and why your future depends on it*, Basic Books, New York, 2014.

69 'And the designer behind the iPhone . . .' Lauren Schwartzberg, 'Why iPod and Nest Creator Tony Fadell Thinks Like a Child', *Fast Company*, 18 March, 2015: https://www.fastcompany.com/3043987/why-ipod-and-nest-creator-tony-fadell-thinks-like-a-child.

69 'Anne Mulcahy, CEO of Xerox . . .' Mark Thomas, '"Don't get smart person's disease." says Anne Mulcahy, former CEO of Xerox', *Global Ed*, 17 December 2013: https://globaleduc.wordpress.com/2013/12/17/dont-get-smart-persons-disease-says-anne-mulcahy-former-ceo-of-xerox/.

70 'For example, in 1995, financial trader . . .' Elliot Smith, "The Barings collapse 25 years on: what the industry learned from the man who broke a bank', *CNBC*, 26 February, 2020: https://www.cnbc.com/2020/02/26/barings-collapse-25-years-on-what-the-industry-learned-after-one-man-broke-a-bank.html.

70 'Recent findings in neuroscience . . .' Manfred F. R. Kets de Vries, 'Creating Safe Places for Executive Play' in *Mindful Leadership Coaching*, INSEAD Business Press, Palgrave Macmillan, London, 2014.

71 'Play is also our most direct . . .' Mihaly Csikszentmihalyi, *Flow: The psychology of optimal experience*, Harper & Row, New York, 1990.

71 'INSEAD's Manfred F.R. Kets de Vries . . .' Manfred F. R. Kets de Vries, 'Get Back in the Sandbox: Teaching CEOs how to play', INSEAD Working Paper No. 2012/125/EFE, 4 December 2012.

72 'In 2003, Ross's Windows Defect Prevention team . . .' Steve Clayton, 'Microsoft's Ross Smith Asks Shall We Play a Game?', *Microsoft AI Blog*, 16 May 2011: https://blogs.microsoft.com/ai/microsofts-ross-smith-asks-shall-we-play-a-game/.

74 'We spend on average 144 minutes a day . . .' 'Average Time Spent Daily on Social Media' (latest 2020 Data), *BroadbandSearch.net*: https://www.broadbandsearch.net/blog/average-daily-time-on-social-media.

74 'As Drucker highlighted . . .' Peter Drucker, *The Essential Drucker: The best of sixty years of Peter Drucker's essential writings on management*, Collins Business Essentials, New York, 2008.

7 Manage energy not time

76 'We think, mistakenly, that success . . .' Arianna Huffington, *Thrive: The Third Metric to Redefining Success and Creating a Life of Well-Being*, Wisdom, and Wonder, WH Allen, New York, 2015.

77 'I first stumbled onto the concept of managing energy . . .' Jim Loehr and Tony Schwartz, *The Power of Full Engagement: Managing energy, not time, is the key to high performance and personal renewal*, Free Press, New York, 2007.

79 'As researcher Christopher Barnes observes . . .' Christopher M. Barnes, 'The ideal work schedule, as defined by circadian rhythms', *Harvard Business Review*, 28 January 2015: https://hbr.org/2015/01/the-ideal-work-schedule-as-determined-by-circadian-rhythms.

82 'According to the World Economic Forum, burnout . . .' Sarah Tottle, 'It's costing the global economy £255 billion, so what can we do to stop workplace burnout?', *World Economic Forum*, 31 October 2016: https://www.weforum.org/agenda/2016/10/workplace-burnout-can-you-do-anything-about-it.

82 'A Gallup study found . . .' Yvette Martin, 'Helping Australia's stressed-out workers', *Gallup*, 24 December 2013: https://news.gallup.com/businessjournal/166355/helping-australia-stressed-workers.aspx.

84 'The experiment was never intended . . .' Spur Projects, 'How is the world feeling: Data: emotions: time of day', http://howistheworldfeeling.wearespur.com/#data.

85 'Stephen Covey, in his seminal work . . .' Stephen Covey, *The Seven Habits of Highly Effective People: Restoring the character ethic* (rev. edn), Free Press, New York, 2004.

86 'James Clear, the author of *Atomic Habits* . . .' James Clear, *Atomic Habits: an easy and proven way to build good habits and break bad ones; tiny changes, remarkable results*, Avery, New York, 2018.

8 Get comfortable being uncomfortable

88 'You don't get to have a meaningful . . .' Susan David, 'The Gift and Power of Emotional Change', TED, November 2017.

88 'During his time at Red Bull . . .' 'Red Bull Stratos', Red Bull, n.d., redbull.com/int-en/projects/red-bull-stratos.

91 'What we fear doing most . . .' Timothy Ferriss, *The 4-Hour Workweek: Escape 9–5, Live Anywhere, and Join the New Rich*, Crown, New York, 2007.

9 Do the work required to hold an opinion

99 'Opinions are like arse-holes . . .' Tim Minchin, 'Occasional Address: 9 Life Lessons', UWA speech, 2013: https://www.timminchin.com/2013/09/25/occasional-address/.

100 'We are continually synthesising . . .' Jim Sollisch, 'The cure for decision fatigue', *Wall Street Journal*, 10 June 2016: https://www.wsj.com/articles/the-cure-for-decision-fatigue-1465596928.

100 'In the last two years alone . . .' Jacquelyn Bulao, 'How much data is created every day in 2020?', *TechJury*, 22 January 2021: https://techjury.net/blog/how-much-data-is-created-every-day/#gref.

100 'In 2020, we created 1.7MB of data . . .' Ibid.; 'Data never sleeps', *Domo*, 2018: domo.com/solution/data-never-sleeps-6.

100 'We are wired to remember . . .' 'Information overload: memory and focus are at risk', Morris Psychological Group, 1 July 2014.

100 'According to David Kirsch . . .' David Kirsch, 'A few thoughts on cognitive overload', *Intellectica*, vol. 30, 2000.

101 'As Evelyn Beatrice Hall said in 1906 . . .' Robert Sharp, '"I disapprove of what you say, but I will defend to the death your rights to say it" – Voltaire, Tallentyre and Hall', 3 May 2018: https://www.robertsharp.co.uk/2018/05/03/i-disapprove-of-what-you-say-but-i-will-defend-to-the-death-your-right-to-say-it-voltaire-tallentyre-and-hall/.

101 'In the 2020 World Economic Forum's list . . .' Kate Whiting, 'These are the top ten skills of tomorrow and how long it takes to learn them', *World Economic Forum*, 21 October 2020: https://www.weforum.org/agenda/2020/10/top-10-work-skills-of-tomorrow-how-long-it-takes-to-learn-them/.

102 'Amal Clooney, the barrister . . .' Rebecca Ratcliffe, 'Journalist Maria Ressa found guilty of cyberlibel in Phillipines', *Guardian*, 15 June 2020: https://www.theguardian.com/world/2020/jun/15/maria-ressa-rappler-editor-found-guilty-of-cyber-libel-charges-in-philippines.

103 'The president, in response . . .' Pia Ranada, 'Duterte calls Rappler fake news outlet', *Rappler*, 16 January 2018: rappler.com/nation/duterte-fake-news-outlet.

103 'Charlie Munger, the long-time business partner ...' 'Charlie Munger on getting rich, wisdom, focus, fake knowledge and more', *Farnam Street*, n.d.; https://fs.blog/2017/02/charlie-munger-wisdom/.

103 'In an amusing (and insightful) experiment...' Thu-huong Ha, 'This April Fool's joke perfectly trolls online trolls', *Quartz*, 2 April 2016: https://qz.com/653018/this-april-fools-joke-perfectly-trolls-online-trolls/.

104 'According to a 2016 study...' Maksym Gabielkov, Arthi Ramachandran, Augustin Chaintreau and Arnaud Legout, 'Social clicks: what and who gets read on Twitter?', *ACM Sigmetrics Performance Evaluation Review*, vol. 44, no. 1, June 2016.

104 'The average Facebook user ...' Nicolas M. Anspach, Jay T. Jennings and Kevin Arceneaux, 'A little bit of knowledge: Facebook's news feed and self-perceptions of knowledge', *Research & Politics*, vol. 6, no. 1, February 2019.

106 'In a famous speech in the 1990s ...' Charles Munger, (ed. Peter Kaufman), *Poor Charlie's Almanack: The wit and wisdom of Charles T. Munger* (3rd expanded ed.), Donning Co., Virginia Beach, 2008.

106 'Models are contextual ...' 'Mental models: the best way to make intelligent decisions (109 models explained)', Farnam Street, n.d.: https://fs.blog/mental-models/.

107 'We must think critically ...' Tim Minchin, 'Occasional Address: 9 Life Lessons'.

107 'As Farnam Street describes it ...' 'Mental models: the best way to make intelligent decisions (109 models explained)', Farnam Street.

108 'As Tina Soika describes ...' Tina Soika, 'Cognitive Dissonance: Overcome What Is Really Holding Back Your Practice', *The Hearing Review*, 20 June 2013: https://www.hearingreview.com/practice-building/practice-management/cognitive-dissonance-overcome-what-is-really-holding-back-your-practice-2?ref=cl-title.

108 'Activist and founder of the #MeToo movement...' Tarana Burke, 'Tarana Burke and Brené on being heard and seen', *Unlocking Us* [podcast]: brenebrown.com/podcast/brene-tarana-burke-on-empathy/.

108 'Spoken word poetry took on a heightened prominence ...' Meliza Banales, 'Slam Poetry', *Encyclopedia Britannica*, 6 April 2018: https://www.britannica.com/art/slam-poetry.

109 'His poem 'Shake the Dust' ...' Anis Mojgani, *Shake the Dust*: https://vimeo.com/73358073.

109 'As Rabbi Ben Hecht described ...' Rabbi Ben Hecht, 'We Need To Be Able To Question Our Own Opinions', *Huffington Post Canada*, 19 July 2016: https://www.huffingtonpost.ca/rabbi-ben-hecht/questioning-oneself_b_11055358.html.

10 Start before you're ready

111 'Start where you are ...' Arthur Ashe.

111 'As Wayne Gretzky famously said ...' Burton W. Kanter, "AARP—Asset Accumulation, Retention and Protection," Taxes69: 717: "Wayne Gretzky, relating the comment of one of his early coaches who, frustrated by his lack of scoring in an important game told him, 'You miss 100% of the shots you never take.'" ... The saying is often attributed to the hockey player Gretzky (sometimes to his father or to a coach). Cf. "You can't score if you don't shoot."

112 'The founder of legendary start-up ...' Read more about this idea in one of my favourite entrepreneurial blogs of all time: Paul Graham, 'How to Get Startup Ideas', November 2012: http://paulgraham.com/startupideas.html.

113 'The region they work in ...' Adara Group, '50,000 Stories of Impact', 'The Adara Businesses, 2017: https://www.adaragroup.org/wp-content/uploads/2017/06/Adara-Ops-Report-LowRes-Pages.pdf.

114 'Whereas a standard CPAP machine ...' Ibid.

118 'The company poured $100 million ...' Jordan Golson, 'Well, that didn't work: The Segway is a technological marvel. Too bad it doesn't make any sense', *Wired*, 16 January 2015: https://www.wired.com/2015/01/well-didnt-work-segway-technological-marvel-bad-doesnt-make-sense/.

119 'One account of its development ...' Matt McFarland, 'Segway was supposed to change the world. Two decades later, it just might', *CNN*, 30 October 2018: https://lite.cnn.com/en/article/h_d831de0838b432f0721964c061c9fe92.

119 'In a *Harvard Business Review* article ...' Tara Sophia Mohr, 'Why women don't apply for jobs unless they're 100% qualified', *Harvard Business Review*, 25 August 2014: https://hbr.org/2014/08/why-women-dont-apply-for-jobs-unless-theyre-100-qualified.

120 'As the saying goes at the go-to design ...' This saying has been widely quoted by a plethora of design companies and articles, attributed to IDEO. See for example: We Are Unstuck, 6 October 2016: https://medium.com/@WeareUnstuck/if-a-picture-is-worth-a-thousand-words-a-prototype-is-worth-a-thousand-meetings-ideo-968ed43a6062#; *The Shortcut*, n.d.: https://theshortcut.org/tag/digital-prototyping/.

121 'The five-stage design thinking model ...' Hasso Plattner Institute of Design at Stanford d.school, 'Design thinking: the beginner's guide', Interaction Design Foundation, n.d., interaction-design.org/courses/design-thinking-the-beginner-s-guide.

11 Unlearn, learn and relearn

125 'The illiterate of the 21st century ...' Alvin Toffler In *Oxford Essential Quotations* (4th edn), ed. Susan Ratcliffe, Oxford University Press, 2016. Also available at: https://www.oxfordreference.com/view/10.1093/acref/9780191826719.001.0001/q-oro-ed4-00010964.

125 'At its peak ...' R. Taagepera, R, 'Size and Duration of Empires: Growth-Decline Curves, 600 B.C. to 600 A.D.', *Social Science History*, vol. 3 no. 3/4, 1979.

125 'In fact, as philosopher ...' Baron de Montesquieu, C. d. S., *Reflections on the Causes of the Rise and Fall of the Roman Empire. Translated from the French of M. de Secondat, Baron de Montesquieu ... In Two Volumes. The Second Edition. With Great Additions and Improvements*, United Kingdom: W. Innys, C. Davis, R. Manby, and H. S. Cox, [1752], 2018.

126 'Across every G20 nation youth unemployment ...' Organization for Economic Co-Operation and Development International Labour Organization, 'Achieving better youth employment outcomes: Monitoring policies and progress in G20 economies,' report prepared for the G20 Employment Working Group Antalya, Turkey, 26–27 February 2015.: https://www.oecd.org/g20/topics/employment-and-social-policy/Achieving-better-youth-employment-outcomes.pdf.

127 'Within the next decade ...' PwC, *The Future of Work: A journey to 2022*, 2014: https://www.pwc.com/ee/et/publications/pub/future-of-work-report.pdf.

128 'To consider that we need look no further ...' 'The Backwards Brain Bicycle: Un-doing understanding – Smarter Every Day', TED Ed, n.d., https://ed.ted.com/best_of_web/bf2mRAfC.

128 'Our brain receives feedback …' Tom Vanderbilt, 'Here's what learning to juggle does to your brain', *Wired*, 4 February 2021: https://www.wired.com/story/heres-what-learning-juggle-does-your-brain/.

129 'As Peter Drucker famously said …' Attributed to Peter Drucker in Marshall Goldsmith, 'Teaching Leaders What to Stop', 2015: https://youtu.be/6NHySKiUJfs /;Marshall Goldsmith, 'Lessons about life and leadership from Peter Drucker', *Corporate Learning Network*, 24 August 2020:https://www.corporate learningnetwork.com/leadership-management/articles/20-behaviors-even-the-most-successful-people-need-to-stop-1.

131 'Atlassian, the Australian 'unicorn' software company …' SBS News, 'Atlassian to list on Nasdaq worth $6b', 2015: https://www.sbs.com.au/news/atlassian-to-list-on-nasdaq-worth-6b.

131 'Atlassian believes in the idea of …' Jack Gramenz, 'Atlassian business software giant pushes out free Chrome extension to help fix bad workplace habits', News.com, 21 January 2020: https://www.news.com.au/technology/innovation/atlassian-business-software-giant-pushes-out-free-chrome-extension-to-help-fix-bad-workplace-habits/news-story/9a32c807b8fd3e3bcb8ca2c5a1e7ede7.

132 'In Josh's bestseller …' Josh Kaufman, *The First 20 Hours: How to learn anything – fast*, Portfolio, New York, 2013.

132 'Kaufman's research shows …' Ibid.

133 'As defined in *Psychological Science* …' Stéphanie Mazza et al, 'Relearn Faster and Retain Longer: Along With Practice, Sleep Makes Perfect', *Psychological Science*, 16 August 2016, vol. 27, no. 10.

134 'Scientists at the Max Planck Institute …' Max-Planck-Gesellschaft, 'Forgotten but not gone: how the brain re-learns', *ScienceDaily*, 22 November 2008: https://www.sciencedaily.com/releases/2008/11/081117110834.htm.

134 'I can't think of a better …' I encourage you to check out Everald's musings at everaldcompton.com or Twitter:@everaldatlarge.

12 Go for goals

137 'The person on top of the mountain …' Marcus Washling, see Matt Maybury, '20 quotes to help motivate you to hustle like never before', *Entrepreneur*, 30 June 2015: https://www.entrepreneur.com/article/247859.

138 'If you write down your goals …' Gail Matthews, 'The effectiveness of four coaching techniques in enhancing goal achievement: writing goals, formulating action steps, making a commitment, and accountability', paper presented at the Ninth Annual International Conference on Psychology, 25–28 May 2015, Athens, Greece. Abstract available from https://www.atiner.gr/abstracts/2015ABST-PSY.pdf; research summary from Sid Savara, 'Writing down your goals – the Harvard goal study. Fact or fiction?', n.d: https://sidsavara.com/fact-or-fiction-the-truth-about-the-harvard-written-goal-study/.

138 'As management consultant Stephen Barnes …' Stephen Barnes, 'Attributes of a successful entrepreneur', *CEO Magazine*, 30 July 2019.

139 'An interesting self-description for someone …' 'Trailblazers: Australia's 50 Greatest Explorers', Australian Museum website, 2021: https://australian.museum/about/history/exhibitions/trailblazers/.

140 'Yachting experts spoke out . . .' Sarah Collerton, 'Plea to parents: don't let Jessica sail', *ABC News*, 5 October 2009: https://www.abc.net.au/news/2009-10-05/plea-to-parents-dont-let-jessica-sail/1091814.

141 'Psychology professor Gail Matthews . . .' Gail Matthews, 'The effectiveness of four coaching techniques'; 'Study confirms smart strategies for achieving goals', *Sciencebeta*, 20 June 2013.

141 'Stephen Covey talks about the temptation . . .' Covey, *The Seven Habits*.

142 'Gail Matthews's study found . . .' Matthews, 'The effectiveness of four coaching techniques'.

142 'It's also good to be strategic . . .' H. J. Klein et al., 'When goals are known: The effects of audience relative status on goal commitment and performance', *Journal of Applied Psychology*, vol. 105, no. 4, 2020.

144 'Eat My Lunch has provided . . .' 'Our story', Eat My Lunch NZ.

144 'Writing is like driving . . .' Nancy Groves, 'EL Doctorow in quotes: 15 of his best', *Guardian*, 22 July 2015: https://www.theguardian.com/books/2015/jul/22/el-doctorow-in-quotes-15-of-his-best.

13 Prepare with discipline

148 'The will to succeed . . .' Juma Ikangaa, quoted in B. Heinrich, *Racing the Antelope*. HarperCollins, New York, 2001.

149 'General Morrison shot to public awareness . . .' 'Chief of Army Lieutenant General David Morrison message about unacceptable behaviour', Australian Army, 13 June 2013: youtube.com/watch?v=QaqpoeVgr8U.

155 'Performance strategist Matt Mayberry provides . . .' Matt Mayberry, 'The extraordinary power of visualizing success', *Entrepreneur Asia Pacific*, 30 January 2015: https://www.entrepreneur.com/article/242373.

156 'The theory is that we say 300 . . .' Cited in Bakari Akil II, 'How the Navy Seals increased passing rates', *Psychology Today*, 9 November 2009: https://www.psychologytoday.com/au/blog/communication-central/200911/how-the-navy-seals-increased-passing-rates?quicktabs_5=0.

156 'So we want those words to be positive and self-encouraging . . .' David Eagleman, *The Brain*, Canongate Books, Edinburgh 2015.

156 'Eric Barker has explained this well . . .' Eric Barker, 'How to be optimistic, according to science', *The Week*, 14 August 2014: https://theweek.com/articles/444812/how-optimistic-according-science.

14 Work 'on' and 'in'

160 'A study by Rich Howarth . . .' Rich Howarth, *The Strategic Thinking Manifesto*, Strategic Thinking Institute, n.d.: strategyskills.com/pdf/The-Strategic-Thinking-Manifesto.pdf?gclid=CIaV2fG0v88CFcVlfgodSBUM8A.

160 'The Einsenhower Matrix . . .' see Covey, *The Seven Habits*, ch. 3.

161 'Our brains are designed . . .' 'Multitasking: Switching Costs', American Psychological Association, 20 March 2006: https://www.apa.org/research/action/multitask.

161 'Psychologists have compared . . .' Ibid.

162 'Multi-tasking, or disrupted attention . . .' Quoted in Renuka Rayasam, 'You probably suffer from scattered brain syndrome', BBC, 12 December 2016: https://www.bbc.com/worklife/article/20161208-you-probably-suffer-from-scattered-brain-syndrome.

162 'As Renuka Rayasam has described . . .' Ibid.

162 'Researchers had people do a series . . .' Adrian F. Ward et al., 'Brain drain: The mere presence of one's own smartphone reduces available cognitive capacity', *Journal of the Association for Consumer Research*, vol. 2, no. 2, 2017.

163 'But according to Sharon Begley . . .' Sharon Begley, *Can't Just Stop: An investigation of compulsions*, Simon & Schuster, New York, 2017.

163 'The emerging idea is that when reality . . .' Quoted in Rachel Hosie, 'The psychological reason you can't stop checking your phone', *Independent*, 10 February 2017, https://www.independent.co.uk/life-style/why-keep-checking-phone-psychology-smartphone-notifications-social-media-a7572916.html.

163 'Consider whether every time . . .' '10 Common Time Management Mistakes', *Mind Tools*, 2021: https://www.mindtools.com/pages/article/time-management-mistakes.htm.

164 'In his bestselling book . . .' Clayton M. Christensen, *How Will You Measure Your Life?*, Harvard Business Review Press, Boston, 2012.

164 'Christensen also looks at . . .' Michael Simmons, 'Bezos, Musk, and Buffett see the world differently, because they see time differently', *Medium*, 14 May 2020: https://medium.com/accelerated-intelligence/these-billionaire-ceos-see-the-world-differently-because-they-see-time-differently-faa2909e8fa2.

165 'It's easier to hold to your principles . . .' Christensen, *How Will You Measure Your Life?*

166 'Dan originally started Thankyou . . .' interview, *Map magazine*: http://theweekendedition.com.au/mapmagazine/daniel-flynn/.

166 'In fact in 2020 they stopped making . . .' Small Business Secrets, 'Thankyou: "Bottled water is kind of dumb"', *SBS*, 2 October 2016: https://www.sbs.com.au/news/small-business-secrets/article/2016/09/27/thankyou-bottled-water-kind-dumb-product.

167 'Fortune 500 business coach Ora Shtull . . .' Quoted in Adrian Granzella Larssen, 'How to get out of the weeds and make time for the big picture', *Fast Company*, 12 June 2019.

167 'For working out what has to go . . .' Ibid.

15   Build your tribe

170 'The values of the world . . .' Malcolm Gladwell, *Outliers*. Hachette Audio, New York, 2008.

171 'According to British anthropologist . . .' R. I. M. Dunbar, 'Neocortex size as a constraint on group size in primates', *Journal of Human Evolution*, vol. 22, no. 6, 1992.

178 'Psychologist and coach Dana Gionta . . .' Quoted in Margarita Tartakovsky, '10 ways to build and preserve better boundaries', *Psych Central*, 17 May 2016: https://psychcentral.com/lib/10-tips-for-setting-boundaries-online#1.

16   Motivate the collective

185 'There is no greater power . . .' Margaret J. Wheatley *Turning to One Another* (Large Print edn, 16pt), Berrett-Koehler Publishers, San Francisco, 2010, p.64.

190 'Secretary Carter became known for . . .' Ash Carter, *Inside the Five-Sided Box: Lessons from a Lifetime of Leadership in the Pentagon*, Dutton, New York, 2019.

190 'From there, Secretary Carter . . .' Ash Carter, 'No Exceptions: The decision to open all military positions to women', Belfer Center, December 2018: https://www.belfercenter.org/publication/no-exceptions-decision-open-all-military-positions-women.

191 'The nation's Catholic identity . . .' 'Huge Republic of Ireland vote for gay marriage', *BBC*, 23 May 2015: https://www.bbc.com/news/world-europe-32858501.

192 'Tiernan explains . . .' Tiernan Brady, 'Marriage equality in Ireland', ABC Big Ideas [radio], 1 February 2017: https://www.abc.net.au/radionational/programs/bigideas/marriage-equality-in-ireland/8033392.

192 'As it turns out, people . . .' Ibid.

195 'A great example of a leader . . .' Simon Mainwaring, 'Purpose At Work: How Clif Bar Drives Business Growth Through Higher Purpose', *Forbes*, 12 March 2019: https://www.forbes.com/sites/simonmainwaring/2019/03/12/purpose-at-work-how-clif-bar-drives-business-growth-through-higher-purpose/?sh=65e317e841a4.

196 'Gary notes proudly . . .' Clif bar, 'The Clif Bar & Company Story', 2013: https://www.clifbar.com/stories/the-clif-bar-and-company-story.

196 'The first "why" was to make . . .' Afdhel Aziz, 'The power of purpose: Gary Ericksen, Founder of Clif Bar Reflects on a Life of Purpose', *Forbes*, 7 May 2020: https://www.forbes.com/sites/afdhelaziz/2020/05/07/the-power-of-purpose-gary-erickson-founder-of-clif-bar-reflects-on-a-life-of-purpose-part-one/.

197 'When I work on a change initiative . . .' Tony Robbins, 'Why We Do What We Do', TED, February 2006: https://www.ted.com/talks/tony_robbins_why_we_do_what_we_do?language=en.

17 Get adaptable with EQ

199 'Our ability to manage . . .' Daniel Goleman, 1 *Working with Emotional Intelligence*, Penguin Random House, New York, 1998.

199 'This skill didn't make the list . . .' Alex Gray, 'The 10 skills you need to thrive in the fourth industrial revolution', *World Economic Forum*, 19 January 2016: https://www.weforum.org/agenda/2016/01/the-10-skills-you-need-to-thrive-in-the-fourth-industrial-revolution/.

199 'The concept of emotional intelligence . . .' Daniel Goleman, *Emotional Intelligence: Why it can matter more than IQ*, Bantam Books, New York, 1995.

202 'Around 1971, the US Navy . . .' Ted M.I. Yellen and Margaret W. Hoover,, 'In-country Experience: Navy Personnel Stationed in Greece', Special Report, Navy Personnel Research and Development Laboratory, Washington, DC, February 1973: https://apps.dtic.mil/dtic/tr/fulltext/u2/a123184.pdf.

202 'The result was the simulation game . . .' Richard L. Dukes, Sandra M. Fowler and Bernie DeKoven, 'R. Garry Shirts: Simulation gaming exemplar', *Simulation & Gaming*, vol. 42, no. 5, 2011, pp. 545–70.

204 'At least one third . . .' Susan Cain, *Quiet: The Power of Introverts in a World That Can't Stop Talking*, Crown Publishers, New York, 2012.

205 'Susan hilariously characterises . . .' Jon Ronson, 'Quiet: The Power of Introverts in a World That Can't Stop Talking by Susan Cain – review', *The Guardian*, 22 March 2012: https://www.theguardian.com/books/2012/mar/22/quiet-power-introverts-susan-cain-review.

205 'But, in Jim Collins' *Good to Great* . . .' Jim Collins, *Good to Great: Why some companies make the leap – and others don't*, HarperBusiness, New York, 2001.

207 **'The five love languages . . .'** Gary Chapman, *The Five Love Languages: How to Express Heartfelt Commitment to Your Mate*, Northfield Publishing, Chicago, 1995.

210 **'EQ is the new IQ . . .'** 'Test your emotional intelligence', Greater Good Science Center, University of Berkeley, greatergood.berkeley.edu/quizzes/ei_quiz/take_quiz.

18   Diversify your dice

211 **'Diversity may be the hardest . . .'** William Sloane Coffin Jr, quoted in 'Remarks following a moment of silence for 9/11', Vassar president speech, 11 September 2017: https://president.vassar.edu/point-of-view/remarks/2017-remarks-9-11.html.

211 **'I should buy a copy of *The Personal MBA* . . .'** Josh Kaufman, *The Personal MBA: Master the art of business*, Portfolio, New York, 2010.

213 **'In Australia, you are 40 per cent . . .'** Matt Liddy and Catherine Hanrahan, 'Fewer women run top Australian companies than men named John – or Peter or David', *ABC*, 8 March 2017: https://www.abc.net.au/news/2017-03-08/fewer-women-ceos-than-men-named-john/8327938.

213 **'According to Black Enterprise . . .'** Patricia Lenkov, 'Beyond commitment: Improving black leadership in corporate America', *Forbes*, 7 June 2020: https://www.forbes.com/sites/patricialenkov/2020/06/07/beyond-commitment-improving-black-leadership-in-corporate-america/?sh=6f316ce4257d.

213 **'Only five world leaders have been openly LGBTQIA+ . . .'** Leaders in Iceland, Belgium, Luxembourg, Ireland and Serbia are openly LGBTQIA+.

213 **'and only 1.9 per cent of the world's . . .'** 'Youth participation in national parliaments: 2016', United Nations Office of the Secretary-General's Envoy on Youth, 2016: un.org/youthenvoy/2016/03/ipu-report-reveals-chronic-representation-young-people-worlds-parliaments/.

213 **'Rent-A-Minority . . .'** Arwa Mahdawi, *Rent-A-Minority*, 2017: http://rentaminority.com.

214 **'For example, according to the World Economic . . .'** *World Economic Forum*, 'Global Gender Gap Report 2020' Insight Report: https://www.weforum.org/reports/gender-gap-2020-report-100-years-pay-equality.

215 **'For example, in a 2006 study of mock juries . . .'** Samuel R. Sommers, 'On racial diversity and group decision making: identifying multiple effects of racial composition on jury deliberations', *Journal of Personality and Social Psychology*, vol. 90, no. 4, April 2006, pp. 597–612.

216 **'In a 2009 analysis of 506 companies . . .'** C. Herring, 'Does diversity pay?: Race, gender, and the business case for diversity', *American Sociological Review*, vol. 74, no. 2, 2009, pp. 208–24.

216 **'In 2017, a Boston Consulting Group study . . .'** Rocìo Lorenzo, et al., 'How diverse leadership teams boost innovation', 23 January 2018, BCG Henderson Institute: https://www.bcg.com/publications/2018/how-diverse-leadership-teams-boost-innovation.

216 **'Vivienne is passionate about . . .'** Brian Honigman, 'Vivienne Ming: How good communication skills can counter workplace bias', *Forbes*, 18 June 2018: https://www.forbes.com/sites/brianhonigman/2018/06/18/vivienne-ming-reducing-workplace-bias/?sh=152831e77332.

217 **'What does Vivienne calculate . . .'** Jenny Anderson, 'A scientist calculated the cost of not being a straight man, and she wants a tax cut', *Quartz*, 7 March 2016: https://qz.com/631455/a-scientist-cacluated-the-cost-of-not-being-a-straight-man-and-she-wants-a-tax-cut/.

220 'Cath got to work fixing . . .' 'TRU Energy in sexual harassment suit', *The Australian Business Review*, 27 August 2013: https://www.theaustralian.com.au/business/business-spectator/news-story/truenergy-in-sexual-harassment-suit/f3b3855f8a993fcdf12061f02717ad69.

19 Look risk in the eye

224 'There is a tremendous bias . . .' Elon Musk and Chis Anderson (interview), 'Elon Musk's Mission to Mars', *Wired*, 21 October 2012: https://www.wired.com/2012/10/ff-elon-musk-qa/.

224 'In 2016, it was estimated that . . .' Ron Carucci, 'Executives fail to execute strategy because they're too internally focused', *Harvard Business Review*, 13 November 2017: https://hbr.org/2017/11/executives-fail-to-execute-strategy-because-theyre-too-internally-focused.

225 'It's not surprising, then, that . . .' Ron Carucci and Eric C. Hansen, *Rising to Power: The journey of exceptional executives*, Greenleaf Book Group Press, Austin, 2014.

226 'It was born out of the 1973 Yom Kippur War . . .' Michael I. Handel, 'The Yom Kippur War and the inevitability of surprise', *International Studies Quarterly*, vol. 21, no. 3, 1977, pp. 461–502.

226 'They initiated a concept called the "Tenth Man" . . .' You can read a more detailed discussion in William Kaplan, *Why Dissent Matters: Because some people see things the rest of us miss*, McGill-Queen's University Press, Montreal, 2017.

228 'As Gary Klein, a psychologist . . .' Gary Klein, 'Performing a project premortem', *Harvard Business Review*, September 2007 [print magazine], Also available: https://hbr.org/2007/09/performing-a-project-premortem.

229 'More helpfully than typical analyses, a premortem . . .' Ibid.

230 'As entrepreneur and Stanford Professor Steve Blank . . .' Steve Blank, 'No Business Plan Survives First Contact With A Customer – The 5.2 billion dollar mistake', *Steve Blank* Blog, 1 November 2010: https://steveblank.com/2010/11/01/no-businessplan-survives-first-contact-with-a-customer-%E2%80%93-the-5-2-billion-dollar-mistake.

231 'It may not be just luck . . .' Joe Hirsh, 'Pixar's secret for giving feedback', *Joe Hirsh website*, 29 March 2017: https://joehirsch.me/2017/03/29/pixar/.

231 'Edwin Catmull, one of Pixar's founders . . .' Edwin E. Catmull, *Creativity, Inc: Overcoming the unseen forces that stand in the way of true inspiration*, Bantam Press, London, 2014; Jenny Anderson, 'A scientist calculated the cost of not being a straight man, and she wants a tax cut'.

233 'In his book *Black Box Thinking* . . .' Matthew Syed, *Black Box Thinking: why most people never learn from their mistakes – but some do*, Portfolio, New York, 2015.

233 'In the early 1900s . . .' Matthew Syed, 'Why you should fail like a pilot, not a doctor', *Time Magazine*, 5 November 2015: https://time.com/collection-post/4098047/matthew-syed-failure-lessons/.

234 'The focus on the individual . . .' Ibid.

234 'Looking at the data . . .' John T. James, 'A new, evidence-based estimate of patient harms associated with hospital care', *Journal of Patient Safety*, vol. 9, no. 3, September 2013.

234 'A paper in the *British Medical Journal* . . .' Martin A. Makary and Michael Daniel, 'Medical error—the third leading cause of death in the US', *British Medical Journal*, 2016; vol. 353, no. 2139.

20 Design for inclusion

239 'Diversity is being invited ...' Verna Myers, presentation to the Cleveland Metropolitan Bar Association, 25 May 2016: https://www.cleveland.com/business/2016/05/diversity_is_being_invited_to.html.

242 'Back here on Earth ...' 're:work', Google, n.d., rework.withgoogle.com/print/guides/5721312655835136/.

242 'Google's findings are consistent with the work of ...' 'Creating psychological safety in the workplace', *Harvard Business Review* IdeaCast episode 666 [podcast], n.d.: https://hbr.org/podcast/2019/01/creating-psychological-safety-in-the-workplace/.

242 'Amy defines the concept as ...' Amy Edmondson, *The Fearless Organization: Creating psychological safety in the workplace for learning, innovation, and growth*, John Wiley, Hoboken, 2018.

243 'As diversity and inclusion consultant ...' Felicity Menzies, 'Inclusion fundamentals: cultivating belonging in diverse settings', Include-Empower.com, n.d.: cultureplusconsulting.com/2019/03/10/inclusion-fundamentals-fostering-belonging-in-diverse-settings/.

243 'In her book *The Fearless Organisation* ...' Edmondson, *The Fearless Organization*.

244 'Here are some yes/no questions ...' Dr Ron Westrum in 'DevOps culture: Westrum organizational culture': https://cloud.google.com/architecture/devops/devops-culture-westrum-organizational-culture.

245 'The US Army uses four ...' Marilyn Darling, Charles Parry and Joseph Moore, 'Learning in the Thick of It', *Harvard Business Review*, July–August 2005: https://hbr.org/2005/07/learning-in-the-thick-of-it.

246 'The game originated from ...' Edward De Bono, *Six Thinking Hats*, Back Bay Books, Boston, 1999.

247 'Steve is the Chief Human Resources Officer ...' Steve Pemberton, n.d.: https://www.workhuman.com/leadership/steve-pemberton/.

248 'If you google Steve ...' Barbara Palmer, 'Steve Pemberton: defying the odds', *PMCA Convene*, 31 October 2018: https://www.pcma.org/defying-the-odds/.

21 Build the case for change

252 'There is nothing more difficult ...' Niccolo Machiavelli, *The Prince*, Dante University Press, Boston, 2002.

252 'A perspective attributed to Darwin ...' *USA TODAY*, GNS Millennium Special, 1 November 1999.

254 'Far more valuable is finding ...' Rose Whyman, *The Stanislavsky System of Acting: Legacy and influence in modern performance*, Cambridge University Press, Cambridge, United Kingdom, 2008.

256 'I find it helpful to think about ...' Tim Creasey, 'A Roadmap for Building an Organizational Change Management Capability', Prosci: https://blog.prosci.com/a-roadmap-for-building-an-organizational-change-management-capability.

257 'Organisational transformation requires empowerment ...' Paula Asher, 'What's the Difference Between a Change Agent and a Change Champion?', IMA, 26 January 2017: https://www.imaworldwide.com/blog/whats-the-difference-between-a-change-agent-and-a-change-champion.

259 'Larry Ellison, of rival Oracle ...' 'Lou Gerstner's Turnaround Tales at IBM' [podcast], *Knowledge@ Wharton*, 18 December 2002:https://knowledge.wharton.

upenn.edu/article/lou-gerstners-turnaround-tales-at-ibm/#:~:text=The%20
Economist%20doubted%20whether%20%E2%80%9Ca,but%20they're%
20irrelevant.%E2%80%9D.

259 'One important lesson . . .' Ibid.

259 'Fostering a culture entails . . .' Jim Collins, *Good to Great*.

261 'In 2019, Atlassian . . .' Sharon Masige, 'Atlassian is weeding out the "brilliant
jerks", changing the way it does performance reviews to reward workers who show
"heart and balance" not just technical skills', *Business Insider*, 19 July 2019: https://
www.businessinsider.com.au/atlassian-is-weeding-out-the-brilliant-jerks-changing-
the-way-it-does-performance-reviews-to-reward-workers-who-show-heart-and-
balance-not-technical-skills-2019-7.

261 'The global head of talent . . .' Frank Chung, 'Atlassian ditches "brilliant jerks" in
performance review overhaul', News.com, 19 July 2019: https://www.news.com.
au/finance/work/at-work/atlassian-ditches-brilliant-jerks-in-performance-review-
overhaul/news-story/82a5e2abba1939f51d68ae81db8f05bd.

262 'IBM recognised this need . . .' 'A Business and Its Beliefs', IBM: https://www.ibm.
com/ibm/history/ibm100/us/en/icons/bizbeliefs/.

262 'The company have a young workforce . . .' Ibid.; 'Culture's role in enabling organisational change', *PWC* Strategy&, 14 November 2013: https://www.strategyand.
pwc.com/gx/en/insights/2011-2014/cultures-role-organizational-change.html.

22 Yes, and

264 'Life is improvisation . . .' Tina Fey, 'Tina Fey's aha! moment', n.d.: https://www.
oprah.com/spirit/tina-feys-aha-moment.

266 'Three MIT Sloane professors . . .' Edivandro Carlos Conforto et al., 'Learning the
art of business improvisation', *MIT Sloan Management Review*, vol. 57, no. 3, 2016:
https://sloanreview.mit.edu/article/learning-the-art-of-business-improvisation/.

266 'As business improv expert . . .' Bob Kulhan, *Getting to 'Yes and': The art of business
improv*, Stanford Business Books, Stanford, 2017.

266 'The origins stem from David Alger . . .' David Alger, 'Rules of improv', Pan
Theatre,n.d.: pantheater.com/rules-of-improv.html.

270 'This exercise (used by the team at CSz Berlin) . . .' Noah Telson,
'ComedySportz Berlin', 22 November 2015: comedycafeberlin.com/uncategorized/
2015-11-22-comedysportz-berlin/.

23 Navigate from polarisation to participation

274 'No one is exempt . . .' Barack Obama, *The Audacity of Hope: Thoughts on reclaiming the American dream*, Crown, New York, 2007.

276 'In the late 1980s and early 1990s . . .' 'Honoring the Killers: Justice Denied For
"Honor" Crimes in Jordan', Human Rights Watch, April 19 2004: https://www.
hrw.org/report/2004/04/19/honoring-killers/justice-denied-honor-crimes-jordan.

280 'One of the things I'm forever . . .' Amazingly, the program is still around: scramwa.
com/about.

282 'The book I have leant on more times . . .' Kerry Patterson, Joseph Grenny, Ron
McMillan and Al Swizler, *Crucial Conversations: Tools for talking when stakes are high*,
McGraw-Hill, New York, 2012.

283 'Clifford Notarius and Howard Markham . . .' Howard J. Markman and Clifford I. Notarius, 'Coding and marital family interaction: current status', in T. Jacob, (ed.), *Family Interaction and Psychology*, Plenum, New York, 1987, pp. 329–90.

283 'When we look at communities . . .' Howard J. Markman and Clifford I. Notarius, 'Coding and marital family interaction: current status'.

286 'To borrow Martin Luther King Jr's words . . .' Martin Luther King, Jr, 'Where do we go from here?' [excerpt]: http://www-personal.umich.edu/~gmarkus/MLK_WhereDoWeGo.pdf.

24 Apply critical curiosity

287 'It's not the answer . . .' 'Eugene Ionesco Quotes', n.d., BrainyQuote.com: https://www.brainyquote.com/quotes/eugene_ionesco_109171.

291 'She quotes from . . .' Martin Luther King Jr, *Letter from the Birmingham Jail* (12 June 1963), Harper, San Francisco, CA, 1994.

293 'Against the backdrop of a social media minute . . .' Ashley Viens, 'This graph tells us who's using social media the most', *World Economic Forum*, 2 October 2019: https://www.weforum.org/agenda/2019/10/social-media-use-by-generation/.

294 'Because trust is oxygen for belief formation . . .' Malcolm Gladwell, *Talking to Strangers: What we should know about the people we don't know*, Little, Brown and Company, New York, 2019.

25 Inspire and empower followership

301 'One measure . . .' Dennis A. Peer, quoted in David R. Kolzow, 'Leading From Within: Building organizational leadership capacity', 2014: https://www.iedconline.org/clientuploads/Downloads/edrp/Leading_from_Within.pdf, p.1.

302 'In his legendary three-minute TED talk . . .' Derek Sivers, 'How to start a movement', TED, February 2010.

304 'Vicki was compelled to set up . . .' Kimberley Weisul, 'Venture capital is broken. These women are trying to fix it', *Inc*, November 2016: https://www.inc.com/magazine/201611/kimberly-weisul/new-face-of-funding.html.

304 'From 2010 to 2019 . . .' Kimberley Weisul, 'A decade-long scorecard for women raising venture capital shows progress, but is it enough?', *Inc*, 4 March 2020: https://www.inc.com/kimberly-weisul/women-venture-capital-ten-years-progress.html.

304 'A minuscule 0.2% goes to women of colour . . .' Davey Alba, 'It's Embarrassing how few black female founders get funded', *Wired*, 2 October 2016: https://www.wired.com/2016/02/its-embarrassing-how-few-black-female-founders-get-funded/.

306 'As it stands in the world right now . . .' 'Figures at a Glance', United Nations Refugee Agency, 18 June 2020: https://www.unhcr.org/en-au/figures-at-a-glance.

306 'Wars and climate change . . .' Kanta Rigaud et al., *Groundswell – preparing for internal climate migration*, World Bank, Washington, 2018: openknowledge.worldbank.org/handle/10986/29461.

307 'The movement's eight guiding principles . . .' 'Techfugees 8 Guiding Principles', Techfugees, n.d.: https://techfugees.com/techfugees-guiding-principles/.

308 'Interestingly, Techfugees found that . . .' Louise Brousset, 'What happens to a tech4refugees project after a Techfugees' Hackathon?', Techufugees, 21 April 2020:

https://techfugees.com/all_news/community/what-happens-to-a-tech4refugees-project-after-a-techfugees-hackathon/.

309 'I first came across her work . . .' 'A master class in organizing', *Vox Conversations* [podcast], 17 March 2020.

26 Sustain momentum

317 'David's bold and long-term approach . . .' Sarah Kimmorley and Paul Cogan, 'David Thodey is leaving Telstra having doubled the value of the company Australia once loved to hate', *Business Insider*, 20 February 2015: https://www.businessinsider.com.au/telstra-ceo-david-thodey-has-resigned-2015-2.

317 'The ten principles . . .' John Jones et al. '10 principles of change management', Leader, 2 July 2010: http://www.leader.co.za/article.aspx?s=6&f=1&a=2108.

318 'The three steps set out by Jones . . .' Ibid.

320 'After all, as Janine Benyus . . .' *What Is Biomimicry?*, n.d., Biomimicry Institute, https://biomimicry.org/what-is-biomimicry-3/.

321 '. . . the Shinkansen Bullet . . .' 'Shinkansen bullet trains', JapanRailPass, n.d: https://www.jrailpass.com/shinkansen-bullet-trains.

321 'By modelling the front end of a train . . .' 'High Speed Train Inspired by the Kingfisher', Ask *Nature*, 2016: https://asknature.org/idea/shinkansen-train/.

322 'Ben and Jerry's Ice-cream, for example . . .' Ben & Jerry's, 'Our Ice, Our Future: Ben & Jerry's on Melting Poles and Rising Seas', 2015: https://www.benjerry.com/values/issues-we-care-about/climate-justice/polar-ice-caps-melting.

322 'When Paul took over Unilever . . .' 'Unilever celebrates 10 years of the sustainable living plan', Unilever, 6 May 2020: unilever.com/news/press-releases/2020/unilever-celebrates-10-years-of-the-sustainable-living-plan.html.

323 'Amazingly, the coalition managed . . .' 'Sanitation unblocked: taking action to make sanitation a global priority', Unilever, 30 November 2020: unilever.com.au/news/news-and-features/2020/sanitationunblocked-taking-action-to-make-school-sanitation-a-global-priority.html.

326 'Ultimately, the message of momentum . . .' Donna M. Mertens, Fiona Cram, Bagele Chilisa, *Indigenous Pathways into Social Research: Voices of a New Generation*, United Kingdom, Taylor & Francis, 2016.

27 Think in systems

327 'One's got to change the system . . .' George Orwell, *Keep the Aspidistra Flying*, Harvill Secker, London, 1987.

328 'As one of the modern fathers . . .' Peter Senge, *The Fifth Discipline: The art and practice of the learning organization*, Doubleday, New York, 1990, p. 53.

328 'As an article from the World Economic Forum . . .' Lisa Drier, 'Systems leadership can change the world – but what exactly is it?', World Economic Forum: https://www.weforum.org/agenda/2019/09/systems-leadership-can-change-the-world-but-what-does-it-mean.

333 'Cyrill's life and career . . .' Dan Howarth, '"Plastic is a design failure", says Parley for the Oceans founder', *dezeen*, 8 June 2016: https://www.dezeen.com/2016/06/08/cyrill-gutsch-interview-parley-for-the-oceans-founder-ocean-plastic/.

333 'Paul painted a grim picture . . .' John Roach, 'Seafood may be gone by 2048, study says', *National Geographic*, 2 November 2016.

334 'The Parley for the Oceans team . . .' 'Cleanup volunteers intercept 800kg of plastic from 35km of coast in the Whitsundays', Ocean Rafting: https://oceanrafting. com.au/parley-australia-ocean-rafting/.

334 'Together, Parley and Adidas . . .' 'The Prototype', Parley for the Ocean, n.d.: https://www.parley.tv/updates/adidasxparley.

335 'Donella (known as Dana) Meadows . . .' 'About Donella Meadows', *The Donella Meadows Project: Academy for Systems Change:* http://donellameadows.org/ about-donella-meadows/.

28 Grow others to grow others

338 'The key to greatness . . .' Peter Drucker, *Classic Drucker: Essential Wisdom of Peter Drucker from the Pages of Harvard Business Review,* Harvard Business Press, Boston, 2006, p. 59.

339 'Jim noticed all high-performing organisations . . .' Jim Collins, *Jim's Seven Questions: Learning From Young Leaders,* 2018: https://www.youtube.com/watch?v=LHs_2tSw-M4.

344 'In the book *Legacy* . . .' James Kerr, *Legacy: What the All Blacks Can Teach Us About the Business of Life.*

345 'When a player makes the All Blacks . . .' Ibid.

Bibliography

Primary sources

Interviews

Gus Balbontin, podcast interview, June 2019

Layne Beachley, podcast interview, September 2017

Genevieve Bell, video interview, August 2020

Alex Bodman, podcast interview, July 2018

Mark Brand, podcast interview, February 2019

Sir Richard Branson, panel discussion, May 2018

Matt Brimer, fireside chat during Going Global with General Assembly, Sydney School of Entrepreneurship, November 2018

Darren Cahill, interview, July 2020

Susan Cain, Capitalising on Disruption panel discussion, Energy Disruptors UNITE, Calgary, Canada, May 2018

Everald Compton, video interview, July 2020

Geena Davis, interview, January 2019

Audette Exel, video interview, September 2020

Daniel Flynn, video interview, September 2017

Malcolm Gladwell, on-stage interview at the Energy Disruptors Forum, Calgary, Canada, September 2019

Cyrill Gutsch, Virgin Disruptors, London, October 2016

Reem Abu Hassan, video interview, August 2020

Gail Kelly, Young Leaders Forum Session 10: Live, Lead & Learn, June 2018

Jane McAlevey, video interview, August 2020

Arwa Mahdawi, video interview, August 2020

Pam Melroy, podcast interview, May 2019

Stephen Moore, podcast interview, February 2018

Barack Obama, interview at University of Queensland, November 2014

Dawn O'Neil, video interview, May 2020

Karen Palmer, podcast interview, November 2018

Steve Pemberton, video interview, August 2020

Dom Price, podcast interview, August 2017

Condoleezza Rice, PCMA Convening Leaders, San Francisco, USA, January 2020

Sir Ken Robinson, Energy Disruptors, September 2018; 2019

Paul Roos, podcast interview, April 2019

Vicki Saunders, podcast interview, August 2018

Bec Scott, video interview, July 2020

Simon Sinek, Convening Leaders Conference, San Francisco, USA, January 2020

Harinder Singh (Sifu), podcast interview, May 2018

Cath Tanna, video interview, August 2020

Jane Tewson, podcast interview, July 2017

Jessica Watson, podcast interview, February 2018

Secondary sources

Books

Ansari, Aziz, and Klinenberg, Eric, *Modern Romance: An investigation*, Penguin, New York, 2015.

Begley, Sharon, *Can't Just Stop: An investigation of compulsions*, Simon & Schuster, New York, 2017.

Berger, Warren, *A More Beautiful Question: The power of inquiry to spark breakthrough*, Bloomsbury, New York, 2014.

Brashares, Ann, *The Second Summer of the Sisterhood*, Delacorte, New York, 2003.

Buchanan, G. M., and Seligman, M. E. P. (eds), *Explanatory Style*, Lawrence Erlbaum Associates, Hillsdale, New Jersey, 1995.

Cain, Susan, *Quiet: The Power of Introverts in a World That Can't Stop Talking*, Crown Publishers, New York, 2012.

Catmull, Edwin E., *Creativity, Inc: Overcoming the unseen forces that stand in the way of true inspiration*, Bantam Press, London, 2014.

Carter, Ash, *Inside the Five-Sided Box: Lessons from a Lifetime of Leadership in the Pentagon*, Dutton, New York, 2019.

Carucci, Ron and Hansen, Eric C., *Rising to Power: The journey of exceptional executives*, Greenleaf Book Group Press, Austin, 2014.

Chapman, Gary, *The Five Love Languages: How to Express Heartfelt Commitment to Your Mate*, Northfield Publishing, Chicago, 1995.

Christensen, Clayton M., *How Will You Measure Your Life?*, Harvard Business Review Press, Boston, 2012.

Clear, James, *Atomic Habits: an easy and proven way to build good habits and break bad ones; tiny changes, remarkable results*, Avery, New York, 2018.

Collins, Jim, *Good to Great*, HarperBusiness, New York, 2001.

Covey, Stephen, *The Seven Habits of Highly Effective People: Restoring the character ethic* (rev. edn), Free Press, New York, 2004.

Csikszentmihalyi, Mihaly, *Flow: The psychology of optimal experience*, Harper & Row, New York, 1990.

De Bono, Edward, *Six Thinking Hats*, Back Bay Books, Boston, 1999.

Drucker, Peter, *The Essential Drucker: The best of sixty years of Peter Drucker's essential writings on management*, Collins Business Essentials, New York, 2008.

Drucker, Peter, *Classic Drucker: Essential Wisdom of Peter Drucker from the Pages of Harvard Business Review*, Harvard Business Press, Boston, 2006.

Eagleman, David, *The Brain*, Canongate Books, Edinburgh, UK, 2015.

Edmondson, Amy C., *The Fearless Organization: Creating psychological safety in the workplace for learning, innovation, and growth*, John Wiley, Hoboken, 2018.

Ferriss, Timothy, *The 4-Hour Workweek: Escape 9–5, Live Anywhere, and Join the New Rich*, Crown, New York, 2007.

Franklin, Benjamin, *The Autobiography of Benjamin Franklin*, Duke Classics, 2020.

Gladwell, Malcolm, *Outliers*. Hachette Audio, New York, 2008.

Gladwell, Malcolm, *Talking to Strangers: What we should know about the people we don't know*, Little, Brown and Company, New York, 2019.

Goldsmith, Marshall, *What Got You Here Won't Get You There*, Hyperion, 2007.

Goleman, Daniel, *Emotional Intelligence: Why it can matter more than IQ*, Bantam Books, New York, 1995.

Goleman, Daniel, *Working with Emotional Intelligence*, Penguin Random House, New York, 1998.

Hagen, Uta, and Frankel, Haskel, *Respect for Acting*, Macmillan, New York, 1973.

Heinrich, B., *Racing the Antelope*. HarperCollins, New York, 2001.

Huffington, Arianna, *Thrive: The Third Metric to Redefining Success and Creating a Life of Well-Being*, Wisdom, and Wonder, WH Allen, New York, 2015.

Kaplan, William, *Why Dissent Matters: Because some people see things the rest of us miss*, McGill-Queen's University Press, Montreal, 2017.

Kaufman, Josh, *The First 20 Hours: How to learn anything – fast*, Portfolio, New York, 2013.

Kets de Vries, Manfred F. R., 'Creating Safe Places for Executive Play' in *Mindful Leadership Coaching*, INSEAD Business Press, Palgrave Macmillan, London, 2014.

Kerr, James, *Legacy: What the All Blacks Can Teach Us About the Business of Life*. Little, Brown and Company, Great Britain, 2015.

King, M. L., Jr, *Letter from the Birmingham Jail*, Harper, San Francisco, CA, 1994.

Kulhan, Bob, *Getting to 'Yes and': The art of business improv*, Stanford Business Books, Stanford, 2017.

Leslie, Ian, *Curious: The desire to know and why your future depends on it*, Basic Books, New York, 2014.

Loehr, Jim, *The Power of Story: Rewrite your destiny in business and in life*, Free Press, New York, 2007.

Loehr, Jim, and Schwartz, Tony, *The Power of Full Engagement: Managing energy, not time, is the key to high performance and personal renewal*, Free Press, New York, 2007.

McCormack, Mark, *What They Don't Teach You at Harvard Business School*, Bantam Books, New York, 1984.

McGonigal, Kelly, *The Upside of Stress: Why stress is good for you, and how to get good at it*, Avery, New York, 2015.

Montesquieu, C. d. S. (1752). *Reflections on the Causes of the Rise and Fall of the Roman Empire. Translated from the French of M. de Secondat, Baron de Montesquieu ... In Two Volumes. The Second Edition. With Great Additions and Improvements*. United Kingdom: W. Innys,. C. Davis, R. Manby, and H. S. Cox.

Moss, Larry, *The Intent to Live: Achieving your true potential as an actor*, Bantam, New York, 2005.

Munger, Charles, (ed. Kaufman, Peter), *Poor Charlie's Almanack: The wit and wisdom of Charles T. Munger* (3rd expanded ed.), Donning Co., Virginia Beach, VA, 2008.

Obama, Barack, *The Audacity of Hope: Thoughts on reclaiming the American dream*, Crown, New York, 2007.

Obama, Michelle, *Becoming: A Guided Journal for Discovering your Voice*, Penguin Random House, New York, 2019.

Orwell, George, *Keep the Aspidistra Flying*, Harvill Secker, London, 1987.

Patterson, Kerry, Grenny Joseph Joseph, McMillan, Ron, and Swizler, Al, *Crucial Conversations: Tools for talking when stakes are high*, McGraw-Hill, New York, 2012.

Scheidel, Walter, Saller, Richard P., and Morris, Ian, *The Cambridge Economic History of the Greco-Roman World*, Cambridge University Press, Cambridge, UK, 2007.

Senge, Peter, *The Fifth Discipline: The art and practice of the learning organization*, Doubleday, New York, 1990.

Stone, Douglas, and Heen, Sheila, *Thanks for the Feedback: The science and art of receiving feedback well (even when it is off base, unfair, poorly delivered, and, frankly, you're not in the mood)*, Portfolio Penguin, London, 2015.

Syed, Matthew, *Black Box Thinking: why most people never learn from their mistakes – but some do*, Portfolio, New York, 2015.

Wheatley, Margaret J. *Turning to One Another* (Large Print edn, 16pt), Berrett-Koehler Publishers, San Francisco, 2010.

Whyman, Rose, *The Stanislavsky System of Acting: Legacy and influence in modern performance*, Cambridge University Press, Cambridge, UK, 2008.

Wooden, John and Jamison, Steve, *Wooden on Leadership*, McGraw-Hill, New York, 2005.

Online: audiovisual

Australian Army, *Chief of Army Lieutenant General David Morrison Message about Unacceptable Behaviour*, YouTube, 13 June 2013, youtube.com/watch?v=QaqpoeVgr8U.

The Backwards Brain Bicycle: Un-doing understanding, Smarter Every Day, n.d., TED Ed, https://ed.ted.com/best_of_web/bf2mRAfC.

Berger, Warren, *What Kills Questioning? (Book trailer for* A More Beautiful Question *by Warren Berger)*, YouTube, 7 November 2013, youtube.com/watch?list=PLm7JQ 0fOI8XCaen6Vu76hdq7BCPX16LFC&v=dey1Rm5gUxw&feature=youtu.be.

Brady, Tiernan, 'Marriage equality in Ireland', ABC Big Ideas [radio], 1 February 2017: https://www.abc.net.au/radionational/programs/bigideas/marriage-equality-in-ireland/8033392.

Brown, Brené, 'Tarana Burke and Brené on being heard and seen', *Unlocking Us* [podcast], brenebrown.com/podcast/brene-tarana-burke-on-empathy/.

Collins, Jim, *Jim's Seven Questions: Learning From Young Leaders*, 2018, https://www.youtube.com/watch?v=LHs_2tSw-M4.

'Creating psychological safety in the workplace', *Harvard Business Review*, HBR IdeaCast, episode 666 [podcast], n.d., https://hbr.org/podcast/2019/01/creating-psychological-safety-in-the-workplace.

David, Susan, 'The Gift and Power of Emotional Change', TED, November 2017.

McGonigal, Jane, 'Gaming can make a better world', TED, February 2010.

McGonigal, Kelly, 'How to make stress your friend', TED, June 2013.

'A master class in organizing', Vox Conversations [podcast], 17 March 2020.

Mojgani, Anis, *Shake the dust*, Vimeo, 2014, https://vimeo.com/73358073.

On Productions, *Tim Don: The Man with the Halo*, YouTube, 2018, youtube.com/watch?v=UhjIchwAkAU.

'Red Bull Stratos', Red Bull, n.d., redbull.com/int-en/projects/red-bull-stratos.

Robbins, Tony, 'Why We Do What We Do', TED, February 2006, https://www.ted.com/talks/tony_robbins_why_we_do_what_we_do?language=en.

Robinson, Sir Ken, 'Do schools kill creativity?', TED, February 2006.

Sivers, Derek, 'How to start a movement', TED, February 2010.

What Is Biomimicry?, n.d., Biomimicry Institute, https://biomimicry.org/what-is-biomimicry-3/.

Wujec, Tom, 'Build a tower, build a team', TED, February 2010.

Journals, reports and papers

Adara Group, '50,000 Stories of Impact', The Adara Businesses, 2017: https://www.adaragroup.org/wp-content/uploads/2017/06/Adara-Ops-Report-LowRes-Pages.pdf.

Anspach, N. M., Jennings, J. T., and Arceneaux, K., 'A little bit of knowledge: Facebook's news feed and self-perceptions of knowledge', *Research & Politics*, vol. 6, no. 1, February 2019, pp. 1–9.

Benjet, C. et al., 'The epidemiology of traumatic event exposure worldwide: results from the World Mental Health Survey Consortium', *Psychological Medicine*, vol. 46, no. 2, 2016, pp. 327–43.

Breuer, H., and Lüdeke-Freund, F., 'Values-based network and business model innovation', *International Journal of Innovation Management*, vol. 21 no. 3, 2017.

Chestnut Global Partners, *2016 Top Trends in EAP and Wellness Report: An analysis of what is occurring in the fields of employee assistance, organizational health and workplace productivity industries*, 2016.

Dukes, Richard L., Fowler, Sandra M., and DeKoven, Bernie, 'R. Garry Shirts: Simulation gaming exemplar', *Simulation & Gaming*, vol. 42, no. 5, 2011, pp. 545–70.

Dunbar, R. I. M., 'Neocortex size as a constraint on group size in primates', *Journal of Human Evolution*, vol. 22, no. 6, 1992, pp. 469–93.

'Figures at a Glance', United Nations Refugee Agency, 18 June 2020: https://www.unhcr.org/en-au/figures-at-a-glance.

Gabielkov, Maksym, Ramachandran, Arthi, Chaintreau, Augustin and Legout, Arnaud, 'Social clicks: what and who gets read on twitter?', *ACM Sigmetrics Performance Evaluation Review*, vol. 44, no. 1, June 2016.

The Geena Benchmark Report: 2007–2017, Geena Davis Institute on Gender in Media, 2019, https://seejane.org/research-informs-empowers/the-geena-benchmark-report-2007-2017/.

Goldsmith, Marshall, 'Teaching Leaders What to Stop', 2015: https://youtu.be/6NHySKiUJfs /.

Green, Paul, Jr, Gino, Francesca, and Staats, Bradley, *Shopping for Confirmation: How disconfirming feedback shapes social networks*, Harvard Business School Working Paper, No. 18–028, 2017.

Handel, Michael I., 'The Yom Kippur War and the inevitability of surprise', *International Studies Quarterly*, vol. 21, no. 3, 1977, pp. 461–502.

Herring, C., 'Does diversity pay?: Race, gender, and the business case for diversity', *American Sociological Review*, vol. 74, no. 2, 2009, pp. 208–24.

James, John T., 'A new, evidence-based estimate of patient harms associated with hospital care', *Journal of Patient Safety*, vol. 9, no. 3, September 2013, pp. 122–8.

Kets de Vries, Manfred F. R., *Get Back in the Sandbox: Teaching CEOs how to play*, INSEAD Working Paper No. 2012/125/EFE, 4 December 2012.

Kirsch, David, 'A few thoughts on cognitive overload', *Intellectica*, vol. 30, 2000, pp. 19–51.

Klein, H. J., Lount, R. B., Jr, Park, H. M., and Linford, B. J., 'When goals are known: The effects of audience relative status on goal commitment and performance', *Journal of Applied Psychology*, vol. 105, no. 4, 2020, pp. 372–89.

Larssen, Adrian Granzella, 'How to get out of the weeds and make time for the big picture', *Fast Company*, 12 June 2019.

Lorenzo, Rocìo, et al., 'How diverse leadership teams boost innovation', 23 January 2018, BCG Henderson Institute: https://www.bcg.com/publications/2018/how-diverse-leadership-teams-boost-innovation.

Makary, Martin A. and Daniel, Michael, 'Medical error—the third leading cause of death in the US', *British Medical Journal*, 2016; vol. 353, no. 2139.

Markman, H. J., and Notarius, C.I., 'Coding and marital family interaction: current status', in Jacob, T., (ed.), *Family Interaction and Psychology*, Plenum, New York, 1987. pp. 329–90.

Matthews, Gail, 'The effectiveness of four coaching techniques in enhancing goal achievement: writing goals, formulating action steps, making a commitment, and accountability', paper presented at the Ninth Annual International Conference on Psychology, 25–28 May 2015, Athens, Greece.

Mazza, Stéphanie et al, 'Relearn Faster and Retain Longer: Along With Practice, Sleep Makes Perfect', *Psychological Science*, 16 August 2016, vol. 27, no. 10.

Organization for Economic Co-Operation and Development International Labour Organization, 'Achieving better youth employment outcomes: Monitoring policies and progress in G20 economies,' report prepared for the G20 Employment Working Group Antalya, Turkey, 26–27 February 2015.: https://www.oecd.org/g20/topics/employment-and-social-policy/Achieving-better-youth-employment-outcomes.pdf.

Palmer, Barbara, 'Steve Pemberton: defying the odds', PMCA Convene, 31 October 2018.

PwC, *The Future of Work: A journey to 2022*, 2014.

'Refugees', United Nations, un.org/en/sections/issues-depth/refugees.

Rigaud, Kanta, et al., *Groundswell – preparing for internal climate migration*, World Bank, Washington, 2018: openknowledge.worldbank.org/handle/10986/29461.

Sommers, Samuel R., 'On racial diversity and group decision making: identifying multiple effects of racial composition on jury deliberations', *Journal of Personality and Social Psychology*, vol. 90, no. 4, April 2006, pp. 597–612.

Smith, Stacy, and Cook, Crystal Allene, *Gender Stereotypes: An analysis of popular films and TV*, Geena Davis Institute on Gender in Media, 2008, https://seejane.org/research-informs-empowers/.

Taagepera, R., 'Size and Duration of Empires: Growth-Decline Curves, 600 B.C. to 600 A.D.', *Social Science History*, vol. 3 no. 3/4, 1979, pp. 115–138.

Ward, Adrian F., Duke, Kristen, Gneezy, Ayelet, and Bos, Maarten W., 'Brain drain: The mere presence of one's own smartphone reduces available cognitive capacity', *Journal of the Association for Consumer Research*, vol. 2, no. 2, 2017.

World Economic Forum, 'Global Gender Gap Report 2020' Insight Report: https://www.weforum.org/reports/gender-gap-2020-report-100-years-pay-equality.

Yellen, Ted M.I. and Hoover, Margaret, W., 'In-country Experience: Navy Personnel Stationed in Greece', Special Report, Navy Personnel Research and Development Laboratory, Washington, DC, February 1973, https://apps.dtic.mil/dtic/tr/fulltext/u2/a123184.pdf.

'Youth participation in national parliaments: 2016', United Nations Office of the Secretary-General's Envoy on Youth, 2016: un.org/youthenvoy/2016/03/ipu-report-reveals-chronic-representation-young-people-worlds-parliaments/.

Online: text

'10 Common Time Management Mistakes', *Mind Tools*, 2021, https://www.mindtools.com/pages/article/time-management-mistakes.htm.

'About Donella Meadows', *The Donella Meadows Project: Academy for Systems Change*, http://donellameadows.org/about-donella-meadows/.

'A Business and Its Beliefs', IBM, https://www.ibm.com/ibm/history/ibm100/us/en/icons/bizbeliefs/.

Akil II, Bakari, 'How the Navy Seals increased passing rates', *Psychology Today*, 9 November 2009.

Alba, Davey, 'It's Embarrassing how few black female founders get funded', *Wired*, 2 October 2016.

Alger, David, 'Rules of improv', Pan Theatre, n.d.: pantheater.com/rules-of-improv.html.

All Blacks website, 'About the Team', 2021, https://www.allblacks.com/teams/all-blacks/#:~:text=The%20All%20Blacks%20are%20the,prolific%20teams%20across%20any%20sport.

Anderson, Jenny, 'A scientist calculated the cost of not being a straight man, and she wants a tax cut', *Quartz*, 7 March 2016: https://qz.com/631455/a-scientist-cacluated-the-cost-of-not-being-a-straight-man-and-she-wants-a-tax-cut/.

Asher, Paula, 'What's the Difference Between a Change Agent and a Change Champion?', IMA, 26 January 2017, https://www.imaworldwide.com/blog/whats-the-difference-between-a-change-agent-and-a-change-champion.

'Atlassian to list on Nasdaq worth $6b', *SBS News*, 2015, https://www.sbs.com.au/news/atlassian-to-list-on-nasdaq-worth-6b.

'Average Time Spent Daily on Social Media' (latest 2020 Data), *BroadbandSearch.net*, https://www.broadbandsearch.net/blog/average-daily-time-on-social-media.

Aziz, Afdhel, 'The power of purpose: Gary Ericksen, Founder of Clif Bar Reflects on a Life of Purpose', *Forbes*, 7 May 2020, https://www.forbes.com/sites/afdhelaziz/2020/05/07/the-power-of-purpose-gary-erickson-founder-of-clif-bar-reflects-on-a-life-of-purpose-part-one/.

Badian, E. et al., 'Ancient Rome: ancient state, Europe, Africa, and Asia', Encyclopedia Britannica.

Banales, Meliza, 'Slam Poetry', Encyclopedia Britannica.

Barker, Eric, 'How to be optimistic, according to science', *The Week*, 14 August 2014.

Barnes, Christopher M., 'The ideal work schedule, as defined by circadian rhythms', *Harvard Business Review*, 28 January 2015.

Barnes, Stephen, 'Attributes of a successful entrepreneur', *CEO Magazine*, 30 July 2019.

Ben & Jerry's, 'Our Ice, Our Future: Ben & Jerry's on Melting Poles and Rising Seas', 2015, https://www.benjerry.com/values/issues-we-care-about/climate-justice/polar-ice-caps-melting.

Blank, Steve, 'No Business Plan Survives First Contact With A Customer – The 5.2 billion dollar mistake', *Steve Blank* Blog, 1 November 2010, https://steveblank.com/2010/11/01/no-business-plan-survives-first-contact-with-a-customer-%E2%80%93-the-5-2-billion-dollar-mistake.

Brousset, Louise, 'What happens to a tech4refugees project after a Techfugees' Hackathon?', *Techufugees*, 21 April 2020.

Bulao, Jacquelyn, 'How much data is created every day in 2020?', TechJury, 22 January 2021, https://techjury.net/blog/how-much-data-is-created-every-day/#gref.

Carter, Ash, 'No Exceptions: The decision to open all military positions to women', Belfer Center, December 2018, https://www.belfercenter.org/publication/no-exceptions-decision-open-all-military-positions-women.

Carucci, Ron, 'Executives fail to execute strategy because they're too internally focused', *Harvard Business Review*, 13 November 2017, https://hbr.org/2017/11/executives-fail-to-execute-strategy-because-theyre-too-internally-focused.

'Charlie Munger on getting rich, wisdom, focus, fake knowledge and more', Farnam Street, n.d., https://fs.blog/2017/02/charlie-munger-wisdom/.

Chung, Frank, 'Atlassian ditches "brilliant jerks" in performance review overhaul', News.com, 19 July 2019.

Clayton, Steve, 'Microsoft's Ross Smith Asks Shall We Play a Game?', *Microsoft AI Blog*, 16 May 2011, https://blogs.microsoft.com/ai/microsofts-ross-smith-asks-shall-we-play-a-game/.

'Cleanup volunteers intercept 800kg of plastic from 35km of coast in the Whitsundays', Ocean Rafting, https://oceanrafting.com.au/parley-australia-ocean-rafting/.

Clif Bar, 'The Clif Bar & Company Story', 2013, https://www.clifbar.com/stories/the-clif-bar-and-company-story.

Collerton, Sarah, 'Plea to parents: don't let Jessica sail', *ABC News*, 5 October 2009.

Compton, Everald, *EVERALD@LARGE*, everaldcompton.com.

Conforto, Edivandro Carlos, 'Learning the art of business improvisation', *MIT Sloan Management Review*, vol. 57, no. 3, 2016.

Creasey, Tim, 'A Roadmap for Building an Organizational Change Management Capability', Prosci, https://blog.prosci.com/a-roadmap-for-building-an-organizational-change-management-capability.

'Culture's role in enabling organisational change', PWC, *Strategy&*, 14 November 2013.

Cunningham, Lillian, 'In a big move, Accenture will get rid of annual performance reviews and rankings', *Washington Post*, 21 July 2015.

Darling, Marilyn, Parry, Charles and Moore, Joseph, 'Learning in the Thick of It', *Harvard Business Review*, July–August 2005, https://hbr.org/2005/07/learning-in-the-thick-of-it.

'Data never sleeps', Domo, 2018, domo.com/solution/data-never-sleeps-6.

'Deloitte joins Abode and Accenture in dumping the annual performance review', *Impraise*, n.d.

'Design thinking: the beginner's guide', Interaction Design Foundation, n.d., interaction-design.org/courses/design-thinking-the-beginner-s-guide.

Drier, Lisa, 'Systems leadership can change the world – but what exactly is it?', World Economic Forum, https://www.weforum.org/agenda/2019/09/systems-leadership-can-change-the-world-but-what-does-it-mean.

Fey, Tina, 'Tina Fey's aha! moment', n.d., https://www.oprah.com/spirit/tina-feys-aha-moment.

'First Nations languages', Common Ground, n.d., commonground.org.au/learn/indigenous-languages-avoiding-a-silent-future

Flynn, Daniel [interview], *Map magazine*, http://theweekendedition.com.au/mapmagazine/daniel-flynn/.

Ganz, Marshall, 'What Is Public Narrative'?, The Community Organizing Website, 2007, https://comm-org.wisc.edu/syllabi/ganz/WhatisPublicNarrative5.19.08.htmGino, Francesca, 'Research: We tend to drop people who give us critical feedback', *Harvard Business Review*, 16 September 2016.

Ganz, Marshall, 'Leading Change: Leadership, organization, and social movements', in Nitin Nohria and Rakesh Khurana (eds), *Handbook of Leadership Theory and Practice: A Harvard Business School centennial colloqium*, Harvard Business Press, Boston, 2010.

'The global state of employee engagement', Officevibe, n.d. https://officevibe.com/guides/state-employee-engagement.

Godin, Seth, 'Urgency and accountability are two sides of the same coin', *Seth's Blog*, https://seths.blog/2013/05/urgency-and-accountability-are-two-sides-of-the-innovation-coin/.

Goldsmith, Marshall, 'Lessons about life and leadership from Peter Drucker', *Corporate Learning Network*, 24 August 2020, https://www.corporatelearningnetwork.com/leadership-management/articles/20-behaviors-even-the-most-successful-people-need-to-stop-1.

Golson, Jordan, 'Well, that didn't work: the Segway is a technological marvel. Too bad it doesn't make any sense', *Wired*, 16 January 2016.

Graham, Paul, 'How to get startup ideas', November 2012, http://paulgraham.com/startupideas.html.

Gramenz, Jack, 'Atlassian business software giant pushes out free Chrome extension to help fix bad workplace habits', News.com, 21 January 2020.

Gray, Alex, 'The 10 skills you need to thrive in the fourth industrial revolution', *World Economic Forum*, 19 January 2016: https://www.weforum.org/agenda/2016/01/the-10-skills-you-need-to-thrive-in-the-fourth-industrial-revolution/.

'Groundswell – preparing for internal climate migration', *World Bank*, March 2018, openknowledge.worldbank.org/handle/10986/29461.

Groves, Nancy, 'EL Doctorow in quotes: 15 of his best', *Guardian*, 22 July 2015, https://www.theguardian.com/books/2015/jul/22/el-doctorow-in-quotes-15-of-his-best.

Ha, Thu-huong, 'This April Fool's joke perfectly trolls online trolls', *Quartz*, 2 April 2016, https://qz.com/653018/this-april-fools-joke-perfectly-trolls-online-trolls/.

Hasso Plattner Institute of Design at Stanford d.school, 'Design thinking: the beginner's guide', Interaction Design Foundation, n.d., interaction-design.org/courses/design-thinking-the-beginner-s-guide.

Hecht, Rabbi Ben, 'We Need To Be Able To Question Our Own Opinions', *Huffington Post Canada*, 19 July 2016, https://www.huffingtonpost.ca/rabbi-ben-hecht/questioning-oneself_b_11055358.html.

'High Speed Train Inspired by the Kingfisher', Ask *Nature*, 2016, https://asknature.org/idea/shinkansen-train/.

Hirsh, Joe, 'Pixar's secret for giving feedback', *Joe Hirsh website*, 29 March 2017, https://joehirsch.me/2017/03/29/pixar/.

Honigman, Brian, 'Vivienne Ming: How good communication skills can counter workplace bias', *Forbes*, 18 June 2018, https://www.forbes.com/sites/brianhonigman/2018/06/18/vivienne-ming-reducing-workplace-bias/?sh=152831e77332.

'Honoring the Killers: Justice Denied For "Honor" Crimes in Jordan', Human Rights Watch, April 19 2004, https://www.hrw.org/report/2004/04/19/honoring-killers/justice-denied-honor-crimes-jordan.

Hosie, Rachel, 'The psychological reason you can't stop checking your phone', *Independent*, 10 February 2017, https://www.independent.co.uk/life-style/why-keep-checking-phone-psychology-smartphone-notifications-social-media-a7572916.html.

Howarth, Dan, '"Plastic is a design failure", says Parley for the Oceans founder', *dezeen*, 8 June 2016.

Howarth, Rich, *The Strategic Thinking Manifesto*, Strategic Thinking Institute, n.d., strategyskills.com/pdf/The-Strategic-Thinking-Manifesto.pdf?gclid=CIaV2fG0v88CFcVlfgodSBUM8A.

'Huge Republic of Ireland vote for gay marriage', *BBC*, 23 May 2015, https://www.bbc.com/news/world-europe-32858501.

'Information overload: memory and focus are at risk', Morris Psychological Group, 1 July 2014.

Jamieson, Darran, 'Making Difficult Fun: How to Challenge Your Players', Envatotuts+, 20 May 2016, https://gamedevelopment.tutsplus.com/tutorials/making-difficult-fun-how-to-challenge-your-players--cms-25873.

Jones, John et al. '10 principles of change management', *Leader*, 2 July 2010, http://www.leader.co.za/article.aspx?s=6&f=1&a=2108.

Kimmorley, Sarah and Cogan, Paul, 'David Thodey is leaving Telstra having doubled the value of the company Australia once loved to hate', *Business Insider*, 20 February 2015.

King, Martin Luther (Jr), 'Where do we go from here?' [excerpt]: http://www-personal.umich.edu/~gmarkus/MLK_WhereDoWeGo.pdf.

Klein, Gary, 'Performing a project premortem', *Harvard Business Review*, September 2007 [print magazine], Also available: https://hbr.org/2007/09/performing-a-project-premortem.

Kolzow, David R., 'Leading From Within: Building organizational leadership capacity', 2014, https://www.iedconline.org/clientuploads/Downloads/edrp/Leading_from_Within.pdf, p.1.

Konnikova, Maria, 'How People Learn to Become Resilient', *The New Yorker*, 11 February 2016, https://www.newyorker.com/science/maria-konnikova/the-secret-formula-for-resilience.

Lenkov, Patricia, 'Beyond commitment: Improving black leadership in corporate America', *Forbes*, 7 June 2020, https://www.forbes.com/sites/patricialenkov/2020/06/07/beyond-commitment-improving-black-leadership-in-corporate-america/?sh=6f316ce4257d.

Lobosco, Mark, 'Four trends changing the way you attract and retain talent', *LinkedIn Talent Blog*, 22 January 2020, https://business.linkedin.com/talent-solutions/blog/trends-and-research/2020/global-talent-trends-2020.

'Lou Gerstner's turnaround tales at IBM', *Knowledge@ Wharton*, 18 December 2002, https://knowledge.wharton.upenn.edu/article/lou-gerstners-turnaround-tales-at-ibm.

McFarland, Matt, 'Segway was supposed to change the world. Two decades later, it just might', *CNN*, 30 October 2018, https://lite.cnn.com/en/article/h_d831de0838b432f0721964c061c9fe92.

Mainwaring, Simon, 'Purpose At Work: How Clif Bar Drives Business Growth Through Higher Purpose', *Forbes*, 12 March 2019, https://www.forbes.com/sites/simonmainwaring/2019/03/12/purpose-at-work-how-clif-bar-drives-business-growth-through-higher-purpose/?sh=65e317e841a4.

Martin, Yvette, 'Helping Australia's stressed-out workers', *Gallup*, 24 December 2013.

Masige, Sharon, 'Atlassian is weeding out the "brilliant jerks", changing the way it does performance reviews to reward workers who show "heart and balance" not just technical skills', *Business Insider*, 19 July 2019.

Max-Planck-Gesellschaft, 'Forgotten but not gone: how the brain re-learns', *ScienceDaily*, 22 November 2008, https://www.sciencedaily.com/releases/2008/11/081117110834.htm.

Maybury, Matt, '20 quotes to help motivate you to hustle like never before', *Entrepreneur*, 30 June 2015, https://www.entrepreneur.com/article/247859.

Mayberry, Matt, 'The extraordinary power of visualizing success', *Entrepreneur Asia Pacific*, 30 January 2015.

Mental Health Australia and KPMG, *Investing to Save: The economic benefits for Australia of investment in mental health reform*, May 2018.

Mental models: the best way to make intelligent decisions (109 models explained)', Farnam Street, n.d., https://fs.blog/mental-models/.

Menzies, Felicity, 'Inclusion fundamentals: cultivating belonging in diverse settings', Include-Empower.com, n.d., cultureplusconsulting.com/2019/03/10/inclusion-fundamentals-fostering-belonging-in-diverse-settings/.

Minchin, Tim, 'Occasional address: 9 life lessons', timminchin.com/2013/09/25/occasional-address/.

Mohr, Tara Sophia, 'Why women don't apply for jobs unless they're 100% qualified', *Harvard Business Review*, 25 August 2014.

Monteiro, Catie, '"Black, queer, disabled and brilliant": Activist hopes to make history in space', *NBC News*, 27 June 2018.

'Multitasking: Switching Costs', American Psychological Association, 20 March 2006.

'Mums asked nearly 300 questions a day by kids', *Business Standard*, 29 March 2013.

Musk, Elon and Anderson, Chris (interview), 'Elon Musk's Mission to Mars', *Wired*, 21 October 2012, https://www.wired.com/2012/10/ff-elon-musk-qa/.

Myers, Verna, presentation to the Cleveland Metropolitan Bar Association, 25 May 2016, https://www.cleveland.com/business/2016/05/diversity_is_being_invited_to.html.

'No Looking Back: Eddie Ndopu makes space for a historic 2018', *African Leadership Academy*, 26 January 2018.

Nwokike, Francis, 'What are your goals? Differentiate your goals from your wishes', The Total Entrepreneurs: For entrepreneurs and startups, n.d.

Ranada, Pia, 'Duterte calls Rappler fake news outlet', *Rappler*, 16 January 2018, rappler.com/nation/duterte-fake-news-outlet.

Oxford Essential Quotations (4th edn), Susan Ratcliffe (ed.), Oxford University Press, 2016.

'The Prototype', Parley for the Ocean, n.d., https://www.parley.tv/updates/adidasxparley.

Ratcliffe, Rebecca, 'Journalist Maria Ressa found guilty of cyberlibel in Phillipines', *Guardian*, 15 June 2020.

Rayasam, Renuka, 'You probably suffer from scattered brain syndrome', *BBC*, 12 December 2016.

're:work', Google, n.d., rework.withgoogle.com/print/guides/5721312655835136/.

'Remarks following a moment of silence for 9/11', Vassar president speech, 11 September 2017: https://president.vassar.edu/point-of-view/remarks/2017-remarks-9-11.html.

Rentaminority.com.

Roach, John, 'Seafood may be gone by 2048, study says', National Geographic, 2 November 2016.

Rogers, R. D., and Monsell, S., 'Costs of a predictable switch between simple cognitive tasks', *Journal of Experimental Psychology: General*, vol. 124, 1995, pp. 207–31.

Ronson, Jon, 'Quiet: The Power of Introverts in a World That Can't Stop Talking by Susan Cain – review', *The Guardian*, 22 March 2012, https://www.theguardian.com/books/2012/mar/22/quiet-power-introverts-susan-cain-review.

'Rules of improv', Pan Theatre, n.d., pantheater.com/rules-of-improv.html

'Sanitation unblocked: taking action to make sanitation a global priority', Unilever, unilever.com.au/news.

Savara, Sid, 'Writing down your goals – the Harvard goal study. Fact or fiction?", Sid Savara [website], n.d. https://sidsavara.com/fact-or-fiction-the-truth-about-the-harvard-written-goal-study/.

Schwartzberg, Lauren, 'Why iPod and Nest Creator Tony Fadell Thinks Like a Child', *Fast Company*, 18 March, 2015, https://www.fastcompany.com/3043987/why-ipod-and-nest-creator-tony-fadell-thinks-like-a-child.

SCRAM Schools Conflict Resolution and Mediation, n.d., scramwa.com.

Sharp, Robert, '"I disapprove of what you say, but I will defend to the death your rights to say it" – Voltaire, Tallentyre and Hall', 3 May 2018, https://www.robertsharp.co.uk/2018/05/03/i-disapprove-of-what-you-say-but-i-will-defend-to-the-death-your-right-to-say-it-voltaire-tallentyre-and-hall/.

Simmons, Michael, 'Bezos, Musk, and Buffett see the world differently, because they see time differently', *Medium*, 14 May 2020.

Small Business Secrets, 'Thankyou: "Bottled water is kind of dumb"', *SBS*, 2 October 2016, https://www.sbs.com.au/news/small-business-secrets/article/2016/09/27/thankyou-bottled-water-kind-dumb-product.

Smith, Elliot, 'The Barings collapse 25 years on: what the industry learned from the man who broke a bank', *CNBC*, 26 February, 2020, https://www.cnbc.com/2020/02/26/barings-collapse-25-years-on-what-the-industry-learned-after-one-man-broke-a-bank.html.

Soika, Tina, 'Cognitive Dissonance: Overcome What Is Really Holding Back Your Practice', *The Hearing Review*, 20 June 2013, https://www.hearingreview.com/practice-building/practice-management/cognitive-dissonance-overcome-what-is-really-holding-back-your-practice-2?ref=cl-title.

Sollisch, Jim, 'The cure for decision fatigue', *Wall Street Journal*, 10 June 2016.

Spur Projects, 'How is the world feeling: Data: emotions: time of day', http://howistheworldfeeling.wearespur.com/#data.

St Anne, Christine, 'Gail Kelly on lessons learnt from Mandela', RFi Group, 27 August 2017.

Stanford d.school, 'Resources: Spaghetti marshmallow challenge', https://dschool.stanford.edu/resources/spaghetti-marshmallow-challenge.

'Steve Pemberton', n.d., https://www.workhuman.com/leadership/steve-pemberton/.

'Study confirms smart strategies for achieving goals', *Sciencebeta*, 20 June 2013.

Syed, Matthew, 'Why you should fail like a pilot, not a doctor', *Time Magazine*, 5 November 2015: https://time.com/collection-post/4098047/matthew-syed-failure-lessons/.

Tartakovsky, Margarita, '10 ways to build and preserve better boundaries', *Psych Central*, 17 May 2016.

'Techfugees 8 Guiding Principles', Techfugees, n.d., https://techfugees.com/techfugees-guiding-principles.

Tedeschi, Richard G., and Calhoun, Lawrence G., 'Posttraumatic growth: conceptual foundations and empirical evidence', *Psychological Inquiry*, vol. 15, no. 1, 2004, pp. 1–18.

Telson, Noah, 'ComedySportz Berlin', 22 November 2015, comedycafeberlin.com/uncategorized/2015-11-22-comedysportz-berlin/.

'Test your emotional intelligence', Greater Good Science Center, University of Berkeley, greatergood.berkeley.edu/quizzes/ei_quiz/take_quiz.

Thomas, Mark, '"Don't get smart person's disease." says Anne Mulcahy, former CEO of Xerox', *Global Ed*, 17 December 2013, https://globaleduc.wordpress.com/2013/12/17/dont-get-smart-persons-disease-says-anne-mulcahy-former-ceo-of-xerox/.

Tottle, Sarah, 'It's costing the global economy £255 billion, so what can we do to stop workplace burnout?', *World Economic Forum*, 31 October 2016.

'Trailblazers: Australia's 50 Greatest Explorers', Australian Museum website, 2021, https://australian.museum/about/history/exhibitions/trailblazers/.

'TRU Energy in sexual harassment suit', *The Australian Business Review*, 27 August 2013, https://www.theaustralian.com.au/business/business-spectator/news-story/truenergy-in-sexual-harassment-suit/f3b3855f8a993fcdf12061f02717ad69.

'Unilever celebrates 10 years of the sustainable living plan', Unilever, unilever.com/news/press-releases/2020/unilever-celebrates-10-years-of-the-sustainable-living-plan.html.

Vanderbilt, Tom, 'Here's what learning to juggle does to your brain', *Wired*, 4 February 2021, https://www.wired.com/story/heres-what-learning-juggle-does-your-brain/.

Viens, Ashley, 'This graph tells us who's using social media the most', *World Economic Forum*, 2 October 2019, https://www.weforum.org/agenda/2019/10/social-media-use-by-generation/.

Weisul, Kimberley, 'A decade-long scorecard for women raising venture capital shows progress, but is it enough?', *Inc*, 4 March 2020.

Westrum, Dr Ron, in 'DevOps culture: Westrum organizational culture', https://cloud.google.com/architecture/devops/devops-culture-westrum-organizational-culture.

Weisul, Kimberley, 'Venture capital is broken. These women are trying to fix it', *Inc*, November 2016.

Whiting, Kate, 'These are the top ten skills of tomorrow and how long it takes to learn them', World Economic Forum, 21 October 2020.

Williams, Benjamin, 'Living life online: Adolescent mental health and social media', *Psychiatry Advisor*, 7 December 2020.

Ye, Leslie, 'The Psychology of Choice: How to Make Decisions Easier', HubSpot, 14 August 2018, https://blog.hubspot.com/sales/the-psychology-of-choice.

Zak, Paul J., 'Why your brain loves good storytelling', *Harvard Business Review*, 28 October 2014.

Acknowledgements

The first word of this book was written in the middle of a COVID-19 lockdown where my fellow Melburnians and I couldn't venture beyond 5 km from our homes, go out after 8 pm or really partake in any semblance of normal life. As an extrovert who enjoys rooms full of people, deciding to write a book in this environment was both a gift, for the deep concentration and lack of distraction, and an introverted curse, as I sat alone with my thoughts, attempting to type thousands of words each day. The forced halt of the pandemic enveloped us in a liminal space of slow-motion perspective, reflection and gratitude. There was no sound of traffic. The birds came back. Communities pulled together. In the smallness of our world, like many people, I was glued to my newsfeed watching challenges consume the globe. But 'out there' is 'in here'. The pandemic taught us how connected we are and how reliant on each other in our fragile ecosystem. It was here I formed a steely resolve that the world needed new leadership and we humans needed positive points of light and hope like never before.

I owe an enormous debt of gratitude to those who inspired this book to be written and to those who helped with the crafting of it. Few things have simultaneously daunted and excited me like writing this book. While public speaking is something I could do underwater, putting my ideas down in a coherent, accessible format leaves me gulping for air and I am so grateful to everyone who has helped me to learn, grow and develop as a writer during this process.

My first acknowledgment goes to Nikki, my furiously creative, indefatigable companion on this writing journey. This book would never have even begun were it not for breakfast in Adelaide one fateful morning, and none of it would have been finished without your encouragement, perseverance, enthusiasm and off-the-charts linguistic wizardry. Thank you for helping me to convey my ideas with such clarity. Our friendship is one of the greatest gifts this book has given me.

Thank you to my tribe, Cat, Kate, Shimmy, Adam, Graeme and Michelle, for the hours you put into reading drafts, giving me feedback and discussing ideas and case studies. I hope you can see how your feedback has shaped the book and I hope you know how much your friendship, love and support over the years has shaped me. Thanks also to BT, who pulled the threads of research into a tighter weave, and the emerging leaders who laid out their honest feedback on the usefulness of the lessons within, particularly Katie and Anton – you two are a force! I can't thank enough my extended 'family', whose encouragement gave me the confidence to write this book in the first place and the boost I needed to get through the challenging moments. To Jan and DJ, Lisa, Julie, Mim, Layne, Pops, Tess, Tal, Maggie, Maria, Julie, Ali, Dan and Mac, thank you for your unwavering belief in me and endless thoughtfulness, love and hugs.

To 'the leading edge' protagonists who fill the pages of this book, thank you for your courage and purpose and for leading by example. While I have done my best to do justice to each of you, in reality your leadership inspires me more than I can adequately convey in words. I hope what I've captured of your stories in these pages will reach and inspire many more. Equally, thank you for the generosity and candour with which you shared of your own experiences so that I and others may learn.

This book, and my career to date, would not have been possible without the mentorship and sponsorship of numerous leaders who saw potential in me, thoughtfully cultivated it and provided me with opportunities to stretch and challenge myself. There are too many to name but you all know who you are and though I try to tell you regularly how much I appreciate you, I don't think I'll ever be able to tell you enough. I want to say a particular thank you to Sam, Andrew, Sally, David, KB, Audette, JK, Jane, Carol, Cath, Kristin, Beth, Andrea, John, Liz and Peter – you have gone above and beyond, and I owe you all a debt of gratitude. Thank you also to Janine and Naomi, two of our nation's best entrepreneurs . . . I'm not sure either of you realise what it meant to me when at twenty-five, feeling like a fish out of water, you told me you'd invest in me should I ever need it. When I took my first tentative steps towards running my own business, your belief was the greatest currency I could ever have been given.

Thank you to my earliest mentors – my school teachers. I reflect often on how blessed I am to have been taught by people who encouraged my curiosity, challenged me to apply my learning outside the classroom and gave me responsibility and leadership roles before I knew what either of those things meant. Thank you for never telling me to colour inside the lines. There is no more selfless task than to devote yourself to raising the next generation. I hope you know that the time I spend every month in schools, working with teachers and students, is in some small way my attempt to pay forward what you invested in me. A particularly big thanks to Mrs Ellison, Mr Wynhorst, Mrs Hudson, Mr Ford, Mrs Palmer, Sheila Flanagan and Professor Robson.

It is deeply unedifying to approach people you admire and ask them to write nice things about you. Thank you to Muhammad, Matt, Richard and Layne for being so generous and so worthy of admiration in the first place.

Despite the book's substantial size, there were many more amazing leaders whose stories I, unfortunately, just did not have the pages to contain. Please know how grateful I am for your work and the time

you gave to our conversations. Please also know how enthusiastically I will find the platforms and opportunities to showcase your leadership in future.

To Denis, Eden and the team at Our Community, thank you for your generosity in letting me take up near permanent residence in your beautiful space as I wrote this book. Never have I been in a more consciously curated space and I could not have asked for a more purpose-anchored and inspiring place to bring the ideas in this book to life. Thanks to all the team at Seven Seeds who kept me caffeinated throughout not just the writing of this book but a whole pandemic! Your banter and smiles (even behind a face mask) gave me more of a daily energy kick than the coffee.

To my team at Penguin Random House, thank you for your guidance and expertise. Izzy Yates, thank you for breathing life into this project in the first place and for your enthusiasm throughout. To Amanda Martin and Susan Keogh, thank you for your healthy mix of encouragement and constructive criticism; your help in sharpening the ideas in this book was invaluable.

To my best friend Charlie, thank you for being my rock and my partner in crazy adventures for more than a decade. There are few things in life I'm more grateful for than our friendship and I wouldn't be the person I am today without you. Thank you for always saying 'yes' and being there for me, even when we're half a world away.

To my beloved, Kate, you are integrity and compassion personified and you inspire me to be a better person every day. Thank you for reading every word of the enormous first draft, running with me every day to clear my writer's block and being my sounding board for *everything*. Your love gives me the confidence and surety to dream big and the resilience to weather any and every challenge. I am endlessly grateful that I get to do life with you. You are, without question, the best thing that's ever happened to me.

Finally, to my grandma Dorothy, words can't express what you mean to me, nor could an entire book (and then some) do justice

to all you've taught me. Your selflessness, empathy, humility, curiosity and joie de vivre have always inspired me. Your innate ability to make people feel heard, appreciated and important is what first made me believe in an individual's power to change the world. I cherish our relationship. You believed in me long before I knew how to believe in myself and the encouragement and the love you and Grandpa show me have been a constant source of strength. I have always admired the symbiosis of the relationship the two of you share and the beauty of the fact that seventy years into your marriage you still both tell me you fall more in love with each other every day. If I can grow up to be a fraction of the woman you are, I'll consider myself to be a success.